2/02

SAVAGE

Savage

THE LIFE AND TIMES OF JEMMY BUTTON

Nick Hazlewood

THOMAS DUNNE BOOKS
ST. MARTIN'S PRESS NEW YORK

THOMAS DUNNE BOOKS
An imprint of St. Martin's Press

www.stmartins.com

ISBN 0-312-25213-7

First published in Great Britain by Hodder and Stoughton, a division of Hodder
Headline

First U.S. Edition: June 2001

10 9 8 7 6 5 4 3 2 1

For Caroline

Contents

List of Illustrations

The dark and brooding captain, Robert FitzRoy sketched some time around 1838.
Reproduced with permission of the Mitchell Library, State Library of New South Wales, Australia.

Fuegian indian as seen by the crew of the Beagle who called him a Yapoo Tekeenica
from *Narratives of the surveying voyages of His Majesty's ships Adventure and Beagle*, reproduced by permission of the Syndics of Cambridge University Library

Feuggians greet a sailor from their wigwams
from *Narratives of the surveying voyages of His Majesty's ships Adventure and Beagle*, reproduced by permission of the Syndics of Cambridge University Library

Sailors trading with Fuegians near Button Island
from *Narratives of the surveying voyages of His Majesty's ships Adventure and Beagle*, reproduced by permission of the Syndics of Cambridge University Library

Yamana indians at Wulaia Cove, with Beagle expedition tents and boats in the background
from *Narratives of the surveying voyages of His Majesty's ships Adventure*

ix

and Beagle, reproduced by permission of the Syndics of Cambridge University Library

Monte Video in the 1830s, the first city the kidnapped Fuegians would ever have encountered
from *Narratives of the surveying voyages of His Majesty's ships Adventure and Beagle*, reproduced by permission of the Syndics of Cambridge University Library
Welcome to England. The November 1830 muster roll for the Royal Navy Hospital in Plymouth with the Fuegians at the head of the list
reproduced by the permission of the Public Record Office, Kew.

FitzRoy's Fuegians, clockwise from top left Fugia Basket in 1833, Jemmy Button's wife in 1834, Jemmy Button in 1833, York Minster profile 1833, York Minster portrait 1832, Jemmy Button 1834 a year after leaving the Beagle.
from *Narratives of the surveying voyages of His Majesty's ships Adventure and Beagle*, reproduced by permission of the Syndics of Cambridge University Library

The infants school as it is today, as seen from St Mary's church.
Nick Hazelwood

Inside St Mary's infant school, Walthamstow, where the walls 'spoke' messages from the scriptures.
Reproduced with permission of the Vestry House Museum, London Borough of Waltham Forest.

England's glory, Sailing Billy or Silly Billy. King William IV

England's Marie-Antoinette, Queen Adelaide
from a portrait by Sir William Beechey, RA, in the National Portrait Gallery.

The young fly-catcher, or stone-pounder, Charles Darwin in 1840, painted by George Richmond.
Reproduced with permission of GP Darwin on behalf of Darwin Heirlooms Trust. Copyright the English Heritage Photographic Library.

An Indian family glide across the still waters of Tierra del Fuego in their canoe.
Reproduced with permission of the South American Missionary Society.

'their hair hanging down on all sides, like old thatch. . .' a Yamana couple pose for the camera.
Reproduced with permission of the Royal Geographical Society.

The ill-fated vessel, the Allen Gardiner
From *Hope deferred not lost*, by GP Despard. Shelfmark 4745.a.40, reproduced with permission of the British Library.

The Patagonian Missionary Society's great hope, the Cranmer mission station on Keppel Island, the Falklands.
From *The Missionary Martyr of Tierra del Fuego: being the memoir of JG Phillips* by GW Phillips. Shelfmark: 4920.cc.32, reproduced with permission of the British Library

The thorn in the side of the Patagonian Missionary Society. William Parker Snow in 1867.
Reproduced with permission of the Trustees of the Trevelyan Family Papers at the Robinson Library, Newcastle University.

Waite Stirling, the first bishop of the Falklands, with the four Fuegians – Threeboys, Uroopa, Mamastugadegenes, (Jack) and Sesoienges – he brought to England in 1865.
Reproduced with permission of the South American Missionary Society.

Fuegian men dressed in European clothes pose while building a traditional wigwam
Reproduced with permission of the South American Missionary Society.

Alakaluf women rounded up to work in the mission station on Dawson Island
Reproduced with permission of the Royal Geographical Society.

A source of amusement. . . a Fuegian man wanders the deck of a European ship, smoking a cigarette.
Reproduced with permission of the Royal Geographical Society.

'Muerto en el terreno de honor' – dead in the land of honour. Fuegians were mercilessly hunted down by European settlers.
Reproduced with permission of the Royal Geographical Society.

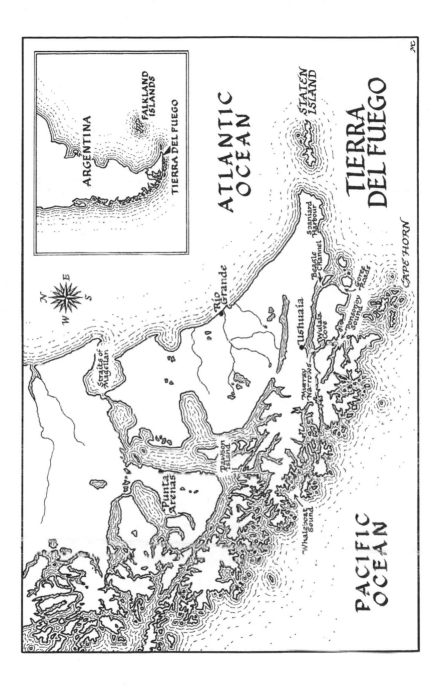

He cried in a whisper at some image, at some vision — he cried out twice, a cry that was no more than a breath —
'The horror! The horror!'

Joseph Conrad *Heart of Darkness*

Court House Port Stanley, 28 May 1860

The names of the dead men were read out . . .

> 'John Johnston, Carpenter
> Hugh McDowall, Able bodied seaman
> John Johnston, Able bodied seaman
> John Brown, Able bodied seaman
> John Fell, Ship's Mate
> August Peterson, Ordinary Seaman
> Robert Fell, Captain
> Garland Phillips, Catechist'

Eight men butchered on Wulaia Cove, Tierra del Fuego. Only the ship's cook, Alfred Coles, survived to point the finger of blame. The man responsible, he said, was the man who had slept in the dead captain's bed after the bloodbath.

That man was the Fuegian, Jemmy Button.

PART ONE

Land of Fire 1830

One night a great number of fires were seen, mostly on their left hand, from which they guessed that they had been seen by the natives of the region. But Magellan, seeing that the country was rocky, and also stark with eternal cold, thought it useless to waste many days in examining it; and so, with only three ships, he continued on his course along the channel, until, on the twenty-second day after he had entered it, he sailed out upon another wide and vast sea.

Maximilian Transylvanus, secretary of the Holy Roman
Emperor Charles V, in a letter to the Cardinal of Salzburg

Chapter 1

In 1520 the Portuguese explorer Ferdinand Magellan became the first European to pass from the Atlantic into the Pacific by way of the straits that would henceforth bear his name. To his north lay the barren wastelands of Patagonia, to the south a harsh and uninviting territory that he thought to be the tip of a huge land mass known as Tierra Australis or Terra Incognita. Here, it was believed, there existed an Anti-Earth, a place where everything was upside down, back to front and inside out. In this mixed-up continent, which stretched as far as Antarctica, snow and rain fell upwards, the sun was black and the people were sixteen fingered beasts known as Antipodeans. Little surprise that Magellan did not stop to explore the territory, although after hearing the roar of a sea on a still farther coast, he surmised that if this was a huge continent, then what he was seeing was a series of islands at its crumbling apex.

Legend has it that from the deck of his flagship, the *Trinidad*, he traced mysterious plumes of smoke across the sky. Only eighteen of the original 290 men arrived back in Spain alive from this first, accursed circumnavigation of the globe, and when the survivors described what were almost certainly Indian signals to the Holy Roman Emperor, Charles V, he replied that there is no smoke without fire, and christened the land Tierra del Fuego – the Land of Fire.

In the popular imagination Magellan's sighting of the strange land of Tierra del Fuego was heralded as a vision of hell, with the distant fires being the pyres on which souls of the dead were incinerated, and the strait itself acting as nothing less than a Styx-like passage to the shores of Hades. Time and exploration were to reveal the truth about the land at the end of the world: the bitter tempests, the fearful williwaws and the swirling seas may have continued to conjure up a picture of the underworld, but only as a metaphor. Sitting between 52° and 56° south, this bleak outpost is a windswept complex of tightly knit channels and islands covering roughly the same area as Ireland. It is separated from the mainland of South America by the Straits of Magellan and dominated by one large island to the east and to the north, the Isla Grande. It is in Tierra del Fuego that the Andes finally tumble, under the pressure of successive glaciations and appalling weather conditions, into a cruel sea. As much as five metres of rain drench its western flank every year, yet in the eastern rain shadow of the colossal mountains annual precipitation can be as relatively low as half a metre. Here gales rip across sombre plains bringing an unpredictability to an otherwise gloomy but surprisingly mild climate. It is a land that inspired awe in its early European explorers, preserved in the names of much of its terrifying geography: Fury Bay and Fury Island, Useless Bay, Desolation Bay, Port Famine, Devil Island and, of course, it is here, at Cape Horn, that the Atlantic and Pacific meet like two Goliaths doing battle.

The sculpting hands of this southern wilderness were huge ice sheets which, acting on the volcanic tail of the Andes chain, advanced and retreated over millions of years. For almost nine-tenths of the last 800,000 years the landscape of Tierra del Fuego has been shaped by the action of massive glaciers nurtured in the high and wet peaks of the Andes in the western half of the archipelago. Powerful rivers of glacial meltwater poured down the steep south and western sides of the mountains into the Pacific, chiselling out fjords and carving complex and jagged islands. To the east, glacial meltwater cut the large basins, the impressive bays and the lakes that pockmark the region, glaciofluvial deposits pushed out the undulating ridges of morainic detritus and the vast plains of outwash gravel that stretch as far as the Atlantic. The sense of the majesty, ferocity and inhospitality of the area was reflected in the writings of the early European explorers. Francis Fletcher, the chaplain who accompanied Sir Francis Drake around the globe in 1577, was clearly in awe of the

> grisly sight of the cold & frozen mountains, reaching their heads yea the greatest part of their bodyes into the cold & frozen region, where the power of reflection of the Sonn never toucheth to dissolve the Ise & Snow: so that the Ise & Snow hang about the Spire of the Mountaine circulerwise as it were regions by degrees one above another & one Exceeding another in breadth in a wonderfull order as may apeare . . . from those hills distilled so sharpe a breath that it seemed to enter into the bowells of nature, to the great discomfort of the lives of our men.

In the sixteenth and seventeenth centuries Tierra del Fuego, with its forests of sourthern beech trees, its wild grassy plains and vast boggy moors, was virgin territory for the European explorers who ventured this far south, but it had long been inhabited by tribes of Fuegian Indians. A number of theories exist regarding the peopling of the archipelago, but the most likely begins back at the time of the initial crossing of the Bering Straits into Alaska, when humans set foot in the Americas for the first time. In the thousands of years that followed, there was a slow demographic movement across the continent as tribes of hunter-gatherers sought out amenable homes. The search, and intercommunal violence, drove groups across and down North and Central America then into the southern continent. Here, during the Ice Age, they found Patagonia and its Fuegian extension inhospitable and barren. About 14,000 years ago, when the ice began to retreat, enabling a southerly spread of flora and fauna, the wandering tribes followed. These were unsophisticated, primitive people, for whom a stretch of water as wide as the Straits of Magellan would have been an impenetrable frontier. Strong evidence shows, though, that as much as 11,000 years ago varying climatic conditions led to long periods when the straits were bridged by land exposed as water levels dropped. Groups of people could pass over onto northern Tierra del Fuego until around 8,000 years ago when warmer global conditions caused sea levels to shoot up. The straits were flooded and those who had crossed them were trapped – the first inhabitants of Tierra del Fuego.

At the very ends of the earth, the island fragmentation, scant resources and awful weather conditions split the native people into isolated groups, who over the intervening millennia were to become distinct, differentiated by technological advances such as canoes and weapons, diet and, most significantly, language. By the early nineteenth century it is estimated that there were 9,000 native Fuegians divided among four tribes, defined by geography, linguistics and mutual antipathy. They were the Selk'nam (alternatively known as the Ona or Oens-men), the fearsome peoples of the main island; the Alakaluf (or Kaweskar) of the western lands; the Haush (or Mannekenk) who lived on the south-eastern tip of Tierra del Fuego; and the Yamana.

Outsiders called them Yahgans, Yapoos or Tekeenicas, but Yamana was the word the canoe Indians of the Beagle Channel region used to describe and distinguish themselves from foreigners, whether

Fuegian or European. In simple translation it meant people and described a race of bronze-skinned Aborigines who dwelt at the extreme of Tierra del Fuego, survivors clinging to the southern-most edge of the habitable world. They lived a fragile existence in small nomadic groups across a territory south of a line mapped by the British from Desolation Bay in the west, to Spaniard Harbour in the east. The men averaged less than five foot two in height and the women, who were even shorter, tended towards obesity, brought on by long periods of inactivity and a diet of seal blubber. Nevertheless they were a powerful race of people, with strong-featured faces, straggling jet-black hair, stout bodies and tapering limbs.

At the heart of their territory was the Yahgashaga, the Yamana word for the channel of a mountain valley, which was known in English as the Murray Narrows. Here, in the waters and on the banks of the Beagle Channel and Ponsonby Sound, the Yamana fished, hunted and scoured the coastline for food. The prizes were birds' eggs, fish and beached whales, mussels and limpets and, in the thickly forested western flank of Navarin Island, berries and the occasional animal. On these shores the Yamana endured makeshift lives, in temporary wigwams with frames of branches and coverings of twigs, grass and leaves. They were built into small hollows that offered little protection against a clattering wind.

Despite the adverse climate and the paucity of their shelter, the Yamana wore little clothing. Hides could be obtained from otters, foxes, seals and occasionally the llama-like guanaco, but these rarely provided much more than an apron and a stole for the shoulders. In what little class distinction existed among these people, an impoverished Yamana — one who had failed to obtain a fur — would be called *api-tupan*, skin only.

There were few rules or laws to Yamana life, and while there is evidence that they were superstitious, it appears they had no concept of a Superior Being or God. According to their folklore, when the first settlers came to Tierra del Fuego the men had all the unpleasant tasks in life: making meals, building huts, minding the children and tending the fires. Women were free spirits who wore masks and practised witchcraft; they led the hunting and fishing, and came and went as they pleased. The men, however, were biding their time. Neglected and oppressed, they rose in rebellion, seized the terrifying masks and killed the women, sparing none but the baby girls. To these they repeated a mantra: their only duty in life was to serve. After years of indoctrination the men were able to relax, their dominance successfully established.

If this story had any basis of truth, though, it was not reflected in the day-to-day dealings of the indigenous people, for while men claimed some authority over their women, they also respected and deferred to their spouses – unlike the Selk'nam, who held women in strict submission. Nevertheless there was a well-defined sexual division of labour. Yamana women had great power and responsibility. They carried out the domestic chores – prepared the food and looked after the children – but they also controlled the canoes, did most of the paddling and caught mullet, smelt and conger eel with strands of their hair, cut and plaited into a fine line and baited with discarded fish tails. Such was their standing that the women kept all the fish they caught and decided with whom they would share it.

Men took greater responsibility for land-based activities: whereas the women were proficient swimmers, their husbands were barely able to float. They therefore took charge of hunting, collecting fuel, repairing canoes and tending fires.

The provision of food was the Yamana's most constant concern. They used slings, snares and spears of finely honed and barbed bone to hunt shags and steamer ducks; highly prized, vicious dogs hounded sea otters out of kelp jungles and chased guanacoes off the coast and into the sea, where they were easy meat for the waiting canoes. Against whales and seals they flung specially designed spears with heads connected to the shaft by leather thongs that would detach when they hit the target. The beleaguered creature would drag the shaft through the water, until its energy dissipated and the the pursuing Yamana overtook it and pounced. Mussels and limpets were scraped off the rocks at low tide. The Yamana's meat intake was supplemented by berries – *belacamaim* (rain berry), *shanamaim* (swamp berry), the bright red clumps of *sepisa* and the grape-like *goosh*.

Meat and blubber were often consumed raw, but sometimes cooked over the family fire, which was perhaps the most valuable element of all: for cooking, as a buttress against cold and, with smoke, a warning signal to others of visitors or danger. The upkeep of a fire was a great responsibility: once built it was rarely allowed to die and then only through carelessness. A fire was watched day and night, and if it went out, glowing embers had to be cadged off a neighbour.

The Yamana were nomads, who passed their days shifting from one location to another in bark canoes or large dug-outs. In these circumstances their fires posed a particular problem: how to keep them alight while at sea. Each canoe was fitted with a plinth of sand and turf upon which a small blaze could be placed and transported without posing any risk to the vessel (canoes were far from watertight anyway, so there was little danger and there was the added bonus of heat during freezing journeys). When a family pulled into a rocky cove for the night and was unable to beach the boat, the woman would paddle the canoe to the shore and the man would lift the fire off the plinth and carry it to land. Once the operation was completed the woman would row out – sometimes hundreds of metres – to a bed of sea kelp, where she would moor the boat with fronds then jump into the icy water to swim back to her family and the warmth of a glowing bonfire.

It was around these fires that the latest news would be spread by passing travellers: sightings of whale or seal; where the *alacush* (steamer duck) was nesting; and the death of distant relations. And it was here that the many tales of Yamana folklore were passed down to new generations: of how canoes were invented, and of the stone man that ate young girls. Amid tales of incest, infidelity, menstruation, violence and anthropomorphism, young children would have heard how the truculent Wasana had been turned into a mouse, of how the rockfish got its flat head, and stories of the wild men who lived in the woods or the monsters that dwelled in the lakes.

The story of Tierra del Fuego has been told many times by exploiters, explorers and settlers – in the chronicles and narratives of the likes of Magellan, Drake, de Sarmiento, van Noort, Anson, Fitzroy, Darwin and Bridges to name but a few. But the Fuegians are absent, save as freaks and novelties or nuisances and obstacles to the advance of the white man and his civilisation. To most of the Europeans and North Americans who ventured into these parts, they were a primitive and wretched group of savages, lawless atheists who lived in squalor – as Darwin was to say, they were 'the most abject and miserable creatures I anywhere beheld' – and thus undeserving of a history. Eventually, when they began to be heard, as in the accounts of the Ushuaia mission station, established in the 1870s, it was both too late and their listeners too plagued by Victorian values and prejudices. Most tragically, by the time historians, anthropologists, archaeologists and ethnographers with a different, more sympathetic approach to the native population arrived on the scene, there was virtually no one left to study. Wiped out in a genocide launched from the barrel of a gun and the spread of alien diseases, much of the history of the Fuegian peoples died with them.

At the time that this story begins, in May 1830, there would have been nothing extraordinary about a Yamana boy called Orundellico. Not long into his teens, he lived on the shores of the Yahgashaga in a loose grouping of father, mother, brothers, sisters and several uncles and their families. As winter was closing in and the skies blackened, news began to filter through of the activities of white men in their area. This would not have troubled Orundellico's people. Their relations with these strange visitors had largely been cordial and when, around 7 May, the white man eventually appeared, it caused little consternation. The arrival of the foreigner opened up opportunities for the bartering of dogs and dried fish, sparkling stones, metal objects, and the lengths of cloth they craved.

Alerted that a large boat bearing Europeans was plying the area, Orundellico's family boarded three canoes and went in chase. They carried fish and skins to trade. Alongside Orundellico were several men he would have known as his uncles. Each would have been anxious to intercept the foreigners before any other group could get to them. That way the spoils of trade were greater. It would, therefore, have been with some satisfaction that, within sight of the coast, they encountered the large boat alone and hailed it with their offerings, waving their arms and banging their chests with clenched fists. All seemed normal, the white men expressed interest, the fish were being examined, trinkets were being received and then something unexpected happened. The basic facts are clear: over the course of the next few minutes Orundellico was removed from his canoe and carried on board the foreigners' boat. A large button was thrown to an uncle as payment. Then the white men sailed away with Orundellico. What is less clear is the level of coercion, the degree of willingness on the Fuegians' part to trade one of their own and how far they understood the transaction. The only account we have of this moment is that of Robert FitzRoy, commander of the *Beagle*,

and in charge of the whale-boat in question. His report of 11
May 1830 reads:

> . . . we continued our route, but were stopped when in sight of
> the Narrows by three canoes full of natives, anxious for barter.
> We gave them a few beads and buttons, for some fish; and,
> without any previous intention, I told one of the boys in a canoe
> to come into our boat, and gave the man who was with him a
> large shining mother-of-pearl button. The boy got into my boat
> directly, and sat down. Seeing him and his friends seem quite
> contented, I pulled onwards, and, a light breeze springing up
> made sail. Thinking that this accidental occurrence might prove
> useful to the natives, as well as to ourselves, I determined to take
> advantage of it. The canoe, from which the boy came, paddled
> towards the shore . . .

There is no way of testing the account's reliability, no means of
knowing whether Orundellico was happy to climb into the large
boat, or if he was torn kicking and screaming from his uncle.
FitzRoy knew no Yamana, and the Fuegians could neither speak
nor understand English. It is highly unlikely that they understood
what was about to befall Orundellico — and had they known would
they really have sold him for a cast-off button? But however the
abduction was achieved, FitzRoy was only too aware that if,
indeed, he had ordered his men to seize the young boy and
hold him against his will on the boat, he had committed an act
of kidnap, for which he could expect to be severely reprimanded.
If this was so he was unlikely to admit to it in his official report.
In further elaboration and justification of his conduct, FitzRoy
wrote that his new captive 'seemed to be pleased at his change
and fancied he was going to kill guanaco, or *wānākäye* as he called
them — as they were to be found near that place'.

The boat sailed swiftly to a beach where camp was made for

the night. Orundellico must have soon realised that it was no guanaco hunt he was engaged in. Whether willingly traded by his parents, or seized by the English barterers, the consequence for him was the same: he had been abducted. And in that critical moment, when Orundellico passed from one boat into the other, he crossed an invisible frontier. In his new existence he would begin to shed his Fuegian identity – his clothes, his habits and his language. But first his captors took his name. As the Fuegian child was hauled into the boat, Orundellico became Jemmy Button.

Chapter 2

By May 1830 Robert FitzRoy had been with the *Beagle* for just eighteen months. His acquaintanceship with Tierra del Fuego was barely a year old. It had been a challenging, frustrating and at times exasperating experience. When he accepted command of the ship, his first captaincy, he was twenty-three years old, and he took on the job in tragic circumstances.

The two ships HMS *Adventure* and HMS *Beagle* had set out from England in 1826 charged with establishing accurate longitudes for the city of Monte Video and the cape of Santa Maria. When that was done they were to survey and map the southern coastline of South America, from Cape St Antonio on the Atlantic coast to the island of Chiloe on the Pacific. Even by the shortest route possible, through the Straits of Magellan, this would have been a survey covering more than 2,500 miles; going the long way around the Horn would have added another 500 miles. The task before the ships, however, included all of this plus plotting the complex coves, bays and channels of Tierra del Fuego and the labyrinthine western coast of Patagonia, many hundreds, if not thousands of miles extra.

The justification for the work was simple: in the days before the Panama Canal, the passage around Cape Horn and Tierra del Fuego constituted one of the world's most important shipping channels, and the major route around the Americas, but countless ships came to grief on these terrible shores — at the end of the nineteenth century up to nine ships a year foundered on Staten Island alone, at the eastern tip of the archipelago. This survey would make the route a far safer proposition. There was more to it, though. This was conquest and influence by mapping. The Royal Navy was the most deadly sea force on the globe, the world's self-appointed policeman: information was not only crucial to maintaining its position of power, but plotting the courses and coastlines of unexplored passages and territories gave it and its officers immense status and intensified prestige.

At the head of the expedition, on board the *Adventure*, was Captain Philip Parker King. The son of the first governor of New South Wales, he had already built a reputation surveying the coast of Australia, yet he was still only in his mid-thirties. His number two, in command of the *Beagle*, was Pringle Stokes, an industrious yet frail sailor whom King was keen to praise for his 'daring, skill and seamanship'. Between them they divided up the workload of the survey: while the *Adventure* concentrated on the area around Port Famine to the east of the Straits of Magellan, the *Beagle* headed off to the straits' western mouth to fix the positions of Cape Pillar and Cape Victory, then to survey the Evangelist Islands. Over the next months each of the ships was to have a number of escapades – including, on the *Beagle*'s part, the rescuing of a ship's crew stranded in Fury Bay – before reuniting and turning back to Rio de Janeiro to refit.

In March 1828 Stokes was instructed to survey Patagonia's Pacific coastline from the western mouth of the straits to the most northerly point of the Gulf of Penas. It proved a difficult and exhausting voyage, covering more than 400 miles and five degrees of latitude. Progress was slow: the weather played cruel tricks – intermingling vicious storms, hurricane squalls, known as williwaws, and prolonged periods of paralysing calm – one man died from 'inflammation of the bowels', sickness debilitated the crew, the ship's deck was constantly awash, rain quashed the men's spirit, days passed with no surveying possible, fatigue set in, and Stokes was overwhelmed by the monotony of the country he found himself consigned to.

Four months after she had left the *Adventure*, the *Beagle* rendezvoused with her sister ship at Port Famine. It was 27 July 1828, the ship was three days late, and there was already concern for her whereabouts. As she passed under the stern of the *Adventure*, Pringle Stokes's deputy, Lieutenant Skyring, shouted bad news from the *Beagle*'s deck — the captain was ill and confined to his cabin. King went on board and found Stokes in a state of near mental collapse brought on by extreme fatigue and demoralisation. 'He expressed himself much distressed by the hardships the officers and crew under him had suffered . . . I was alarmed at the desponding tone of his conversation.' Hoping for explanations, King read Stokes's journal and found the roots of his colleague's melancholia spelled out in its description of the journey he had just completed:

> Nothing could be more dreary than the scene around us. The lofty, bleak and barren heights that surround the inhospitable shores of this inlet were covered, even low down their sides, with dense clouds, upon which the fierce squalls that assailed us beat, without causing any change: they seemed as immovable as the mountains where they rested.
>
> Around us, and some of them distant no more than two thirds of a cable's length, were rocky islets, lashed by a tremendous surf; and as if to complete the dreariness and utter desolation of the scene, even birds seemed to shun its neighbourhood. The weather was that in which (as Thompson emphatically says) 'the soul of man dies in him'.

Over the next few days Stokes alternated between periods of

delirium and clarity. King wrote, 'Suspicions arose in my mind that all was not quite right with him . . .' They were well founded. On 1 August a boat slipped across from the *Beagle* with the news that Stokes had fallen into a deep depression and, alone in his cabin, had put a gun to his head and pulled the trigger. Efforts to save him were forlorn, and the surgeons found they could do little to save his life.

> During the delirium that ensued, and lasted four days, his mind wandered to many of the circumstances, and hairbreadth escapes of the *Beagle*'s cruize. The following three days he recovered so much as to be able to see me frequently and hopes were entertained by himself, but by no-one else, that he would recover. He then became gradually worse, and after lingering in most intense pain, expired on the morning of the 12th.

Thus it was that in November 1828, Robert FitzRoy, flag lieutenant on HMS *Ganges*, based on the Brazilian station, found himself appointed to the command of the *Beagle*, which had recently limped into Rio to report its sad news.

It was a difficult commission for the young man. The continuing work of the survey was demanding, he had been promoted above Stokes's expected successor, Skyring, and there was an air of gloom on the ship following the demise of the captain. One of FitzRoy's first tasks would be to restore morale and mend fences. Nevertheless, despite his youth, he was well qualified for the task ahead. A gold-medal graduate of Portsmouth naval college, his career had thundered along a fast track, aided by influential relatives, hard work and his undoubted seamanship. It had taken just nine years to rise from lowly midshipman to the command of his own ship. But he was a man of stark contrasts. His background was aristocratic. Grandson of the third Duke of

Grafton, he could trace a direct lineage back to Charles II and his mistress Barbara Villiers, as the name FitzRoy implies – the bastard son of a king. His politics were those of the highest, archest Tory: he was bigoted, morally confident, asserted the authority of the Church and the power of the landed interests. He was also convinced of the innate necessity of slavery.

FitzRoy was a strict disciplinarian, who trusted in firm but fair justice. He believed that punishments should always be in proportion to the offence committed. Many men endured floggings during the course of the two *Beagle* voyages under his command, but he prided himself that all understood the purpose of the punishment and its equity. If he was not loved by the men around him, he was certainly respected as a man of principle and a man of his word. Add this to his indefatigable energy, and his crew found in FitzRoy a man who led by example, a commander who never shirked his responsibility and who was always first to take on the hard work of keeping a ship afloat and on course.

None the less, if he exhibited all the confidence and self-assurance that went with his social standing, he also showed much of the fragility of temperament that went with it. Here was a man of volatility and unpredictability that in later life would descend into instability. 'Blue evils' was how he referred to the dark moods that endowed him with self-doubt, discontent and depression. In 1822 his uncle, the Foreign Secretary Lord Castlereagh, had slit his own throat, and this played heavily on FitzRoy's mind. Now he was headed for one of the world's bleaker outposts to take over the command of a man who had also taken his life. The result was unexpected vitriol, a whiplash temper that could tear a strip off the sturdiest of sailors. This capricious rage led to unease among his immediate coterie of officers, who not infrequently questioned his sanity. To gauge the mood of the man, they created little codes and warning signs.

Most notably officers coming on duty would discover the captain's humour by asking 'whether much hot coffee had been served out this morning'.

The *Beagle* and its new commander arrived back in the Straits of Magellan in April 1829, and later that month FitzRoy encountered his first Fuegians. They made an immediate impact with

> . . . their hair hanging down on all sides, like old thatch, and their skins of a reddish brown colour, smeared over with oil, and very dirty. Their features were bad, but peculiar; and if physiognomy can be trusted, indicated cunning, indolence, passive fortitude, deficient intellect, and want of energy. I observed that the forehead was very small and ill-shaped, the nose was long, narrow between the eyes and wide at the point; and the upper lip, long and protruding . . .

Aided by the newly purchased schooner HMS *Adelaide* – which had been bought in Rio to add versatility to the expedition – the *Beagle* was to pass through the Straits of Magellan and explore the western waters and sounds of Tierra del Fuego, before heading north to the island of Chiloe for a reunion with HMS *Adventure* and new instructions from Captain King. The nature of the geography, the tortuous inlets, shallow coasts and impassable channels, meant that the greater part of this work was done not from the decks of the ship, but from its more versatile cutter and whale-boat. Parties were despatched for days, sometimes weeks, with provisions and equipment to sound the coasts, plot their courses and report back. As a consequence they made contact with the native populations scattered across the archipelago.

In the 300 years since Magellan's voyage, there had been no fewer than eighty-one expeditions to Tierra del Fuego, with a mixed history of brutality and tolerance in European–Indian dealings. Drake's chaplain, Francis Fletcher, had described the archipelago as 'frequented by comely & harmless Poeple [*sic*] but naked men & women & children . . . gentile and familiar to strangers'. However, in November 1599 the Dutch Admiral Olivier van Noort took exception to a group of native men at Cape Nassau who shook their weapons in defiance at the passing ships. Van Noort pursued them to a cave, 'which they stubbornly defended to the last Man, dying every one of them upon the Spot. The Dutch, being got in, found their Wives and Children in that Dark Receptacle; and the Mothers, who expected nothing but present Death to themselves and their Infants, covered the little ones with their own Bodies, resolving to receive the first Stab themselves.' The slaughter was over, though, and the Dutch crew left with four boys and two girls as hostages.

Another Dutch explorer, Sebald de Weert, who was stranded in Tierra del Fuego for nine months in 1599, speculated that the Fuegians were descendants of a lost tribe of Welsh because, he wrote, 'penguin in the British (vulgarly called Welsh) signifies white Head, and these birds have white Heads, it has been argued from hence, that these Savages are descended from a Colony of Britons, supposed to be settled in America by Madoc, Prince of North Wales, about the year 1170.' De Weert kidnapped a young girl, aged about four years old, whom he took back to Amsterdam where she died.

The violence was not always one-sided, and shipwrecked sailors could rarely expect sympathy from the Indians they encountered. Where help was forthcoming it often brought unpleasant surprises. When the British ship the *Wager* was wrecked on the shores of Tierra del Fuego in 1741, survivors were helped for a while by a Fuegian they called Martin. One day Martin went with his wife to collect sea-eggs in their canoe. They filled a basket and on their return were welcomed by their young son who ran into the sea to greet them. Martin passed the boy the basket, but he dropped it. The Fuegian man picked up his son and flung him against the rocks. The boy died in a pool of blood. Martin walked off unconcerned. The stranded seamen looked on, incredulous.

Europeans rarely treated the Fuegians as anything more than savages; descriptions of early communication between the crew of the *Beagle* and the various Fuegian tribes leave one in no doubt as to the disgust that these 'civilised', educated and house-trained Europeans felt as they watched the locals feast on their favourite meal, whale blubber: '. . . The whole affair from first to last is most offensive to the sight; and the countenance of the carver is beyond description, for his eyes being directed to the blubber, squint shockingly and give his ugly face a hideous appearance.' The blubber was drawn through the teeth, sucked, warmed in the fire, cut into small pieces and swallowed without chewing.

Around the same time Captain King reported that, during an apparently friendly meeting, one of the Fuegians 'who seemed more than half an idiot, spit in my face; but as it was apparently not done angrily, and he was reproved by his companions, his uncourteous conduct was forgiven'. Little wonder that 'civilised' visitors dismissed the interests of the Fuegians and treated them with contempt. American sealers who worked the area frequently abused its inhabitants; on one occasion an American captain even amused himself by firing grapeshot at the Indians on the beach.

Yet, on the whole, the early meetings between FitzRoy's survey and the native people were banal, tedious and somewhat irritating. Native canoes would follow the British boats with scrawny fish and even scrawnier furs for barter. Their pursuit was persistent and their clamours of '*Yammerschooner*', which the British took to mean 'give me', were unrelenting and often deafening. Where they could, the Fuegians would climb on board the boats, pat the foreigners vigorously on their chests, and insist on trades for trinkets, glass beads, rags, cloth. Sometimes they stayed for hours.

Trades were sometimes amusing and informative, as when FitzRoy astonished the Indians with his watch, which he put to their ears: '. . . each came in his turn to hear it tick. I pointed to the watch and then to the sky; they shook their heads and suddenly looked so grave, that from their manner in this instance, and from what I could understand from their signs, I felt certain they had an idea of a Superior Being, although they have nothing like an image, and did not appear to us to have any form of worship.' The visits were also bewildering. When FitzRoy bought a dog for a pinch of tobacco, he then found its former owners demanding it back. The Fuegian man hurled abuse at the captain, calling on the wind to destroy him. The wife cried and scolded. The man's 'gestures were very expressive and animated. I was surprised to see so much feeling for a wretched little half-starved puppy, and made them happy by returning it to them without asking for the tobacco.' These sessions, which were characterised by petty theft on the part of the Fuegians, might also affront the prim sensibilities of the captain and his officers. Early on in the *Beagle's* expedition, Captain King had been offered a surprising barter. One Fuegian man was so desperate that, King commented, he 'at last offered his wife, as a bribe, who used all her fancied allurements to second his proposal . . . So highly did they esteem beads and buttons that a few of each would have purchased the canoe, his wife and children, their dogs and all the furniture.' Such inducements were not uncommon. On another occasion FitzRoy received a similar proposition:

One of the men having parted with all his disposable property, tendered one of his daughters, a fine girl of 14 or 15 years of age, for some mere trifle, and, being refused, became very pressing and importunate to close the bargain for the price that was jestingly offered; nor was it without difficulty that he was convinced we were not in earnest.

The frequent encounters, however, were becoming worrying. They were slowing down the work of the survey, and the constant vigilance needed to counter the incessant pilfering was wearisome. There was a more serious problem, too. Many of the early parleys between members of the *Beagle* crew and the Fuegians had been charged with an underlying tension, an implicit threat of violence on both sides. The British would claim that there was a purely defensive reflex to their suspicions that many of the natives they encountered wished them ill. Whenever crew members camped on land, they routinely placed sentinels around tents, organised musketry demonstrations and marked boundaries in the sand with rope, which Fuegians were forbidden to pass. Occasionally tempers flared. In June 1828, a Fuegian who persistently crossed a boundary line threw a boulder at one of the guards. He was manhandled back over the line by a marine 'upon which he ran to his canoe and took out several spears . . . but the appearance of two or three muskets brought him to his sense, and the spears were returned to the canoe; after which he became familiar and apparently friendly'.

By the end of 1829 the situation was more troublesome. Matters were coming to a head. Four days before Christmas, a party of sailors was sent out in a boat to map the eastern end of Landfall Island. The task should have taken a few days, but with the weather worsening, FitzRoy watched apprehensively from the ship's deck for their return. Christmas and Boxing Day passed. By now the small party would have run out of food. FitzRoy grew anxious. Just before noon on 27 December, the *Beagle*'s lookout spotted the missing mate and coxswain waving from the shore. A boat was sent to collect them. They were exhausted and weak, not having eaten for three days and having spent the previous afternoon and night walking to the ship. The rest of their party, they reported, were in a cove at the back of the island. They had tried to get back every day, but each attempt had been abandoned in the face of driving gales. The appalling weather had ruined their ammunition and tinder – not only had they been without food since Christmas Eve, they had also been unable to build a fire. On a more sinister note, when they had gone down to the seafront, twenty Fuegians had taken advantage of their enfeebled state to assault the coxswain and steal his clothes.

FitzRoy took the boat and collected the missing crew. His plans to take vengeance on the truculent Fuegians were thwarted by their disappearance from the scene. The weather, the work, the isolation were starting to play on the young captain. As if conditions were not harsh enough, he also had to contend with what he saw as the perpetual larceny of the native peoples, their constant jabbering, their untiring pursuit and now their assault on one of his men. His tolerance was slipping, his nerves beginning to fray.

Chapter 3

It was a whale-boat that caused FitzRoy to snap.

At the end of January 1830, the ship's master, its coxswain and a small crew departed on a three-day expedition to chart the waters around the western fringe of Tierra del Fuego.

Over the next few days the weather closed in, gales lashed the *Beagle* at anchor and the expedition's deadline for returning passed. Hour followed hour without any sign from them. A week went by and still no word. Then, at three in the morning of 5 February, FitzRoy was roused from his sleep. The missing coxswain and two men had reached the ship in a clumsy coracle-like basket, made from the boughs of a tree and the remnants of a canvas tent, lined with clay.

The whale-boat was gone, reported the coxswain, filched by Indians. The rest of the crew were safe in a cove on Cape Desolation, but they were cold and had no food, most of it having disappeared with the boat. Threatened by starvation and the local people, the master had ordered the construction of the frail vessel. Then with only a biscuit each to sustain them, the three men had paddled all day and all night until, with exhaustion threatening to overwhelm them, they had been alerted by the barking of the ship's dogs.

FitzRoy was furious. Part of him could not believe that the Fuegians would steal the boat. Part of him suspected a ruse, a cover-up for carelessness on the part of his own men. But most of him sensed that this was not so, that what they said was true. He was concerned at the threat to his men, and appalled by the loss of the boat. The *Beagle* had already lost one earlier in the voyage, and this one had been built while they had rested up in Chiloe. It was, FitzRoy claimed, a particularly fine piece of work. Things had come to a fine pass. What little tolerance he had left for the Fuegians was spent. One senses that, in this haze of fury, a moment of clarity was reached in the mind of the commander. Months of exasperation, of tolerating the intolerable, of pussy-footing around the natives were all blown away. He would rescue his men then deal appropriately with the offending savages.

A boat was prepared for immediate departure. A fortnight's victuals for eleven men, two tents and fresh dry clothing were loaded aboard and, in the face of intermittent rain and a fresh wind, the rescue party pushed off. Thus began a chase that lasted months, that became an obsession, a bizarre pursuit in a speck of a boat against a backdrop of towering, snow-capped mountains, vast plains and roaring seas. It would result in terror, bloodshed, kidnapping and hostage-taking. FitzRoy wanted his boat back and he wanted justice.

After a vigorous seven-hour pull, the boat reached the stranded men waiting on the shore of Cape Desolation. While they changed clothes and dug into their first meal in days, FitzRoy cross-questioned the master, Mr Murray, about the disappearance, and scrutinised the mooring where the boat had been secured. This was such an isolated site that the normal practice of keeping guard at night had been thought unnecessary. Clothes, theodolite and chronometer had been unloaded and stored in the tent, but mast, sails and food had been left where they lay in the boat's hold. At two o'clock in the morning one of the men had been sent to check how the boat was riding at her mooring. All was well, he reported. At four o'clock another man went, but the craft had gone. In panic, the men fanned the shoreline looking for it. They found no boat, but within a mile of their camp they discovered the remains of two wigwams and a fire with still-smouldering ashes. The next morning Murray had organised the construction of the coracle.

The interrogation over, the eleven men climbed into the rescue boat and headed for an island two miles away. Here they found their first clue: the boat's chopped-up mast near the remains of a recently occupied wigwam. That evening they passed a canoe with a man and 'the best-looking' Fuegian woman FitzRoy had seen, even though she 'was uncommonly fat, and did justice to a diet of limpets and muscles [sic]'. From them the commander learned that several canoes had recently passed to the north.

Two days later they pounced on canoes belonging to a native family, and found the lead line of the missing whale-boat. FitzRoy was overjoyed. 'This was a prize indeed,' he wrote in his *Narratives of the Voyage of HMS Adventure & Beagle*. One man was taken hostage and made to understand that for his own sake he must lead them to the Fuegians who had given him the line.

By early afternoon they had surprised a group of six women in canoes moored in a cove. With them were their children, a teenage boy and an old man. While they huddled in fear, FitzRoy conducted a search. There was a sail, an oar, an axe and a tool-bag all belonging to the boat.

> The women understood what we wanted, and made eager signs to us to explain to us where our boat was gone. I did not like to injure them, and only took away our own gear, and the young man, who came very readily, to show us where our boat was, and, with the man who brought us to the place, squatted down

in the boat apparently much pleased with some clothes and red caps, which were given to them.

The crew rowed for four hours before making camp on a beach. The two Fuegians were allowed to sleep by the fire, but under cover of the dark, they fled — with a couple of tarpaulin coats. FitzRoy was infuriated. After a hopeless search for the escaped prisoners, he pointed his hard-pressed crew back to the native settlement. As they approached the Fuegians ran. The sailors pursued, but their prey escaped. In an act of spite, the commander ordered the Fuegians' canoes to be torched.

Three more days were spent in aimless island hopping before they returned to this native settlement. FitzRoy had been away from the *Beagle* for eight days now, time was moving on, and on 12 February he raised the stakes. They arrived at the cove late in the day, but there was still time for planning. Half the party was given a rest, while the others tracked down the much-harassed Indians to a far-off bay. After they had scouted the land and counted the Fuegian numbers, they returned to their base 'and prepared for surprising the natives and making them prisoners. My wish was to surround them unawares, and take as many as possible, to be kept as hostages for the return of our boat, or else to make them show us where she was . . .'

The next day, each man armed himself with a pistol, a cutlass and a length of rope. They sailed nearer to the wigwams and crawled through the brush, encircling the native camp. Dogs barked, the sailors jumped up, the Indians bolted. Seaman Elsmore was the swiftest of the attacking party, but in attempting to leap a stream he stumbled and fell at the feet of three hidden Fuegians, who pinned him down and pummelled him with rocks. Sharp blows to the head rendered him insensible, a crunching blow to the temple shattered an eye. His head sank under the waters of the stream. From out of the bush came a flash and a bang. Murray had fired. The floundering sailor broke free. The wounded Fuegian staggered back, then threw a boulder with great power and accuracy, hitting Murray in the chest and snapping a powder horn that hung from his neck. Two more rocks forced sailors to dive for cover. The Fuegian hurled one last missile, then sank into the stream and died.

Fighting broke out along the bank, and several Fuegians escaped, but FitzRoy began to accumulate his hostages. He and the coxswain pinned down one woman who had the strength of a horse, and another, the oldest woman of the tribe, 'was so powerful, that two of the strongest men of our party could scarcely pull her out from under the bank of the stream'. At a muster on the beach, FitzRoy discovered that the dead Fuegian was one of the two who had escaped a few nights back; he also found that he had the missing coats back, and that he had eleven Indians – two men, three women and six children – in captivity. There were now twenty-two people on board the boat, and his project was becoming unwieldy. Next morning they began the journey back to the *Beagle*. The ship weighed anchor and with the Fuegians on board they sailed off towards Cape Castlereagh from where FitzRoy and Murray set off again, this time in two boats. They took with them three Fuegian guides – two women and a young man – hoping that they would feel that the lives of their loved ones, left on the *Beagle*, depended on their complicity. However, on making camp for the night FitzRoy found his concept of fidelity sorely tried.

He had fed his prisoners mussels, limpets and pork, and let the three curl up together by the warm glow of the fire. 'I would not tie them, neither did I think it necessary to keep an unusual watch,' the commander wrote, for he presumed that 'their children being left in our vessel was a security for the mothers far stronger than

rope or iron'. Instead he covered the captives with old blankets
and his own poncho, under which they were concealed. His was
first watch and, at midnight, as he stood staring out to sea, he
heard a rustling noise. He turned round, but the Fuegians slept
on. He crouched down to peer at his watch in the firelight. It was
just before midnight. There was another rustle. His dog jumped
up and barked. The blankets looked the same, but when he
investigated them he found them propped up by bushes. The
Fuegians were gone.

The crews split up over the course of the next couple of days
for a solemn and increasingly demoralised scout of Gilbert Island,
Adventure Sound and Thieves' Cove. By 22 February both boats
had arrived back at the *Beagle* only to find that the night before all
but three of the prisoners had jumped overboard and swum away.
All FitzRoy had now to show for his efforts was the wardship of
three abandoned children and no whale-boat. But he had learned
some important lessons:

> This cruise had also given me more insight into the real character
> of the Fuegians, than I had then acquired by other means. I
> became convinced that so long as we were ignorant of the
> Fuegian language, and the natives were equally ignorant of ours,
> we should never know much about them, or the interior of their
> country; nor would there be the slightest chance of their being
> raised one step above the low place which they then held in our
> estimation.

The decision was made to abandon the chase, to sail to a
sheltered harbour and make a new whale-boat. At the end of
the month they hove-to in Christmas Sound with the spectacular
promontory of York Minster – named after the cathedral – in the
background. While the new boat was under construction, Murray

was instructed to carry out more surveying, and to take with him the three children, whom he would leave with any Fuegians he came across. However, at the last minute, there was a change of plan. Only two of the children climbed into the departing boat. 'The third, who was about eight years old, was still with us,' wrote FitzRoy. 'She seemed to be so happy and healthy, that I determined to detain her as a hostage for the stolen boat, and try to teach her English.'

This girl, who FitzRoy said was as broad as she was high, had been named by the men Fuegia Basket – in honour of the wicker canoe built on Cape Desolation. Always referred to as a merry, happy child, she had become a favourite among the crew, 'a pet on the lower deck'. How much choice she really had in the matter of going home can only be speculated on; whether she knew what she had let herself in for is doubtful.

Less than twenty-four hours after Murray left, the *Beagle* was visited by more Fuegians anxious to climb on board. FitzRoy would have none of it: he was done with the annoyance, the theft and the noise. He instructed the mate to scare them off by firing a gun over their heads. The effect was but temporary, for although they retreated, FitzRoy knew that they did not comprehend the power of firearms and would be back before long. He therefore instructed the mate to chase them out of the vicinity. However, as he did so, he toyed with one more idea: the possibility of getting another Indian on board, another potential intermediary between Englishman and Fuegian. He joined the chase, and on catching up with the native canoes, pulled one alongside. Looking at the youngest man, he demanded that he get into the boat which, according to FitzRoy, he did 'quite unconcernedly and sat down, apparently contented and at his ease. The others said nothing, either to me or to him, but paddled out of the harbour as fast as they could.' This man, whom they called York Minster after the local geography, was a sullen brute, to British eyes, in his mid to late twenties, whose spirits only picked up when the now scrubbed and dressed Fuegia took it upon herself to console and amuse him. The new passenger had a mighty appetite and a habit of burying food for later in a secret cubby-hole. According to FitzRoy, 'as soon as he was well cleaned and clothed, and allowed to go about where he liked in the vessel, he became much more cheerful'.

The commander might have felt at this point that he now had his full complement of native captives for whatever purpose he was formulating. His intentions towards them were still unclear and the idea of taking either or both of them to England remained unvoiced. But if he had thought his specimen collecting was over he was only half correct. Less than a week after welcoming York Minster on board he was involved in a pitched battle with a party of Fuegians on cliffs near where the carpenter was building the new boat. Shots were fired and stones hurled. One of the crew went down, seriously wounded, and when it was all over FitzRoy found bottles of beer and a part of the missing whale-boat's gear in one Fuegian canoe. The commander had not found his boat yet, but the new discoveries revived his appetite one last time.

From the deck of the *Beagle*, smoke was spotted rising from nearby Whittlesbury Island. Next day he took a small raiding party across the sound and found a piece of King's white line near to some deserted wigwams. He sensed that his quarry was close and, looking from a hilltop vantage-point, he saw two canoes making a dash for it. The sailors scrambled into their boat and pushed off. Their superior numbers meant that within minutes they had caught hold of one canoe while the other escaped. A young man and a girl plunged into the sea and attempted to swim away. Fifteen minutes of fierce flailing followed as the man put up a mighty struggle in the water before being dragged, beaten and exhausted, onto the boat.

In contrast to the stout, rather squat appearance of both Fuegia Basket and York Minster, this new prisoner, who was called Boat Memory, was the best-looking Fuegian FitzRoy had ever seen, 'a very favourable specimen of the race'. As they rowed the captive back to the *Beagle*, FitzRoy reflected on his encounters with the locals and speculated that 'kindness towards these beings, and good treatment of them, is as yet useless . . . Until a mutual understanding can be established, moral fear is the only means by which they can be kept peaceable.' There was no hope for them, and no hope for relations with them, he concluded, while they could not understand European languages, European ways and European power.

Boat Memory was unsurprisingly frightened when they pulled him on board the *Beagle*. The bewilderment he must have felt at what was happening to him would not have been helped by the frosty welcome given him by York Minster, who refused either to talk or even acknowledge the presence of the new arrival. Boat was given a large meal then allowed to sleep it off.

As FitzRoy watched over him his thoughts crystallised. 'Three natives of Tierra del Fuego, better suited for the purpose of instruction, and for giving, as well as receiving information, could not, I think, have been found,' he noted in self-congratulation. Soon he was seeing confirmation of this in his Fuegians' behaviour. Within a few hours of his coming on board the ship, Boat Memory and the other two Fuegians were getting on famously.

This morning, having been well cleaned and dressed, 'Boat' appeared contented and easy; and being together, kept York and him in better spirits than they would probably otherwise have been, for they laughed, and tried to talk, by imitating whatever was said. Fuegia soon began to learn English, and to say several things very well. She laughed and talked with her countrymen incessantly.

Yet the constant presence of Fuegians on the *Beagle* highlighted FitzRoy's true ignorance of these people, and revealed the poverty of his earlier statements about communicating ideas, threats, directions and trades with them.

As March slipped away the ship moved slowly towards Cape Horn and the territories of eastern Tierra del Fuego. Only now, after a year spent charting the region, did he realise that there were more than superficial differences between the various groups of native peoples they were encountering. Early in April he observed a meeting between the captive natives on the ship and those who came to barter, and perceived distinctions that he found both distressing and shocking. 'I was sadly grieved at finding that some Fuegians who arrived were not of the same tribe as our captives, nor even spoke the same language. On the contrary, much enmity appeared to exist between them; though their colour, features and habits were similar.'

York Minster and Boat Memory's initial response to the native traders had been to snub them. Through signs and by pointing at their scars, they helped FitzRoy recognise that they had had many violent fights with these Indians and that there was no love lost between them. Then, however, York and Boat decided there was a better policy than the cold shoulder, and 'took delight in trying to cheat them out of things they offered to barter; and mocked their way of speaking and laughing; pointing at them and calling them "Yapoo, yapoo"'.

Fuegia's reaction was more violent. As soon as she saw them she went frantic with panic, and when one of the crew jibed that she was to be disembarked with the visitors, she burst into floods of tears and ran away screaming to hide below deck. FitzRoy's understanding of a homogeneous Fuegian tribe had been shattered.

As the *Beagle* continued its passage south and east, the days the Fuegians spent on board became weeks.

FitzRoy set the *Beagle* on a course that took it from Orange Bay, past West Cape and Cape Spencer to Horn Island where a party climbed the Cape, built an eight-foot-high pile of stones to commemorate the occasion, and drank the health of the King.

On the last day of the month the *Beagle* rounded the Horn in glorious weather. A big push was organised on the surveying front. Mr Murray was despatched to the Cape of Good Success with three weeks' provisions. Another boat departed to chart the eastern coasts of Nassau Bay and New Island, and FitzRoy took the opportunity to explore the filigree passages and channels of the interior. In particular he was interested in a fine, wide channel that Murray had reported seeing on an earlier sortie.

Over the course of the next week, FitzRoy penetrated the Murray Narrows and sailed along what was to become known as the Beagle Channel. His days were a mix of hard work and hot pursuit, as he tried to avoid the frequent demands of the local population. From his notes, he was clearly wearied by their unwarranted attentions. He ordered his men to paddle harder as Fuegian canoes came in sight and on a number of occasions abandoned camp to avoid them. Of one such incident he wrote, 'Just as we had moored the boat, kindled a fire, and pitched our tent a canoe came into the cove; another and another followed, until we were surrounded with natives. Knowing we must either drive them away by force, or be plagued with them all night, we at once packed up our things, and wished them good evening.'

However, his realisation that there were several tribes of Fuegians opened his eyes to other disparities. On 7 May, in the Murray Narrows area, he noted another encounter with a group of Indians: 'When we stopped to cook and eat our dinner, canoes came from all sides, bringing plenty of fish for barter. None of the natives had any arms, they seemed to be smaller in size and less disposed to be mischievous than the western race: their language sounded similar to that of the natives whom we saw in Orange Bay.' It was with observations of tribal differences playing in his mind that, four days later, FitzRoy found himself trading with three canoes of chattering old men and a young boy they called Orundellico. It was with these same thoughts in mind that his 'spontaneous' trade in flesh was contracted.

Chapter 4

FitzRoy's haul of Fuegians had reached four.

After camping ashore with his captors, the boy was taken to the *Beagle* for a humiliating meeting with the three other Fuegians, who mocked him and hurled abuse at him. He found the meeting distressing, but FitzRoy was amused: 'Our Fuegians were in high spirits, and the meeting between them and Jemmy Button was droll enough: they laughed at him, called him Yapoo, and told us to put more clothes on him directly.'

Jemmy was clothed and fed, and attempts were made to make him feel comfortable, but despite their best efforts these early days of captivity must have been difficult for the Yamana boy. He had already spent several days away from his family in the company of strange men, in strange clothes, with an incomprehensible language and odd habits. Now he was on board their ship and expected to live in close quarters not only with the foreigners but also with three mocking members of an enemy tribe.

Jemmy's presence brought a new clarity to FitzRoy's thinking. He decided to take the four to England, 'trusting that the ultimate benefits arising from their acquaintance with our habits and language, would make up for the temporary separation from their own country'. It had not been, he conceded, his original idea, but the captives' apparent happiness, their continuing good health and the discovery of the grave inter-tribal animosity among the Fuegians had alerted him not only to the potential advantages of the abduction – educating them and bringing them back to Tierra del Fuego to act as advocates of civilisation and interpreters for passing English ships – but also the inherent dangers of not doing so. He acknowledged that he could not

in common humanity, land them in Nassau Bay or near the Strait of Le Maire. Neither could I put the boy ashore again, when once to the eastward of Nassau Bay, without risking his life; hence I had only the alternative of beating to the westward, to land them in their own districts, which circumstances rendered impracticable, or that of taking them to England . . . In adopting the latter course I incurred a deep responsibility, but I was fully aware of what I was undertaking.

FitzRoy endeavoured to look after his prisoners. They were dressed in sailors' clothes and given high priority in the queue for fresh food, after the sick, but before the officers and crew. On 17 May, the four feasted on three gulls and two redbills that had been shot by the carpenter Mr May and George West. Two days later, after FitzRoy had bartered with Indians, they shared thirty-six fish with the sick. Over the next few months, Jemmy and his colleagues dined on a diet of penguin, albatross, goose, shag and bittern. FitzRoy stressed that his prisoners were happy and somehow, through signs and gesticulations, and the occasional bastardised Fuegian word, he made a promise that he would return them to their homes at a 'future time, with iron, tools, clothes, and knowledge which they might spread among their countrymen'. He believed this helped them come to terms with their fate and, as the *Beagle* continued a slow trawl up the eastern coastline of Tierra del Fuego, it appeared that the Fuegians were quick to adapt. In the picture that FitzRoy painted, all four helped the crew with the daily tasks of the ship and even 'took pains to walk properly, and get over the crouching posture of their countrymen'. While the ship had been at anchor in Good Success Bay, they had accompanied him ashore on several occasions, without making any attempt to escape, even taking an oar in the boat (though in truth they would have realised, more acutely than anybody else on board, the inadvisability of jumping ship in enemy territory). When Indians visited the passing *Beagle*, two of FitzRoy's prisoners were quick to grasp the nature of these encounters:

> It was amusing to witness York and Boat taking in these people, by their bargains. The same men who, two months back, would themselves have sold a number of fish for a bit of glass, were seen going about the decks collecting broken crockery-ware, or any trash, to exchange for the fish brought alongside by these 'Yapoos' as they called them, not one word of whose language did they appear to comprehend . . .

As they moved away from Tierra del Fuego and along the coast of mainland South America, a two-way learning process began. From the Fuegians the English built a rudimentary vocabulary, Yamana from Jemmy and Alakaluf from the other three. From their captors the Fuegians began to learn English. The Indians were gifted mimics, quickly picking up and copying all sorts of phrases, inflections and noises. From this FitzRoy had anticipated a natural bent for the spoken word, but quite soon he was forced to acknowledge that their progress was surprisingly slow.

Another surprise for the captain was the Fuegians' collective lack of curiosity, which to him marked them out as intellectually idle.

The *Beagle* headed for Monte Video and reached the river Plate on 22 June, anchoring beside the city six days later. Monte Video was busy and bustling, with a harbour full of ships from every corner of the world and a brass band that played boisterous tunes on the quayside. Along the harbour front there were government offices, customs houses and port authorities, and, further in, square blocks of flat-roofed houses along roughly paved but mathematically precise gridiron streets. There was a cathedral, a theatre, hotels and a prison, and on the Calle del 25 Mayo a lively market of stalls and shops dominated by French traders.

There was nothing in the Fuegians' background that could have prepared them for their first experience of a modern city – the agglomeration of people, the hubbub, the dirt and the smells. Yet FitzRoy noted that where he had expected them to be nonplussed they were undisturbed. 'The apparent astonishment and curiosity excited by what they saw, extraordinary to them as the whole scene must have been, were much less than I had anticipated; yet their conduct was interesting, and each day they became more communicative.' It was to be the same in seaports all the way to England:

> Animals, ships and boats seemed to engage the notice of our copper-coloured friends far more than human beings or houses. When anything excited their attention particularly they would appear at the time almost stupid and unobservant; but that they were not so in reality was shown by their eager chattering to one another at the first subsequent opportunity, and by the sensible remarks made by them a long time afterwards, when we fancied they had altogether forgotten unimportant occurrences which took place during the first few months of their sojourn among us. A large ox, with unusually long horns, excited their wonder remarkably; but in no instance was outward emotion noticed . . .

Yet there might have been other reasons for their behaviour. After the cold and wet of Tierra del Fuego, Monte Video days were heavy and oppressive. Perhaps they were struggling with the change of climate, or perhaps, even, they were more resilient than the British gave them credit for. Possibly they expressed surprise in ways alien to the European mind, or were frightened and kept their feelings to themselves. It is feasible too that everything that was happening to them was too much to take in: they were dumbstruck. They had no framework, and as yet no vocabulary, to explain what they were going through. The effect, perhaps, was numbing, disconcerting and too difficult to handle.

The *Beagle* had been due to rendezvous with the *Adventure* and *Adelaide* in Monte Video, but found that they had already left for Rio de Janeiro. FitzRoy cut short the time he had planned to spend in the city. Fuegia was put into the care of an expatriate English family living on shore, while the men spent their days with him. Concerned about the possibility of infection, FitzRoy organised vaccinations against smallpox for the Fuegians at a local hospital.

During this period of relative relaxation, FitzRoy learned more about his charges, and most startlingly, the details of their people's cannibalism. This was a nineteenth-century hobbyhorse for English adventurers. As they opened up new and unexplored territories, tales of man-eating natives added frisson and fear to their expeditions. Lurid stories of missionaries boiled in pots, or wild savages gnawing on the bones of dead seafarers, gripped the public imagination. FitzRoy's Fuegians did not disappoint. They told him that women ate the arms and men the legs of captured enemies, with the trunk and head being discarded in the sea, and of how, in times of famine, they consumed the old women of the tribe. This 'strange and diabolical atrocity' served only to confirm in his mind the prescience of his mission. 'I no longer hesitate to state my firm belief in the most debasing trait of their character . . .' he wrote in his narratives of the voyage.

Nevertheless, the slow journey to England, through Rio and on across the Atlantic to Plymouth, gave him time to draw a largely favourable impression of the Fuegians. Only York Minster proved something of a let-down:

> During the time that elapsed before we reached England, I had time to see much of my Fuegian companions; and daily became more interested about them as I attained a further acquaintance with their abilities and natural inclinations. Far very far indeed were three of the number from deserving to be called savages – even at this early period of their residence among civilized people – though the other, named York Minster, was certainly a displeasing specimen of uncivilized human nature.

PART TWO

Inglan

Chapter 5

An old ledger is stored deep in the vaults of the Public Records Office in Kew, the 1830 Muster Roll for the Royal Naval Hospital in Plymouth. Turn the browning leaves to a November page that lists the names of syphilitic sailors, and seamen with boils, gonorrhoea, ulcers and pneumonia, and at the top can be found the following scribbled entries:

	Person's Names	Quality	When Received	Quality of the disease or hurt
Commissioners Order	York Minster	Fuegian	7th Nov 1830	Vaccine
ditto	Boat Memory	ditto	ditto	Small Pox
ditto	Jemmy Button	ditto	ditto	Vaccine
ditto	Fuegia Basket	a little girl	ditto	Vaccine

The Fuegians were in hospital. It was an inauspicious start to FitzRoy's project.

The *Beagle* arrived at Plymouth in mid October 1830. It was reported in many local and national newspapers, some even picking up on the presence of the Fuegians. Under the headline INTERESTING VOYAGE OF DISCOVERY the *Morning Post* said:

The *Beagle* has brought to England four natives of Tierra del Fuego . . . taken prisoners, during the time that the *Beagle* was employed on the southwest coast of that country . . . [Captain Fitzroy's] intentions are to procure them a suitable education, and in the course of a few years, to send or take them back to their own country. Captain Fitzroy maintains them, and holds himself responsible for their comfort while absent from, and for their safe return to their own country. He hopes that by their assistance the condition of the savages inhabiting the Fuegian Archipelago may be in some measure improved, and that they may be rendered less hostile to strangers. At present they are the lowest of mankind, and, without a doubt, cannibals . . .

The final leg of the journey had been long and frustrating. The Fuegians had kept up their stoical lack of interest until the *Beagle* made a mail call at Falmouth, where for the first time they saw a steamship entering the harbour. The huge, fuming vessels, a recent development in industrial Britain, were described in one music-hall joke as 'a saw mill on one side, a grist mill on t'other, a blacksmith's shop in the middle, and down cellar there's a tarnation pot boiling all the time'. For Jemmy and his compatriots the steamer that roared across their path roaring was a terrifying monster. As it chugged close by the *Beagle* on the night of 13 October, all four Fuegians cowered. The *Beagle*'s crew tried to put their minds at ease, but FitzRoy understood their apprehension and later wrote,

I think that no one who remembers standing for the first time near a railway, and witnessing the rapid approach of a steam-engine, with its attached train of carriages, as it dashed along, smoking and snorting, will be surprised at the effect which a large steam ship passing at full speed near the *Beagle*, in a dark night, must have had on these ignorant, though rather intelligent barbarians.

As the *Beagle* approached the Royal Dockyard at Devonport

the sight that greeted the Fuegians was dramatic. In the harbour lounged the might of British sea power: out-of-service men-of-war moored by immense chains, yardarms, masts and rigging stripped, painted yellow and protected against the elements by temporary roofs. On the quayside sat the convict hulk *Captivity*, with 400 prisoners awaiting transportation. In a former incarnation it had been called HMS *Bellerophon* and had fought at the battles of the Nile and Trafalgar. It had been the site of Napoleon's surrender and had brought the defeated French emperor to Plymouth, where he had been greeted by crowds of jeering locals. Above it all, rising over the eastern bank of the Hamoaze, spread the town.

Images of busy, crowded dockyards, piles of wood and iron, the smells of pitch, tar, varnish, paint, and deafening noise inform our received picture of the ports of the nineteenth century, but Devonport was not like that: it had an ordered Britishness that disguised the flurry of activity that went with the constant arrival of new ships. One journalist of the day described himself as 'pleasantly undeceived' on entering the highly organised world.

> At first he does not see even the ships in dock, nor the storehouses, and unless some extraordinary operation, such as that of raising a vessel, is going on, he does not even hear, or scarcely hears, the sound of a hammer. The broad avenue from the Dockyard gates has not a chip on its surface – it is as clean as the indefatigable broom can make it . . . An air of serenity, of order, of cleanliness, pervades the whole spot.

The Fuegians were whisked away into the town to 'comfortable, airy lodgings' where they spent the next two days.

Devonport was a populous city of around 35,000 inhabitants, with straight, wide, rather monotonous streets paved with variegated marble. It had expanded rapidly in size, boosted in recent times by the defensive and offensive needs of the Napoleonic wars. Until 1824 it had been called Plymouth Dock, but amid great ceremony and the erection of an 124-foot Doric column the town adopted its new name.

If its appearance was lacklustre it nevertheless had a number of buildings that demonstrated the English trait of looting the world for architectural styles. Here on these mundane streets were a Calvinist meeting house, built in the 'fantastic Hindoo style', a library in the Egyptian fashion and a town hall with a Doric portico and four fluted columns.

How much Jemmy, Fuegia, York and Boat saw of this is not recorded. They travelled at night and once in their lodgings it is almost certain that they remained inside as far as possible. As a large seaport Devonport was an entrance point for disease and FitzRoy was 'anxious to protect the Fuegians, as far as possible, from the contagion of any of those disorders, sometimes prevalent, and which unhappily have so often proved fatal to the aboriginal natives of distant countries when brought to Europe'. On their first morning in town he took them for another vaccination against smallpox.

On their second day in England the Fuegians were removed to Castle Farm just outside Plymouth, where they would be able to 'enjoy more freedom and fresh air', and where, the *Hampshire Telegraph and Sussex Chronicle* explained, they seemed 'to be satisfied with their present situation. As soon as they are sufficiently acquainted with the language, and familiarized with the manners of this country, they will begin a course of education adapted to their future residence in their native country.'

Happy that the four were being well cared for, under the supervision of the *Beagle*'s coxswain James Bennet, FitzRoy returned to the ship and sailed on, calling at Portsmouth then berthing at Woolwich where the *Beagle* was paid off.

He had many arrangements to make. There was all the business normally attendant on decommissioning a ship that had been away for five years, there was the social whirl in which a young man, long absent from home, liked to indulge, and he had also to sort out the lives of the Fuegians.

Back in September, as the *Beagle* approached Britain, he had written to Philip Parker King on the *Adventure*, reminding him of his human cargo and pointing out that he had maintained them entirely at his own expense. 'I have now to request,' he wrote, 'that, as senior officer of the Expedition, you will consider of the possibility of some public advantage being derived from this circumstances; and of the propriety of offering them, with that view, to his Majesty's Government.'

FitzRoy had known that Captain King would forward the letter to the Admiralty. He had therefore detailed the ages of each Fuegian and explained why they were on board, emphasising all the time their happiness and contentment. He concluded,

> Should not his Majesty's Government direct otherwise, I shall procure for these people a suitable education, and, after two or three years, shall take them back to their country, with as large a stock as I can collect of those articles most useful to them, and most likely to improve the condition of their countrymen, who are now scarcely superior to the brute creation.

On 19 October John Barrow at the Admiralty responded:

> I am commanded to acquaint you that their Lordships will not interfere with Commander Fitz-Roy's personal superintendence of, or benevolent intentions towards these four people, but they will afford him any facilities towards maintaining and educating them in England, and will give them a passage home again.

In other words the Admiralty did not object to the presence of the Fuegians and FitzRoy could do what he wanted with them, but the commander was in no doubt that he would receive little assistance. He sought help elsewhere, turning first to the powerful Church Missionary Society. Although the Society's focus was mainly in Africa they had a long-running, though not necessarily successful, track record of bringing native peoples to England. As far back as 1816 one of their first African converts in Sierra Leone had been brought to London. When he died suddenly in Church Missionary House he was judged by the Society 'the first ripe ear gathered into the heavenly garner from the Society's missions'.

FitzRoy tried an indirect approach, through the vicar of Plymstock. 'I am very anxious to place the two young men, whom I have brought from Tierra del Fuego, with some person or persons who would instruct them, and enlighten their minds as much as might be practicable during the two or three years they will probably pass in England,' he told the Reverend J.L. Harris on 30 October. Would he, asked FitzRoy, write to the Church Missionary Society and ask them to provide an education for York Minster and Boat Memory? 'My principal object is to enable them to act as interpreters and to give to their countrymen some of the new ideas they will experience while under the care of a sensible person.' His intentions at this point for Jemmy and Fuegia are not recorded.

The next day Mr Harris posted a letter to the Society explaining that his friend Robert FitzRoy had taken four Fuegians prisoner and that he 'has discovered they are Cannibals but now they show a ready appetite for Vegetables. I should be glad of the receipt of your advice as to the most desirable institution to place these in and as to the expense of so doing . . .'

The Society considered the matter on 16 November. The minute of the discussion records,

54

Resolved, That Mr Harris be informed that the Committee do not conceive it to be within the province of this Society to take charge of the Individuals mentioned in this Letter.

FitzRoy's plans were faltering: he was not receiving the help he had expected. However, by the time he received the Society's response he had much bigger problems on his hands.

Smallpox had been the scourge of mankind since 10,000 BC. It had wiped out millions of people across Europe and the so-called New World and brought three empires – Roman, Aztec and Inca – to their knees. As that other great killer, bubonic plague, disappeared from Europe in the seventeenth century, smallpox became the most feared disease. Cesspits of cities, with squalid, filthy streets, festered and propagated vicious epidemics. At the end of the eighteenth century 400,000 people died of smallpox every year in Europe, driven to their graves by a virus that debilitated its victims with fever, nausea and a pus-filled rash. Those who survived were scarred by the lesions the disease left.

But battle was being waged against it. After learning that Gloucestershire milkmaids were said to be immune to smallpox, Edward Jenner took a sample of the mild disease cowpox from a milkmaid and injected it into the arm of a boy called James Phipps. When Jenner subsequently exposed Phipps to smallpox, he was found to be immune to it. Vaccination – from the Latin *vacca* for cow – had proved successful and the tide was turning.

Within two years of Jenner publishing his findings in 1798, over 100,000 people had been vaccinated and the new cure had spread across Europe and was rapidly reaching all corners of the globe. In 1803 Charles IV of Spain sponsored the world's first mass overseas vaccination campaign when his country's Expedición de la Vacuna set sail for Spanish outposts in the Americas and Asia. Twenty-two orphan children were taken on the three-year voyage and each was vaccinated in sequence to keep the vaccine alive. In 1805 Napoleon ordered his whole army to be vaccinated and followed it up a year later with the full-scale vaccination of the French population. The procedure was made compulsory in Bavaria in 1807, and in Denmark three years later.

By 1830 the disease, if not eradicated, was in retreat. The National Vaccine Establishment reported in April 1831, 'We have furnished the means of protection to the Army and Navy, to every county in England and Scotland, to Ireland, to the Colonies, and moreover to several of the capitals of Europe; and nearly 12,000 of the poor of the Metropolis and its immediate neighbourhood have been vaccinated in the course of last year.'

But in early November 1830, Robert FitzRoy received 'sad intelligence' from Devonport: Boat Memory had contracted the disease and was in a critical condition. Back in Plymouth FitzRoy sought the advice of Navy physicians, who advised that all four Fuegians should be placed in the Royal Naval Hospital's smallpox ward as soon as possible. Here they would be in the care of the renowned doctor David Dickson, superintended by Sir James Gordon.

FitzRoy returned to London where he wrote to the First Secretary of the Admiralty, Sir John Croker, requesting *post facto* permission for Jemmy, Boat, York and Fuegia to be admitted into the hospital, 'until this dangerous period of their existence is passed'. In addition, he asked that the *Beagle*'s coxswain James Bennet be allowed to attend to them, 'as he partly understands their language and has always had the care of them'.

Consent was immediately forthcoming, but it was too late. The next day, on 11 November, FitzRoy received the following letter from Dr Dickson:

Dear Sir

I am sorry to inform you that Boat Memory died this afternoon in the eruptive stage of . . . Smallpox. He was perfectly covered with the eruption; but the pustules did not advance to maturation as they should have done and as the breathing was much impeded, I had little, or no expectation of his recovery . . . he has been saved much suffering — and those about him from attending a loathsome Disease.

In the boy Button the appearance of the vaccine bacilli is satisfactory — and as the others have been revaccinated . . . I am in hope they will be saved from the fate of their countryman

Yours faithfully

D.H. Dickson

Boat's death was a severe blow for FitzRoy and he felt, quite rightly, personally implicated. He informed the Admiralty at once, blaming the 'badness of the Vaccine Virus' and claiming that the contagion had hit too hard and too early for the final shot to take effect.

By the time Boat died, the Fuegians had been vaccinated four times, but this did not make FitzRoy immune to criticism. On 20 November the *Royal Devonport Telegraph* commented:

TERRA DEL FUEGO — The four natives of this island, who were brought home by Captain Fitzroy, in his Majesty's ship *Beagle*, have taken the small pox, and are at present in the Naval Hospital. One of them (named Boatwilliam by the crew of the *Beagle*) has fallen a victim to the disease in the course of the past week, but the others are expected to recover. — It is to be regretted that the propriety of vaccination did not suggest itself to Captain Fitzroy, nor to the Surgeon of his ship, as the generally fatal effects of this disorder to foreigners might have frustrated the praiseworthy intentions of the Captain in bringing them to England.

The news took longer to reach the national press but on 7 December the *Morning Advertiser* informed its readers that it understood that the Fuegians 'were vaccinated previously to their sailing for England, but it is supposed they did not properly imbibe the virus'.

That FitzRoy felt the loss of Boat is beyond doubt. He commented in his narratives that the young man was a great personal favourite with a 'good disposition, very good abilities, and though born a savage, had a pleasing, intelligent appearance. He was quite an exception to the general character of the Fuegians, having good features and a well proportioned frame.'

Boat was buried on 18 November in a lonely little ceremony near Plymouth. The other three remained in hospital until the end of the month. In what now seems a remarkable act of risk-taking, especially in the context of her compatriot's death, Fuegia Basket was removed from the hospital and taken to the home of Dr Dickson where his children had measles. In Dickson's opinion it was a chance to expose Fuegia to the disease and strengthen her immune system. So, in the words of FitzRoy 'he prepared her for it, and then took her into his house, among his own children; where she had a very favourable attack, and recovered thoroughly'.

The effect of Boat's death on the other three Fuegians is not recorded. That such a popular character should die in what were, for them, confusing and tragic circumstances must have shocked and upset them, if only because they would miss his gregarious presence. They might have been afraid of contracting the disease themselves or because they did not understand the cause of his death: they would have seen a strapping man transformed into a feverish wreck.

Yet their most likely reaction to Boat's demise was self-absorption and no visible response. Fuegians of all tribes had a strange relationship with death. It made them sad and intro-spective. When visitors came to Fuegian settlements after a long time away, it was considered impolite to ask after missing people in case they had died in the intervening period, for this would force those present to explain the absence. When a Yamana died his or her body was burned on a small pyre and the encampment abandoned for good. When stories of life and death were told around Fuegian fires, Indians of all ages would become quiet, weep, and even leave for their wigwams mid-story. It was an attitude that was dismissed by the British as brusque and brutish, a sign of a Fuegian's lack of emotional depth and understanding of spirituality.

Whatever their feelings, though, they were now inmates of the Royal Naval Hospital. It was not a prison, but it was not the English countryside either. Its ten buildings, which looked down on an exercise quad, could hold up to 1,200 patients. It was peace-time, so it is doubtful that many men were there. Still, FitzRoy would have been aware that hospitals not only cure disease but propagate it. As soon as he could, he had to get them out of there and move his plan on to the next stage – their education and civilisation.

Chapter 6

The three survivors spent a miserable twenty-four days in the naval hospital before Dr Dickson felt confident enough to give them the all-clear. It was time enough for FitzRoy to pick up the tattered pieces of his grand benevolent plan.

If the Church Missionary Society had not been overly helpful, its energetic lay secretary, Dandeson Coates, nevertheless tapped into his extensive personal network of contacts and pointed FitzRoy in the direction of the Reverend Joseph Wigram, secretary of the National Society for Providing Education of the Poor in the Principles of the Established Church. Wigram was an influential man, not just through his position — he later became the Bishop of Rochester — but also by virtue of being the son of one of the country's most powerful merchants. He introduced FitzRoy to William Wilson, the vicar of Walthamstow, Wigram's home village, and founder of the oldest church school in the country. Wilson was only too happy to help. FitzRoy would remain responsible for the Fuegians and pay handsomely for their education, but the burden of their day-to-day care would be shouldered by the schoolmaster Mr Jenkins and his wife. FitzRoy noted that Wilson

at once relieved my mind from a load of uncertainty and anxiety, by saying that they should be received into his parish, and that he would talk to the master of the Infant School about taking them into his house, as boarders and pupils. In a short time it was arranged that the schoolmaster should receive, and take entire charge of them, while they remained in England, and should be paid by me for their board and lodging, for his own trouble, and for all contingent expenses.

Mr Wilson proposed to keep a watchful eye over them himself and give advice from time to time to their guardian and instructor . . .

At the beginning of December 1830, Jemmy, York and Fuegia were discharged from hospital and loaded into a London-bound stage-coach, with James Bennet and the *Beagle*'s old master Mr Murray. Six coaches left Devonport every day for London, a journey of between twenty-three and thirty hours. However, the coach that they took would have been a privately hired one, to avoid drawing attention to themselves, but it would have followed a well-established route across the West Country to Piccadilly, where it would have pulled in at either the Black Bear or the Old White Horse Cellars – around the corner from FitzRoy's Stratton Street home.

Most frequent travellers found the vehicles bumpy and uncomfortable, but the Fuegians, Murray reported, 'seemed to enjoy their journey in the coach, and were very much struck by the repeated changing of horses'.

If the physical landscape that the Fuegians' stage-coach traversed was well established, then the political, social and cultural landscapes of the country they crossed were far less certain. Indeed, as agitation for political reform spilled onto the streets and mixed with unprecedented social tension, Britain was nearer to revolution now than at any time in her history.

The industrial revolution had transformed British society.

Although the landscape was not yet dominated by gargantuan mills and smoke-spewing chimneys — except perhaps in some of the textile areas of Lancashire — swelling urbanisation was having an incalculable effect on it. Britain's population in 1801 had been 10.6 million, double what it had been a century before. By 1831 it had reached 16.6 million. In 1750 only London and Edinburgh had had more than 50,000 inhabitants. By 1851 there were 29 cities of this size. Between 1760 and 1830 the population of Manchester grew from just 17,000 to 180,000. And in 1831 London supported more than 1,700,000 inhabitants.

The cities were crucibles of inequality and discontent. While the industrial revolution feathered the beds of the upper classes and created a whole new thrusting middle class, it condemned the labouring masses to misery and degradation on a hitherto unimaginable scale. In *Great Expectations*, when Pip comes up from the countryside for the first time, he comments, 'We Britons had at that time particularly settled that it was treasonable to doubt our having and our being the best of everything: otherwise, while I was scared by the immensity of London, I think I might have had some faint doubts whether it was not rather ugly, crooked, narrow and dirty.'

These were mean streets of pestilence, pollution and disease. Cholera and typhoid thrived in the cities of the 1830s, crime flourished, and the urban poor crowded into some of the most wretched slum housing ever created. Throughout the whole of the decade one in every ten people was a pauper.

Little surprise, then, that the streets seethed with agitation under the influence of political unions, radical organisations, embryonic socialist movements, anarchic gangs and a disaffected proletariat. Pressure for reform, and in particular electoral reform, was coming to a head in the autumn of 1830, sponsored as much by the aspirations of the middle class as by the rage of the mob. The

Great Reform Bill, which would address some of the problems of voting rights and the indecency of rotten boroughs, was before Parliament and resisted by both the Prime Minister, who was the Duke of Wellington, and the House of Lords.

Debates in Parliament acted as a catalyst for the rabble-rousers on the streets. In the first week of November the new King, William IV, and his wife Adelaide, abandoned plans to visit the City of London for fear that they would be assassinated.

On 9 November, the day that Boat Memory lay dying in Plymouth, the *Morning Advertiser* reported, under the headline 'ALARMING STATE OF THE METROPOLIS', that during the day gangs of pickpockets had run amok in the City and Westminster only to be replaced in the early evening by throngs of people who blocked avenues leading to the Palace of Westminster, many of whom assailed the carriage carrying the soon to be Prime Minister, Sir Robert Peel.

As dusk approached, the report went on, shops closed down to avoid looting and then, as darkness fell, crowds of up to 10,000, many waving tricolour flags, fought with police around Parliament, in the Strand and in Charing Cross Road. Pitched battles with stave-wielding policemen around Temple Bar were described as 'frightful: the combatants, amounting to hundreds, were engaged hand to hand, and man to man, and now and then a paving stone might be seen flying in the air . . . The blood flowed in streams from many a luckless head.' In one mêlée, the reporter said, several lives were lost.

The conflagrations did not all take place in the cities. In 1830 the countryside from Kent to Wiltshire was battered by the mythical hordes of Captain Swing. Threshing machines were destroyed, hayricks and farm buildings burned to the ground, and squadrons of dragoons sent to quell minor uprisings. Hundreds were arrested, but the man who signed the letters forewarning of attacks or taking credit for them – Captain Swing himself – was never apprehended.

This, then, was civilisation: tumultuous towns, impoverished masses and a rich élite. It is not without some irony for this story that when the French political philosopher Alexis de Tocqueville visited Manchester he wrote, 'Civilisation works its miracles and civilised man is turned back almost into a savage.'

The British people had their own idea of what constituted a savage. Foreign explorers, warriors and merchants had been bringing home exotic trophies ever since they had first ventured from their home shores. Their reasons for doing so were manifold, ranging from enslavement through scientific, philosophical and religious motives, to public amusement and commercial exploitation.

Human 'freaks' and animals were treated with equal vigour, as fairground showmen and London theatre promoters sought to make a financial killing. In 1636 Sir Edmund Verney told his son,

A merchant of lundon wrote to a factor of his beyoand sea, desired him by the next shipp to send him 2 or 3 Apes; he forgot the r, and then it was 203 Apes. His factor has sent him fower scoare, and sayes hee shall have the rest by the next shipp, conceiving the merchant had sent for two hundred and three apes; if yorself or frends will buy any to breede on, you could never have had such a chance as now.

Five decades later a rhinoceros that had been brought from Africa was giving two-shilling rides at the Belle Sauvage Inn on Ludgate Hill, and earning for its owner a massive £15 a day.

So it was with human specimens. In 1501 three Eskimos were landed at Bristol, and in later years Henry VIII had a private viewing of a Brazilian chieftain. Once the North American continent was opened up, a succession of indigenous visitors included three Cherokee chiefs, who in 1762 were overwhelmed by a crowd of 10,000 sightseers in Vauxhall Gardens.

In the years that followed, the pace of the living exhibitions arriving in the country picked up: Sartje the Hottentot Venus displayed herself in Piccadilly; Tono Maria, the Venus of South America, appeared in Bond Street; a troupe of Laplanders with reindeer attracted 58,000 spectators. As the empire expanded, so did the variety of exhibits: Eskimos, Zulus, Bushmen, Aborigines all graced the stage of nineteenth-century Britain.

They came, though, in a period when the public's attitude had undergone a cynical change. The century before, Britain had been influenced by the French philosophers, like Rousseau, who had extolled the virtue of the Noble Savage — the innocent native, free from original sin, the noble naïveté from which civilisation had sprouted. Now there was a gloating, preening approach to the imported 'savages', an attitude that said, 'Look how far we have come from these basest of instincts.'

Science stepped in too. Systematic research — the measuring of heads and brains and limbs, the development of ethnology and anthropology — was conducted on specimens brought from abroad. There can be no doubt that this was a period of greatly increased scientific understanding and knowledge, and the showmen now claimed that their exhibitions were in the interests of scientific advancement.

It is important to remember, too, that in 1830 when Jemmy and his compatriots arrived in Britain slavery still existed. There had been a ferocious clamour for its abolition, and in 1806 the slave trade was made illegal, but slavery itself survived legally in British colonies for a further three years.

FitzRoy, of course, as a man of reasonable wealth and aristo-cratic background, had no need of the commercial gains to be made from his Fuegian captives. There would be no degrading public exhibitions for the surviving three and no attempt to make money from them. His objectives were, if naïve, certainly logical. He would have them educated in 'English, and the plainer truths of Christianity, as the first objective; and the use of common tools, a slight acquaintance with husbandry, gardening and mechanism, as the second'. This would allow them to return to their homeland and educate their fellow countrymen. The nomadic lifestyle would give way to agricultural settlements, the Fuegians would become Christians and open to business with traders from Britain. As a bonus they would act with kindness towards the many sailors shipwrecked on the shores of Tierra del Fuego, who were usually butchered by Indians.

There were precedents for FitzRoy's actions. We have already seen the fate of the first convert from Sierra Leone. If FitzRoy had been reading the *Morning Advertiser* on 29 November, just days before the Fuegians were due to join him, he would have seen a court report from the Mansion House that might have served as a warning. Under the headline 'A REVOLTED MISSIONARY', it related the case of Pierre, another young man from Sierra Leone. Pierre had been brought to England years ago by a Quaker woman. He had turned out to be a good scholar and a likeable person, and the Society of Friends had funded a proper school education for him. Then he was sent back to his homeland to preach Christian values to his countrymen. Unfortunately he 'underwent a very sudden and important change, and rather than attending to the duties of his situation, he took a fancy to rum drinking . . .'. He gave up preaching and became a sailor. Pierre went before the mast to China, but the ready supply of liquor was too much temptation for him. On a voyage to England he tried to visit his old benefactors, but 'happened, on his way to the Quakers, to meet a messmate, and to get drunk, so that when he made his appearance, it was some time before he was recognised as the coloured Quaker'. His patrons forgave him, thinking that 'kindness and advice might still reclaim him'. They gave him more money, but he got drunk again. Finally he was charged before the Lord Mayor, who severely admonished him.

In conclusion Pierre announced 'he would go before the mast, or do anything of that kind with all his heart, but he did not like preaching and flogging mixed. – (Laughter). There was a ship in which he could get employment at once. This was agreed to and the Missionary departed.'

The Fuegians found FitzRoy waiting for them at the coach office in Piccadilly. He had had his own personal carriage prepared and whisked them away through the West End and onwards to the East and Walthamstow. This vision they caught of the capital city was fleeting, but the city's gigantic size, its noise and its bustle, were startling: FitzRoy comments that they 'seemed bewildered by the multitude of new objects'. Outside Charing Cross, York Minster gave a shocking cry: "Look!" he said, fixing his eyes on the lion upon Northumberland House, which he certainly thought alive, and walking there. I never saw him show such sudden emotion at any other time.'

The journey to Walthamstow was otherwise brief and uneventful, and when they arrived at the house of the new schoolmaster there was relief all around: the Fuegians loved their new rooms, and the schoolmaster and wife were 'pleased to find the future inmates of their house very well disposed, quiet, and cleanly people; instead of fierce and dirty savages'.

Chapter 7

'Walthamstow Gtr London
Wilcumestowe c. 1075, Wilcumestou 1086
"Place where guests are welcome"
or "holy place of a woman called Wilcume"'
Dictionary of English Place Names

Today Walthamstow is a thirty-minute trip by Underground from the West End of London. Exit up the ramp and a few yards on there's a big, modern pub – the Goose and Granite. If you turn left here, to run the gauntlet of estate agents, kebab shops and McDonald's, you will reach the high street, with its lengthy market lined with greasy-spoon cafés, charity bargain stores, KFC, Pizza Hut and tandoori restaurants. Everywhere the debris of fast food and market commerce is trodden underfoot, the smell of burning fat is in the air and you will hear raised voices and car radios. This is the hub of Walthamstow, a bustling, slightly grimy working-class suburb of London's Essex periphery.

Or take a different route from the station. Cross Hoe Street into St Mary's Road, walk up this quiet little avenue, past Hair Routes Unisex Salon and Pete's Fish Bar and Indian Takeaway, past neat terraced houses with grey wheelie-bins in their front gardens and eventually you will come to the tight little alleyway of Church Path. But this is more than an alleyway: it is a thread to the past, for as you walk along it you are transported back to 1830. On the left are small ivy-clad houses with blue, black and red doors, and to the right is a large brick building, Walthamstow's old workhouse.

When the passage opens out, you will find a village preserved against the vagaries of the passing years, a time capsule at the edge of metropolitan London. Footpaths radiate from the dull sandstone walls of St Mary's church, to the Squire and the Monoux almshouses, the infants' school and overgrown graveyards where cracked tombstones vie with the weeds. On the corner of Church Lane and Orford Road sits a fifteenth-century wattle-and-daub house. Around the corner the National School, founded in 1819, faces the workhouse, built almost ninety years earlier. Some of the buildings have changed their use – the National School has become a Spiritualist Church, the Georgian infants' school is a Welcome Centre, the workhouse a museum – the Monoux almshouses have been rebuilt since being bombed in 1941, the footpaths are now illuminated by electric light, and the housing of a later age now swamps the border. In essence, though, what exists here in this tiny village is the Walthamstow of 1830, and of Jemmy, Fuegia and York.

The journey the Fuegians made with FitzRoy that first day would have been less straightforward. Walthamstow sat just seven miles to the north-east of the capital city, but it was a pleasant contrast to the smog-ridden metropolis. On the east of the river Lea, this was a handsome parish in Epping Forest, noted for the richness of its woodland and the stunning views of the City of London across the marshes. In the early eighteenth century the only real route into Walthamstow would have been through Stratford and along Leyton Road over the Bow Bridge. Here at this major gateway from London into Essex – where dogs' right forefoot claws were removed to stop them chasing the King's deer — highwaymen and footpads still stalked the roads and the woods. However, as rich merchants and bankers began to make Walthamstow their home, there was a growing demand for improved communications. In 1757 an Act of Parliament allowed for the building of a new bridge over the Lea, and for 'making, repairing and widening roads from thence into the great roads at Snaresbrook in the county of Essex, and at Clapton in the county of Middlesex'.

As a result, on 13 May 1758, a major route from Hackney to Epping Forest was opened, which was improved in 1819 with the construction of a new metal bridge with a 70-foot span. The engineer James McAdam commended the road as one of the best in the vicinity of London. 'Its general form is upon the most approved principles . . .' he wrote, adding that it was 'in a very good state: better means have been adopted for draining this road than any other road in the metropolis . . .' It was almost certainly along this road that FitzRoy and the Fuegians entered Walthamstow for the first time.

They would have experienced a sudden break with the city, a sharp leap from the urban to the rural. There had been a settlement at Walthamstow since before the Roman Empire. Stone Age, Bronze Age, Iron Age and Roman remains have all been unearthed here. Boudicca led the Iceni in the surrounding forests. In 1830 it maintained its rural setting, and though London was looming on the horizon, it had yet to expand into this rustic vacuum. The Eastern Counties Railway did not reach this far until the 1840s when it brought with it the essential elements of modernity: gas-lighting, sewers and a water supply. But for the moment the village had a tranquil beauty amid fields, hills and woods. The census of 1831 tells us that 4,258 people were living here in a mixed community that included agricultural labourers, journeymen, artisans, shopkeepers, chandlers, clerks and merchants.

There were also many well-to-do families in Walthamstow, with their attendant entourages of servants. In 1831 more than one in ten of the local population was employed in domestic service, and directories show a profusion of luxury services for the wealthy, with lace menders, hairdressers, perfumers, straw-hat vendors, stay and umbrella makers, music teachers and piano tuners. The village was at a convenient travelling distance from London but, nevertheless, a handsome escape from its smog.

The wealthy were a blend of landed gentry and men who had made small and large fortunes in the City, the law courts, commerce or enterprise. Joseph Wigram, who had found the Fuegians their place in Walthamstow, was the son of Sir Robert Wigram, one of the richest merchants in the country. He had come to England from Wexford in Ireland in 1762 and, after apprenticing with a surgeon, became an entrepreneur of the highest order, owning twenty-one East Indiamen. He had also been the major shareholder in the Blackwall yard of shipbuilders, a partner in Reid's Brewery, now Watney, Combe, Reid, the chairman of the East India Docks and an MP. He died in November 1830.

Joseph Wigram was one of Sir Robert's twenty-three children, all of whom lived at some time in the grand setting of Walthamstow House. Theirs was new money, accumulated through hard work and speculation, not the sophisticated old money of the landed gentry. On meeting one of Joseph's brothers, Jane Austen wrote to her sister that he was 'not agreeable. – He is certainly no addition . . . They say his name is Henry. A proof how unequally the gifts of Fortune are bestowed. – I have seen many a John and Thomas much more agreeable . . . Mr Wigram does no good to anybody.'

But just as there were rich, there were also poor in Walthamstow. The village almshouses catered for the 'widows of decayed tradesmen', and charitable organisations made small donations or gifts of coal and bread to the neediest, and also eased the consciences of the flourishing bourgeoisie and squirearchy – Robert Wigram, for example, arranged the release of a prisoner from the local gaol every time there was a birth in the family.

Charities aside, though, the inequity in local society meant that crime was a growing problem. It was not as grievous or as all-pervasive as that which confronted the citizens of London, but large houses were tempting targets for those who could not make ends meet. In 1854, when Walthamstow's population had risen to 5,000, 147 people were arrested: 51 for felonies, 39 for wilful damage, 17 for assault and 40 for drunkenness.

To combat crime, an early form of police force, known colloquially as 'Charlies', or watchmen, would have been familiar to the Fuegians. From 1819 to 1831 a police committee, supported by local subscription, employed armed Charlies to patrol the winter nights. During the uneasy days of 1830–31 they were augmented by day patrols. In 1831, following the Lighting and Watching Act, the parish appointed inspectors to oversee the employment of a sergeant and a squad of constables. These men roamed the streets and their cries of 'Twelve o'clock midnight and all is well', echoed through the night air.

For those on the lowest rung of Walthamstow's ladder there was an alternative to crime: the workhouse. Like every other parish in the country, Walthamstow tried to palm off its poor to other districts, but here in this dark, foreboding building at the edge of the village, up to eighty people lived and were employed on a strict regime of oakum picking, brewing and gardening. Above the door of the workhouse a plaque warned:

THIS HOUSE ERECTED
AN DOM MDCCXXX
if any would not work
neither Should he eat

It was a message that would return to haunt Jemmy Button in the last years of his life.

Jemmy, Fuegia and York were greeted in Walthamstow by Mr and Mrs Jenkins, the master and mistress of the infants' school they were to attend. As well as being their teachers, the Jenkinses would double as their hosts for the next eleven months. They took an immediate liking to the Fuegians and Fuegia became the special responsibility of Mrs Jenkins, but little else is known about the couple. The 1831 census has a William Jenkins 'professional' living in Church Lane, as head of a household of three men and four women, and it is possible that this was him.

The infants' school they ran had been established by William Wilson in 1824. Wilson was an evangelical preacher of some renown. The son of a wealthy Cheapside silk manufacturer, he was a father of eight who had come to the village in 1822. He had a large personal wealth which was inflated by two livings: he was vicar of Walthamstow in winter and of Worton, near Woodstock, in the summer. The migration from one ecclesiastical money-pot to another involved servants, wagons and geese in a logistical exercise that was a byword for complexity and military precision.

Wilson had been encouraged, even goaded, by the famous nineteenth-century educator Samuel Wilderspin into opening an infants' school in Walthamstow. In the early part of the century National Schools took children from the age of six or seven, but Wilderspin believed that this wasted both time and opportunity.

He felt a gulf in education could be bridged by preparing children as young as two for a life of learning. Valuable time could be saved in the higher schools, he argued, if children arrived at them already familiar with the alphabet and elements of arithmetic, as well as an understanding of the behaviour expected of them in the classroom. He also believed that this early period in a child's life was crucial for impressing upon them social and moral values that might otherwise be lost or debased by the beliefs and actions of crudely educated parents.

Wilderspin approached Wilson and asked for help. After some initial reluctance the vicar agreed to open what became the country's first Church of England infants' school in a barn at the back of his house. It was so successful that by the time the Fuegians arrived in Walthamstow it had been transferred to a permanent, specially constructed Georgian building on glebeland adjoining the graveyard of the church, paid for out of Wilson's own pocket

The experience of St Mary's infant school for the three Fuegians must have been fascinating, exhilarating, at times frustrating and frequently bewildering. The school consisted of a large room and two smaller classrooms off to the side. There was living accommodation upstairs for the master and mistress, but it appears that the Jenkinses did not need this part of the building for themselves. Perhaps this was where the Fuegians lived, for the Jenkinses' social standing was hardly so great that they would have had a large home, able to accommodate three visitors for a long time. Besides, the overwhelming convenience of having the Fuegians living above the schoolroom might have been too strong to resist.

The school was busy six days a week, with up to 150 children attending lessons. What they thought of their new classmates is nowhere recorded, but young children are often quicker to accept and absorb differences than adults. Nevertheless if Jemmy and Fuegia seemed odd to their classmates, one wonders what the children made of the twenty-six-year-old York Minster, a surly and increasingly antisocial man.

The lessons the Fuegians joined were active: clapping, singing, walking and chanting were the order of the day. When we look back on education in the nineteenth century we do so with a notion of its tyranny and abusive practices, harsh discipline and cowed children. But this was not so with the Walthamstow infants' school: lessons had a high religious, scriptural and moral content, but the ethos was liberal and child-centred, even by today's standards.

In his book *The System of Infants Schools* William Wilson laid out the guiding principles of his Walthamstow enterprise. It was essential to get children as young as possible, in the

most impressible years of our existence. The evil which is within us is then fomented, or the principles of religion and moral excellence were then first inculcated and encouraged . . .

[Education] must be conducted under the conviction, that it does not require a more judicious care to select the food of the body, on its entrance into life; to check the disease which threatens it; or to guide its earliest efforts into action, than it does to choose what may afford the best nourishment to the mind, and to watch over and regulate the first energies which it may put forth.

His system, he claimed, was designed to look at the child as a whole, to instil powers of judgement, discrimination and memory at the same time as putting a check on passions and moral uncertainty. It was designed to create 'a class of persons, who . . . would have their minds imbued with the love of moral excellence and religion, and their heart prepared under the influence of the best principles for all the changes and chances of this mortal life'.

And the way to achieve this was not to make children fear and loathe either their schools or their teachers, but the opposite: they should want to come in every day. Classrooms were to be light and airy, with plenty of space, to provide a contrast with the children's home conditions. The school walls were to 'speak' with pictures of animals, drawings illustrating Bible stories and short passages from the scriptures:

FEAR GOD — I Peter ii 17
HONOUR THE KING — I Peter ii 17
GOD IS LOVE   I John iv 8
THOU SHALT NOT STEAL — Eighth Commandment
GOD IS A SPIRIT — John iv 24
A CHILD IS KNOWN BY HIS DOINGS — Proverbs xx ii

Singing and clapping were powerful tools in learning, both to help children enjoy their lessons and to help their teacher keep order. Punishment was judicious and not brutal: it was understood that if a two-year-old committed an offence, the teacher was as culpable as the child. In his book Wilson gives the following example of punishment meted out in his Walthamstow school, to which the Fuegians would have been accustomed. A five-year-old who was caught stealing is placed on the central rostrum:

Master: Do you all see this little boy?
School: Yes, sir.
Master: Who is he?
School: John ——, sir.
Master: What has he been doing?

School: He has been stealing, sir.

Master: What is it to steal?

School: To take what is not your own.

Master: I am very sorry for him. It makes me quite unhappy to see him. Are you not sorry for him?

School: Yes, sir.

Master: I will try to make him a good boy again; will not you?

School: Yes, sir.

Master: What will you do if you see him take what is not his own?

School: We will tell him not to steal, sir.

Master: Try to do so, my dear children; and then if he is a good boy again we shall all love him.

The child was then made to stand alone for a short while and told to pray.

Lessons lasted a quarter of an hour — not long enough for young minds to wander — and were taught with the children sitting in a semi-circle by either a teacher or a monitor. Girls and boys would be placed apart at different ends of the room. They learned reading, writing, arithmetic and the scriptures. There was also a major emphasis on the health of the child. Wilson wrote that

Muscular action is made a component and necessary part of the system. Every lesson is accompanied with some movement of the person . . . the whole frame is at different periods called into action and restored to rest. The beat of the foot, the clap of the hands, the extension of the arms, with various other postures, are measures of the utterance of the lesson as they proceed. The position is also frequently changed. The infants learn sitting, standing or walking . . .

Hygiene was taught by a morning 'purification' in which children sang 'This is the way we wash our hands; this is the way we wash our face' accompanied with gestures.

Chapter 8

As already noted, FitzRoy's instructions to the Jenkinses were to teach the Fuegians 'English, and the plainer truths of Christianity . . . and the use of common tools, a slight acquaintance with husbandry, gardening and mechanism . . .' and for eleven months that is what they did, with varying degrees of success.

The younger two, Jemmy and Fuegia, achieved much and made many friends. York Minster, on the other hand, was a problem. He didn't want to be in this foreign land and was uncooperative, bad-tempered and hard to influence. Only the extra-curricular mechanical lessons, such as woodwork and animal husbandry, roused him. Lieutenant Bartholomew Sulivan, an officer of the *Beagle*, said of him that he was 'too old to take to reading, but he was quick at discerning and catching practical hints'. FitzRoy confirmed this when he wrote that the older Fuegian 'took interest in smith's or carpenter's work, and paid attention to what he saw and heard about animals; but he reluctantly assisted in gardening work, and had a great dislike to learning to read'.

There were other problems with York: his age, curt attitude, lack of manners and resistance to change all combined to create, in English eyes, a rather charmless package. He had also developed an unhealthy interest in Fuegia. The twenty-eight-year-old man had fallen for the ten-year-old girl, and whether it was love or simply a man asserting property rights over the only suitable female, he followed her everywhere, watched her every move, guarded her from the attentions of other men and hid behind her social ease in public situations. At this stage there is no suggestion of anything sexual occurring between the two – it seems that York treated her in the way that he might have cared for a new spear or canoe, but his jealousy occasionally flared, with harsh stares and grunted words of admonition aimed at those he deemed rival suitors.

However, if York was potential trouble, then the other two made a stark contrast. Once again age seems to have been the important factor. Both Jemmy and Fuegia were less abrasive, less fixed in their attitudes and, perhaps, more eager to please. They were still young enough to be flexible in their approach, to absorb new influences and to fit in at the school. Many of York's problems arose from his being forced to spend his days with children, all more than twenty years his junior. His growls and scowls must have been threatening and disturbing, but the youthful enthusiasm of Jemmy and Fuegia made them the darlings of all who met them.

What is more, there seem to have been many aspects of their new lives that they found genuinely agreeable. Both loved the attention and affection they received, and there was one particular aspect of their time in England that they adored: dressing up.

In eleven months the two went, in British eyes, from primitive beasts content with a scrap of fur as a shoulder cover to well-dressed poseurs. Jemmy, in particular, loved the indulgence of fine clothes, gleaming shoes and kid gloves. He could not pass a mirror without preening. The transformation was remarkable. Giving a speech to a rally in Bedford twenty-five years later, Lieutenant Sulivan still remembered the boy's vanity when, at the end of his time in England, he returned to the ship: 'Jemmy was the favourite . . . and his progress in civilization was most conspicuous in his excessive dandyism. In his own country two years previously he was a naked savage, but then, even in weather that made the officers thankful for their rough coats and greased boots, he would make his appearance on deck with polished boots and well brushed broad cloth . . .'

This enthusiasm was reflected in the speed with which the two youngsters learned. FitzRoy notes their 'considerable progress', and from what is known of conversations with them over the next forty years it is clear that Jemmy and Fuegia had made great leaps in their understanding. In a letter dated fifteen years after the Fuegians had left England, Mr Wilson wrote of the boy's ability in English and his improvement in moral understanding:

Button was by far the most intelligent, he managed to pick up a few English words, and before he left, I was able to communicate, but in a very imperfect way, a few simple ideas: 'Button;' 'Mr Jenkins made that wheelbarrow;' 'Mr Barber made that house;' 'Who made the sky and the trees?' 'Not know, our land, Mr Wilson.'

He seemed to have no idea of God. He confessed that he had eaten human flesh, but having once acknowledged it, appeared pained if the subject was mentioned to him again; he had some ideas of moral rectitude, and said of a man who had stolen, 'He bad man.' 'Button, shall I go to your land and preach to them?' 'No, Mr Wilson, not go our land, bad people in our land.' They used to attend at our church, and once he said, 'Mr Wilson go our land, we build large church for him.'

This sounds like faint praise, but it was almost certainly not intended as such. These words reflect instead that while they were in Walthamstow the Fuegians probably had little regular contact with Wilson. He arranged their place in the school and took some of the credit for overseeing their general care, but he did not have a day-to-day relationship with them. His contact was most likely restricted to the occasional snatched conversation at the church door, or across a crowded school hall. However, the real quality of Jemmy and Fuegia's advances would be measured in the years to come.

Education changed the Fuegians. In FitzRoy's eyes it was not just their intelligence that the experience enhanced. At the end of a long passage in the *Narratives*, describing in detail the general appearance of Fuegians he finishes, 'The nose is always narrow between the eyes and, except in a few curious instances, is hollow in profile outline, or almost flat. The mouth is coarsely formed . . .' but then swiftly adds, '(I speak of them in their savage state, and not of those who were in England, whose features were much improved by altered habits and by education . . .)'

Of course, in many senses he was right. They wore expensive clothes, they were washed, their hair was trimmed neatly and their faces had filled out. With their growing English vocabulary they became more presentable and inevitably their contacts increased.

The church would have been a place of some significance to them. In addition to the scriptural and catechistic lessons they received at the infants' school, the three attended St Mary's every Sunday. This was one of the centres of Walthamstow's social scene and William Wilson was a preacher who packed the pews. The rich had permanent rented seats, and a further 432 were set aside for the poor families of the parish. There was a waiting list for them and Wilson had proclaimed, 'If you neglect public worship, your seat will be given to the next poor inhabitant of the parish . . .'

We do not know what stares of curiosity greeted the Fuegians across the aisles in early December 1830, but the fact that the people of the village took them to their hearts is beyond doubt.

FitzRoy noted the 'utmost kindness by the benevolent men . . . by their families, and by many others in the neighbourhood, as well as casual visitors, who became much interested in their welfare, and from time to time gave them several valuable presents'. The casual visitors he speaks of were well-wishers and curious sightseers who came to take a peek at the Fuegians.

Some who have written of the Fuegians in England give the impression of frenetic excitement surrounding them, the constant stream of callers, rich and poor, knocking at the door of the school. In 1906 Mark Twain wrote in an article published in the collection *Letters from the Earth* that York Minster was invited to a ball at the court of St James.

> He got himself ready for that. For the sake of convenience and comfort he resumed his national costume, thinking no harm; and at 11pm, he appeared in the midst of that gorgeous assemblage clad only in his awful innocence and that pathetic shoulder-skin.
>
> Do you know, he emptied that place in two minutes by the watch? Then the guards turned him into the street. When he reached his hotel he was denied admission. The other hotels refused him. It looked as if he was nevermore going to find shelter, but at last he was rescued from his difficulties by compassionate friends.

The story is clearly nonsense – Twain was not a contemporary of the Fuegians and was probably repeating a story he had been told. The Fuegians never caused such a stir, they were not featured heavily in the press, and what references there were to them refer largely to their connection with either the arrival or departure of the *Beagle*. It is plausible that the three were a common discussion point in Walthamstow. It is possible that they inspired the following Christmas dish, reported in the *Essex Standard* in 1831:

PATAGONIAN PIES. – The Christmas pie made by Mr Roberts, of the Sportsman's Group in Fargate, we are informed, contained 30 rabbits, three stones of pork, two legs of veal, and four stones of flour. It measured in length upwards of three feet, and its weight about 16 stones. The other pie served up by Mr Kirk, of the Cross Daggers, Rotherham, was composed of four geese, 12 rabbits, six brace of partridges, three stones of veal, two stones of pork, eight fowls, three turkeys, seven pounds of sausages, four hares, four pounds of flour etc. – Heliogabalus might have been satisfied with such a plenitude of savoury ingredients.

On the whole, though, interest in the Fuegians was low-key. FitzRoy wanted it that way: his Fuegians were in Walthamstow to learn, to help the advance of civilisation and Christianity and to increase the safety of sailors in the South Atlantic. What he most feared was that they would be treated like objects in a freak show, so he restricted their access outside Walthamstow to a close coterie of friends and family. He wrote,

They gave no particular trouble; were very healthy; and the two younger ones became great favourites wherever they were known. Sometimes I took them with me to see a friend or relation of my own, who was anxious to question them, and contribute something to the increasing stock of serviceable articles which I was collecting for their use, when they should return to Tierra del Fuego.

His sister, twenty-nine-year-old Fanny Rice-Trevor – the future Lady Dynevor – became a firm favourite of the three and a frequent benefactress with whom they spent valuable time and who they called 'Cappen's sisser'. Another who met them was Rodney Murchison – the future Sir Rodney, President of the Royal Society – and his wife, who enquired after them for at least three years after they had sailed for home.

FitzRoy was also aware that the Fuegians should be part of a dialogue: while it was of paramount importance that Jemmy, Fuegia and York learned English, he understood that it was also crucial that he picked up some of their language. Over the course of his time with them he therefore constructed a small vocabulary that recognised the differences between the tongues of what he called the Alikhoolip (Alakaluf) and Tekeenica (Yamana) Indians. It was a beginning, though little more. The surviving fragment of his vocabulary lists almost 200 words and their Fuegian translations. It consists largely of nouns and demonstrates no knowledge of Fuegian grammar, though it did point out the difficulty of pronunciation: 'One Fuegian expression, something like the cluck of a hen, can scarcely be represented by our letters; its meaning is "no".'

The Fuegians were not treated as scientific specimens: no record remains of any physical or anatomical examination of Jemmy, York and Fuegia, though a pickled body brought back from Tierra del Fuego, in the hold of the *Adventure*, was dissected. FitzRoy was particularly keen on the pseudo-science of phrenology – the belief that the size, shape and bumps of the head betray a person's character and mental state – so in late 1830 he had all three examined by a phrenologist. The results were as follows:

YOKCUSHLU [Fuegia Basket], a female, ten years of age.
– Strong in attachment.
– If offended, her passions strong.
– A little disposed to cunning, but not duplicity.

— She will manifest some ingenuity.

— She is not at all disposed to be covetous.

— Self-will at times very active.

— Fond of notice and approbation.

— She will show a benevolent feeling when able to do so.

— Strong feelings for a Supreme Being.

— Disposed to be honest.

— Rather inclined to mimicry and imitation.

— Her memory good of visible objects and localities, with a strong attachment to places in which she has lived.

— It would not be difficult to make her a useful member of society in a short time, as she would readily receive instruction.

ORUNDELLICO [Jemmy Button], a Fuegian, aged 15.

— He will have to struggle against anger, self-will, animal inclinations, and a disposition to combat and destroy.

— Rather inclined to cunning.

— Not covetous, not very ingenious.

— Fond of directing and leading.

— Very cautious in his actions: but fond of distinction and approbation.

— He will manifest strong feelings for a Supreme Being.

— Strongly inclined to benevolence.

— May be safely intrusted with the care of property.

— Memory, in general, good; particularly for persons, objects of sense and localities.

— To accustomed places he would have a strong attachment.

— Like the female, receiving instruction readily, he might be made a useful member of society; but it would require great care, as self-will would interfere much.

EL'LEPARU [York Minster], about 28.

— Passions very strong, particularly those of an animal nature; self-willed, positive and determined.

– He will have strong attachment to children, persons and places.

– Disposed to cunning and caution.

– He will show ready comprehension of things, and some ingenuity.

– Self will not be overlooked, and he will be attentive to the value of property.

– Very fond of praise and approbation, and of notice being taken of his conduct.

– Kind to those who render him a service.

– He will be reserved and suspicious.

– He will not have such strong feelings for the Deity as his two companions.

– He will be grateful for kindness, but reserved in showing it.

– His memory, in general, good: he would not find natural history, or other branches of science, difficult, if they can be imparted to him; but, from possessing strong self-will, he will be difficult to instruct, and will require a great deal of humouring and indulgence to lead him to do what is required.

In the several statements that FitzRoy made concerning his Fuegian charges, both in letters and in the press, it was said that they would be in the country for two or three years, or that their education would take place 'over the course of a few years'. By the early summer of 1831, however, he was already planning to take them home. On 23 May he wrote to George Elliott at the Admiralty:

The proper season for the return of the Fuegians is now drawing near. They have been with me for 14 months, and at least five months more must elapse before they can reach their own shores.

They have always expected to return during the ensuing winter (summer of their country), and should they be disappointed, I fear that discontent and disease may be the consequence.

Clearly he had undergone a change of heart, though it is not clear why. By May a number of factors would have been preying on his mind, though the behaviour of the Fuegians was not one of them. The work resulting from the previous voyage of the *Beagle* was now completed and to a certain extent he was kicking his heels; the lack of support he had received with his charges' upkeep was galling and resulted in him having to spend more time and money looking after their needs than he had anticipated. Bringing them to England and educating them had already cost him personally £1,500. The loss of Boat Memory had been a shock, and now the morning papers were full of stories of the spread of cholera through English cities.

The deciding factor must have been the confirmation of rumours that plans to recommission the survey of Tierra del Fuego had been mothballed. This was a blow to his personal prestige, and it also opened the possibility of Jemmy, York and Fuegia being permanently marooned in England. His letter to the Admiralty continued with a tinge of bitterness and a reminder of why it was important to resettle the Fuegians:

> Having been led to suppose that a vessel would be sent to South America to continue the survey of its shores, and to explore parts yet unknown, I hoped to have seen these people become useful as interpreters, and be the means of establishing a friendly disposition towards Englishmen on the part of their countrymen, if not a regular intercourse with them.
>
> By supplying these natives with some animals, seeds, tools, etc and placing them, with some of their own tribe, on the fertile country lying at the east side of Tierra del Fuego, I thought that, in a few years, ships might have been enabled to obtain fresh provisions, as well as wood and water, during their passage from the Atlantic to the Pacific Ocean, on a part of the coast which can always be approached with ease and safety . . .

He concluded with a terse request for a year's leave 'in order to enable me to keep my faith with the natives' using his own 'very limited means'.

The Admiralty acceded to his request, and also offered to give the Fuegians passage on the first man-of-war going to South America. But by June, with no sign of a naval vessel going in the right direction, 'and feeling too much bound to these natives to trust them in any other kind of vessel, unless with myself – because of the risk that would attend their being landed anywhere, excepting on the territories of their own tribes . . .' FitzRoy took exceptional action that reflected well on him. He accepted the offer of twelve months' annual leave and entered into a contract with a merchant of Stepney, John Mawman, to have himself, the Fuegians, James Bennet and one other shipped to South America aboard Mawman's brig the *John*.

With an advance cost of £1,000 and the further expense of provisions and pilotage fees all coming from FitzRoy's pocket, this was a startling demonstration of his commitment to the Fuegians. But shortly after Bennet had bought a herd of goats, with which the party would stock Tierra del Fuego, one of FitzRoy's 'kindly' and politically powerful uncles stepped in. The survey was reinstated, FitzRoy was appointed to the *Chanticleer*, and when this was found to be unfit, he was commissioned to the *Beagle*.

On 2 July 1831 the *Royal Devonport Telegraph* was able to make the following announcement:

His Majesty's sloop *Beagle*, which was paid off at this port in October last . . . is to be again commissioned by her late gallant and indefatigable Commander Robert Fitzroy, esq. for the purpose of completing his examination of that vast continent . . . The natives of Terra del Fuego, brought home by Commander

Fitzroy, having been taught some of the most useful arts, are, we understand, to return to their native country in the *Beagle*.

At around this time, Robert FitzRoy received a special visitor. Colonel John Wood, acting as extra messenger in the King's Household, brought an invitation from Their Majesties King William IV and Queen Adelaide. Word of the Fuegians had reached St James's Palace and they were wanted for a private audience.

When and how this occurred is nowhere recorded. The daily comings and goings of the Court, so fastidiously reported by the morning press, make no mention of the visit of the Fuegians. The Court Circular carries no reference, and neither does the Annual Register for 1831. The Royal Archives at Windsor contain few surviving papers from the short reign of William IV, and there are no references to Robert FitzRoy or the Fuegians attending any of the many levees and balls at which the King and Queen were present that year.

It is most likely that the meeting came about through FitzRoy's sister, Fanny. In the 1830s the royal court was far less formal than it later became, and it was not unusual for the King to meet 'interesting' foreigners who were in town and of whom he would have heard through court gossip. In the early months of 1831 Fanny was attending important events at the palace and on 24 February she was among those present on the Queen's birthday. The *Morning Post* even described her attire: 'A satin dress, shot with gold, trimmed with bands of gold; the train velvet with gold.' Two months later she was at the palace again, attending one of the great royal social occasions, the Queen's Drawing Room.

FitzRoy therefore had an insider at court. Tongues would have wagged and news would have reached the monarch's ears. William

IV, newly installed on the throne and yet to be crowned, was considered by some a lovable buffoon and by others a licentious boor. To the former, anyone was an improvement on his brother, George IV, known to many as Swellfoot the Tyrant. The latter felt that as William had brawled and drunk his way around the whorehouses of the world as a sailor in the Royal Navy he too was unfit for the Crown. However, the King's navy days had given him a taste for adventure and an interest in the exotic, and the idea of meeting the Fuegians would have appealed to him.

There were few airs and graces about the King. Aged sixty-five when he came to the throne, he was a ruddy-faced, jocund soul with a tendency towards plumpness. As the third son of George III he had never expected to ascend to the throne and had spent much of his life ignoring the pomp of princehood. After a short career in the navy he had fallen in love at the age of twenty-five with the famous actress Mrs Jordan with whom he had ten children over thirteen years. However, when gambling debts mounted he deserted her and moved on to the daughter of the Duke of Saxe-Meiningen, Princess Amelia Adelaide.

Even on the throne William was unable to change his ways. One day, when tired of swearing in new privy councillors and lords lieutenants, he took a stroll down Pall Mall where he was recognised by a lively and enthusiastic crowd. Horrified members of White's jumped from a club window to pull him away as he was kissed by a prostitute. On another occasion in 1830 he threw a party for 3,000 of the poor of Windsor. In 1834, 36,000 bottles of wine were drunk at St James's Palace alone.

William was an essentially bourgeois king, and the audience with the Fuegians was less stiff than might otherwise have been expected. The occasion was nevertheless a great feather in the caps of FitzRoy and his charges. It looked at last as though FitzRoy's investment of £1,500 in his protégés might have been recognised. Sometime in the summer of 1831, Jemmy and his colleagues were taken by carriage from Walthamstow to London and through the gates of the palace. From here they were escorted through grandeur beyond their imagining to where their presence was eagerly awaited in one of the State Apartments.

Against all protocol, the King would probably have extended a hand to the four and asked, 'How d'ye do?' They would have been shown to seats around a small table and offered tea and biscuits.

FitzRoy was anxious to record the intelligent interest that both the King and the Queen took in his project:

> His Majesty asked a great deal about their country, as well as themselves; and I hope I may be permitted to remark that, during an equal space of time, no person ever asked me so many sensible and thoroughly pertinent questions respecting the Fuegians and their country also relating to the Survey in which I had myself been engaged, as did his Majesty.

Queen Adelaide was very different from her husband. An austere and implacable opponent of reform, in a short time she had made herself the most unpopular woman in England. A great supporter of the Duke of Wellington, she was, to many, England's Marie-Antoinette. But she also had an amiable, self-effacing, less public side to her character. She had lost two children – one through miscarriage and a day-old daughter – and thus the chance to present her husband with an heir. It coloured the way she treated the Fuegians and was manifested in 'acts of genuine kindness which they could appreciate, and never forgot . . .'. She was particularly taken with Fuegia. At one point during the audience the Queen left the room briefly. She returned with one of her own bonnets, which she placed on Fuegia's head.

'Her Majesty then put one of her rings upon the girl's finger,' FitzRoy remembered, 'and gave her a sum of money to buy an outfit of clothes when she should leave England to return to her own country.'

The meeting was short, but not rushed. It made a lasting impression on the Fuegians, who in years to come remembered it and talked about it.

Chapter 9

The recommissioning of the *Beagle* in early July 1830 was the beginning of a difficult few months for FitzRoy. There were repairs to sort out, provisions to purchase, scurvy-preventing antiscorbutics to accumulate and a crew to appoint. If the *Chanticleer* had been unseaworthy, then the *Beagle* was hardly better. The previous voyage had taken a great toll on the barque and an inspection in dock revealed that substantial portions of her were rotten. With so much woodwork to replace, FitzRoy seized the opportunity to make large-scale improvements to the ship.

A new upper deck was built and raised several inches higher than the previous one, giving valuable head room for those living and working below. This, with a new sheathing of planks, felt, and copper nailed to the hull, added 15 tons to the ship's weight and had the extra effect of making her safer in stormy weather. A new rudder was added, along with a patent windlass, a stove and an oven. To the masts were fixed experimental lightning conductors. Ropes, sails and spars were, FitzRoy claimed, 'the best money could buy', and in his cabin, he stored twenty-two chronometers, which would facilitate the survey's new instructions – not only to carry out an accurate survey of the southern coastlines of South America, but also to complete a running chain of chronometric readings around the world.

Depending on whom one believes, the work was either easy

or exhausting. The newly appointed ship's surgeon, Robert McCormick, an abrasive character, complained in his autobiography that by the time the ship left Plymouth 'six months had been dawdled away in fitting a small 10-gun brig for sea'. More credible, because he had no axe to grind, were the memories of Lieutenant Sulivan. An anecdote in his son's biography of him tells how, at the end of one day's labour, he fell asleep. Before putting his head down he demanded that the steward wake him in two hours' time so that he could have tea before going to a prestigious ball in Plymouth. When he awoke the sun was streaming onto his face. He called the steward and asked the time.

    — Eight o'clock, sir.
    — What do you mean?
    — Eight in the morning, sir.
    — What, have I missed the ball? Why did you not call me?
    — I did, sir.
    — Then when I did not appear at tea, why did you not call me again?
    — You did have tea, sir.

Laughter broke out around him. Sulivan had arrived in the mess room in his nightshirt and cap, with a duck-gun over his shoulder. He sat down at the table, drank his tea and marched back to bed. Tiredness had turned him into a sleepwalker.

Many of the newly commissioned crew, including Lieutenants Wickham and Sulivan, the carpenter, Jonathan May, and the assistant surgeon, Benjamin Bynoe, had sailed on the *Beagle* during its previous voyage. There was a total crew of sixty-five and, with supernumaries, the figure rose to seventy-four people living on the tiny craft. They included the artist Augustus Earl, paid £200 a year to record the sights and adventures of the ship, the instrument-maker George Stebbings, brought along to tend FitzRoy's chronometers, the three Fuegians, and a young naturalist, companion for the commander.

FitzRoy feared more than ever the 'blue evils'. His uncle's suicide, the death of Stokes and the prospect of a long, arduous voyage, played cruel games in his head. His aloof manner and a fear that overfamiliarity with the crew would lead to a breakdown in discipline meant that there was little or no social contact between him and the lower decks. Loneliness might crack him. He needed somebody with whom he could converse, share a meal and from whom he had no fear of mutiny. It was essential that this person was of the right background, sophisticated, intelligent, and preferably, though not essentially, well versed in science and able to take advantage of the many opportunities for research that the voyage would present. Throughout July and August he searched for such an individual.

The Cambridge naturalist John Stevens Henslow was asked to help. For a short while he considered the opportunity for himself, but when his pregnant wife objected to the possibility of a five- or six-year absence, he recommended a student and friend: a twenty-two-year-old named Charles Darwin.

I have stated that I consider you the best qualified person I know of who is likely to undertake such a situation [Henslow told Darwin in August 1831]. I state this not on the supposition of your being a finished Naturalist, but as amply qualified for collecting, observing and noting anything worthy to be noted in Natural History . . . Captain Fitzroy wants a man (I understand) more as a companion than a mere collector, and would not take anyone however good a Naturalist who was not recommended to him likewise as a gentleman . . . Don't put on any modest doubts or fears about your disqualifications, for I assure you I think you are the very man they are in search of, so conceive yourself to be tapped on the Shoulder by your Bum-bailiff and affectionate friend.

FitzRoy had other ideas and other people to consider. Darwin was rather young, the phrenology of his nose suggested 'a lack of energy and determination' and, what was more, he was a Whig, with a fervent distaste for slavery. Nevertheless, in September, after a somewhat fraught interview and a far more congenial meal together, FitzRoy offered the young man a place on the ship.

There were other negotiations to occupy FitzRoy's time. On 5 August Mr Wilson wrote to him from Walthamstow, suggesting the despatch of two missionaries with the Fuegians. This would give the opportunity of continuing the good work that had already begun, and help them and their people towards a 'gradual civilization'.

FitzRoy leaped at the idea and asked the Admiralty for its approval. Until now his plan had been simply to take the three back to their respective homelands and leave them with their compatriots. He would have known that the odds were stacked against them being able to pursue his original plan successfully. Wilson's proposal offered the potential of backup, structure and continuing development. It also provided a watchful eye over his Fuegian charges and even, perhaps, protection.

FitzRoy must have been particularly cheered by the final paragraph of Wilson's letter, in which the Beagle's commander was informed that 'A subscription has been set in foot by Gentlemen who are extremely desirous that this opportunity of extending the benefits of civilization should not be lost . . .'

Wilson approached the Church Missionary Society for help, but once again found it unable to meet his request. Despite the offer of funds from the subscription, the Society could not afford the expense of a missionary. Besides, there was a lack of trained men willing to go to Tierra del Fuego. Feelers were put out and, with the date of embarkation approaching, a man was found: Richard Matthews, a mechanic missionary, still in his late teens. Despite his age, he had a good pedigree: his brother was a successful missionary at Kaitaia in New Zealand so he would have an idea of the severity of the proselytising life. Still, the idea of a single man cut adrift in a 'savage' landscape raised many early doubts. Was it really possible that Matthews would cope? FitzRoy thought him 'rather too young, and less experienced than might have been wished . . .' but, he added, 'his character and conduct had been such as to give very fair grounds for anticipating that he would, at least, sincerely endeavour to do his utmost in a situation so difficult and trying as that for which he volunteered'.

While Matthews prepared mentally, physically and intellectually for the job in front of him, William Wilson, Joseph Wigram and Dandeson Coates, of the Church Missionary Society, moved ahead with the subscription fund. Their aim was to provide the Fuegians and the missionary with the tools of both survival and advancement. Coates persuaded the CMS to donate £10 worth of books. The people of Walthamstow, and others who had befriended Jemmy, Fuegia and York, added a large quantity of European clothing, tools, ironmongery and earthenware. Many of them evidently had no clue about the conditions and adverse circumstances of the mission, for as well as the practical implements of survival they sent a multitude of fashionable London luxuries: toilette services, cut-glass decanters and glasses, soup tureens, butter bolts, tea trays, fine white linen, beaver hats, silk handkerchiefs, a mahogany dressing-case and chamber-pots.

On the eve of the missionary's departure for Plymouth, Dandeson Coates wrote Matthews a long letter of 'suggestions and counsel'. In it he told his acolyte that he was to follow

FitzRoy's every instruction and to look to him for directions. Matthews's aims were to 'promote the glory of God and the good of your fellow creatures'. To speed this he was to endeavour to do them all the good in his power, to gain their confidence and to be 'strong in the grace which is in Jesus Christ'.

Matthews's first object, Coates informed him, was to get to know the Fuegian languages; he should use the voyage to talk with the three, note down all the new words he heard, work out which was the most commonly used language and concentrate on it. He was to use the Bible as the basis of all his lessons, but should 'bear in mind that it is the temporal advantages which you may be capable of communicating to them that they will be most easily and immediately sensible of. Among these may be reckoned the acquisition of better dwellings, and better and more plentiful food and clothing . . .' For this reason he was to make husbandry and agriculture a priority. He should take it upon himself to instruct the Fuegians in the cultivation of 'potato, cabbage and other vegetables; to rear pigs, poultry, etc and to construct a commodious habitation'.

Example was to be Matthews's watchword, Coates concluded. By fencing off a piece of land for himself, with a clean, orderly house, a well-stocked garden and a flourishing supply of live-stock, the natives would learn the advantages of changing their traditional ways.

On the evening of 13 November the Fuegians, accompanied by their teacher Mr Jenkins and Richard Matthews, arrived in Plymouth from London by the steam vessel *Shannon*. Thirteen months earlier they had been frightened out of their wits by a passing steamer in Falmouth harbour, now they were travelling on one – 500 tons burthen, driven by powerful 160 horsepower engines. They had brought with them the 'outfit' of necessaries and not so necessaries raised by their supporters. An already overcrowded *Beagle* looked set to burst at the seams, but as the items were loaded the crew's irritation at having to find even more space turned to mirth. 'In the small hold of the *Beagle*, it was not easy to find places for the stowage of so many extra stores,' noted FitzRoy. 'When dividing the contents of large chests, in order to pack them differently, some very fair jokes were enjoyed by the seamen, at the expense of those who had ordered complete sets of crockery-ware, without desiring that any selection of articles should be made.'

As he waded through it all, he could not have failed to marvel at the irony of a letter brought by Matthews from Dandeson Coates:

My dear Sir . . .
We have provided Matthews with all such articles as appear to be necessary for him, and which could most advantageously be supplied from this country. These had all been completed before I learned from Mr Wilson that you are short of stowage. I hope, however, they will not be found to amount to a quantity to occasion you inconvenience; and I think you will be of opinion that no part of his outfit could, with propriety, be disposed with, in case Matthews becomes a permanent resident in Tierra del Fuego . . .

That evening FitzRoy brought the Fuegians onto the *Beagle* for introductions to the crew, some of whom were familiar, others not. Next day Robert MacCormick noted in his diary, 'Monday Nov 14th. Saw Fuegia Basket at Weakley's Hotel.' This was a smart inn in Devonport's Fore Street, run by Robert Weakley, and the reference suggests that the Fuegians, like many of the officers, were staying ashore until the ship was ready to sail.

Departure must have seemed imminent. All was set fair –

the arrival of the Fuegians and the missionary, stowage of their goods, the presence of Darwin, the muster of the crew – except the weather. Over the next few weeks adverse winds and storms conspired to peg the ship in harbour. As frustration mounted, Darwin commented, 'These two months at Plymouth were the most miserable that I ever spent.'

The *Beagle* moved out from its dock on 23 November to the holding point at Barnet Pool. All eyes were on the skies. A proposed departure date of 5 December came and went in the face of a pummelling gale. Five days later the crew unfurled the sails and the *Beagle* moved out. Within twenty-four hours she was back in port, defeated once again by the furious wind.

Days passed, and superstitious members of the crew believed that their stay was being prolonged by somebody on shore keeping a black cat under a tub. On 21 December they set sail again, only to strike a rock near Drake's Island where they were lodged for half an hour while the crew ran from side to side of the ship to break it free. Just off Cornwall's Lizard Point they were forced back to Plymouth once again.

Several lively parties on board, and a number of balls and dinners on shore, ameliorated the frustration of the officers, but all were getting restless. On Christmas Day the crew went on the rampage. Darwin described the day in his diary, with regret, as 'one of great importance to the men: the whole of it has been given up to revelry, at present there is not a sober man in the ship: King is obliged to perform duty of sentry, the last sentinel came staggering below declaring he would no longer stand on duty, whereupon he is now in irons getting sober as fast as he can . . .'

Whether Jemmy, Fuegia and York were on the ship while this was all going on is unknown. FitzRoy had no part in the revelries and, from the sound of it, had abandoned the ship for the day. It is probable that, knowing his men's love of alcohol, he had removed the Fuegians and the missionary to the safety of the shore.

The greatest annoyance of the celebrations was that the following day was glorious, blue skies, gentle breeze, a placid sea and, unfortunately, a missing crew. Darwin's displeasure spilled onto the next page of his diary:

The ship has been all day in a state of anarchy. One day's holiday has caused all this mischief; such a scene proves how absolutely necessary strict discipline is amongst such thoughtless beings as Sailors. Several have paid the penalty for insolence, by sitting for eight or nine hours in heavy chains. Whilst in this state, their conduct was like children, abusing everybody and thing but themselves and the next moment nearly crying . . .

FitzRoy restored discipline by ordering the flogging of several ringleaders when they were at sea. On 27 December the weather was perfect: a fresh easterly wind, a lightly rippled sea and a high barometer. By noon the *Beagle* was outside the breakwater and on its way. In Lieutenant Sulivan's opinion, never had a vessel left England better equipped for her special service, but as the Fuegians looked back on Mount Edgecumbe as England disappeared from view, they were doubtless reflecting on the strange fourteen months they had spent there. To be sure they were also looking forward to rejoining their own people.

PART THREE

Twenty Dwarf Hairs

Chapter 10

The voyage of the *Beagle* became known as one of the great seafaring journeys, imbued with the romance of adventure and discovery, but at the outset, with a crew exhausted from overwork and too much drink, the likely results seemed less than promising. Nevertheless, FitzRoy set his course for the slow but eventful trip to Cape Horn.

They called at Tenerife, Madeira, the Cape Verde Islands, Porto Noronha, Bahia, Rio, Buenos Aires and Monte Video. At Tenerife the ship was barred entry for refusing quarantine conditions; at St Paul's Rocks, a boat expedition was surrounded by sharks. At Buenos Aires a harbour guardship fired a blank shell at the *Beagle* in an attempt to enforce quarantine regulations and an international incident was barely averted. In Monte Video the crew marched the streets with guns and cutlasses drawn, helping police to suppress a mutiny among local soldiers. At Maldonado, York Minster experienced what might have been the defining moment of his time away from Tierra del Fuego – an encounter with an ostrich. Darwin noted in his *Journal of Researches* that nothing seemed to have astonished the Fuegian more than the sight of the bird: 'Breathless with astonishment he came running to Mr Bynoe, with whom he was out walking – "Oh, Mr Bynoe, oh, bird all same horse!"'

The *Beagle* was cramped, full to the gunwales – seventy-three men, one girl and a well-stocked hold, on a ship barely 100 feet long — and this lack of space aggravated tensions to which the Fuegians were not immune. York was still besotted with Fuegia and kept an eye on her every move. He suspected that all those around him were potential rivals and, as Lieutenant Sulivan later commented, he became 'so jealous at times, as to require the interference of the captain . . .'. York's distrust was mainly directed at Jemmy, for whom Fuegia, it seems, held a candle: 'Jemmy was evidently her favourite,' reported one source. 'But the strength and ferocity of York gained him the victory.' Fearing that York might even murder Jemmy, the ship's officers threw their weight behind the older man. 'So Fuegia Basket was betrothed to York Minster,' commented the same source, and she was 'savagely watched by him the whole time afterwards'.

Jemmy tried to remain aloof from such wrangling. He had become a well-rounded, pleasant and charming young man, a favourite with one and all. His excessive foppishness was ludicrous, but also the toast of the ship: the smallest blemish on his shoes 'would send him immediately to his cabin, where Day and Martin's services would be in request,' remembered one shipmate. 'His collar was kept scrupulously clean. He preferred a dress-coat to the rough sou'westers of the officers, and seldom walked on deck without a pair of gloves.'

But if the positive side of Jemmy's heightened sense of fashion was that it symbolised his progress away from savagery, then the negative side was the vanity that accompanied it. So conceited did he become over his appearance that he could be quite churlish. In his *Journal of Researches*, Darwin wrote that the Fuegian boy was 'short, thick and fat, but vain of his personal appearance . . . He was fond of admiring himself in a looking glass; and a merry-faced little Indian boy from the Rio Negro, whom we had for some months on board, soon perceived this, and used to mock him.' Jemmy hated this and would say with disdain, 'Too much skylark.'

These occasional fits of petulance emerged in other ways too. The crew of the *Beagle* were astounded by the strength of Fuegian eyesight, which they reckoned was the equivalent of a European with a telescope. Jemmy would often stand on lookout, watching for other ships, land and rocks. Several times he and York had spotted a speck in the distance and declared it was such and such an object to a sceptical crew, only to have been proved correct. If Jemmy ever quarrelled with any of the *Beagle*'s officers, Darwin wrote in his diary, he would sulk and threaten 'me see ship, me no tell'.

Tantrums aside, however, Jemmy got on well with everyone except York. The voyage was an opportunity to reacquaint himself with friends from the previous trip, notably with the cox-swain Bennet and his 'confidential friend', the assistant surgeon Benjamin Bynoe (who, after the troublesome Robert MacCormick was removed from the ship in Rio, became acting surgeon). Bynoe was held in special trust by all three Fuegians, possibly because he kept a close eye on their health, and on many occasions acted as a direct link between them and the ship's captain. Out on hunting expeditions with FitzRoy, the acting surgeon would give his commander important accounts of his latest findings on the lives and superstitions of the Fuegian people.

Darwin, too, became a friend. In one revealing passage of his *Journal*, he painted a very human picture of his Fuegian shipmate: though Jemmy could be passionate, he noted, 'the expression of his face at once showed his nice disposition. He was merry and often laughed, and was remarkably sympathetic with anyone in pain . . .' The naturalist had first-hand experience of this compassion. As a landlubber, he had suffered terribly almost from the moment the *Beagle* weighed anchor: 'When the water was rough, I was often a little sea-sick,' he wrote, '[Jemmy] used to come to me and say in a plaintive voice, "Poor, poor fellow!" but the notion, after his aquatic life, of a man being sea-sick was too ludicrous, and he was generally obliged to turn on one side to hide a smile or laugh, and then he would repeat his "Poor, poor fellow!"'

Darwin's records are a useful marker of the Fuegians' progress. Though he had never met them before and could not, therefore, provide a comparison with their former selves, he nevertheless came to them with the fresh, interested perspective of a naturalist. In the hours that he spent with them, both on the ship and ashore, he had time to pin down and note their important characteristics with brevity, clarity and humanity. To him York 'was a full-grown, thick, powerful man . . . reserved, taciturn, morose, and when excited violently passionate; his affections were very strong towards a few friends on board . . .' and despite everything that others wrote of him, Darwin added that his intellect was good. Of Fuegia Basket, he said she was 'a nice, modest, reserved young girl, with a rather pleasing but sometimes sullen expression, and very quick in learning anything, especially languages'.

On the last issue Darwin's observations are especially important. The Fuegians' understanding of English was a crucial benchmark in their progress from 'savage'. Darwin was complimentary of their abilities, but found that although the three 'could both speak and understand a good deal of English, it was singularly difficult to obtain much information from them concerning the habits of their countrymen . . .' This, he felt, came because they did not understand the concept of alternative answers: for example, when a toddler is asked if an object is black or white, the possibility of two answers might overwhelm him. Notwithstanding this, the fact that the Fuegians had a good grasp of English, and that they

The dark and brooding captain, Robert FitzRoy sketched some time around 1838.

Fuegian indian as seen by the crew of the Beagle who called him a
Yapoo Tekeenica.

Fuegians greet a sailor from their wigwams.

Sailors trading with Fuegians near Button Island.

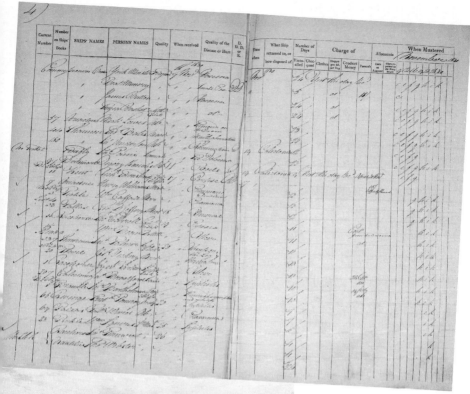

Above: Welcome to England. The November 1830 muster roll for the Royal Navy Hospital in Plymouth with the Fuegians at the head of the list.

Above left: Yamana indians at Wulaia Cove, with Beagle expedition tents and boats in the background.

Left: Monte Video in the 1830s, the first city the kidnapped Fuegians would ever have encountered.

FUEGIA BASKET. 1833.

JEMMY'S WIFE. 1834.

JEMMY IN 1834.

JEMMY BUTTON IN 1833.

YORK MINSTER IN 1833.

YORK IN 1833.

FUEGIANS.

Above: The infants school as it is today, as seen from St Mary's church.

Right: Inside St Mary's infants school, Walthamstow, where the walls 'spoke' messages from the scriptures.

Left: FitzRoy's Fuegians, clockwise from top left, Fuegia Basket in 1833, Jemmy Button's wife in 1834, Jemmy Button in 1833, York Minster profile 1833, York Minster portrait 1832, Jemmy Button 1834 a year after leaving the Beagle.

England's glory, Sailing Billy or
Silly Billy. King William IV.

England's Marie-
Antoinette, Queen
Adelaide.

had the capability to acquire new languages, was demonstrated several times on the voyage south, most notably by Fuegia Basket. Shortly after the *Beagle* docked in Rio de Janeiro, on 4 April 1832, FitzRoy discovered a problem in the readings for longitude and had to return north to Bahia to check his chronometers. While Jemmy and York remained on the ship, Fuegia was placed in the care of an expatriate English family, with whom she spent the majority of the next three months, acting as a nanny to the children of the household. Between April and July 1832, she not only taught them English – they had been away from Britain so long that they had forgotten their mother tongue – she also learned Portuguese well enough to converse in it freely and fluently. More remarkable still was that when the *Beagle* later pulled into Monte Video she learned Spanish with equal success.

The journey to Tierra del Fuego, with all its longueurs, gave the officers time to continue their informal study of the beliefs and customs of the Fuegians. One morning Jemmy told Bynoe that he had been visited in the night by a man who had come to his hammock and whispered in his ear that his father was dead. It had disturbed him, and when Bynoe tried to laugh the story off, Jemmy shook his head saying it was 'bad – very bad'.

Ghosts were nothing new on the *Beagle*: the crew had long been afraid that the ship was haunted. Stories circulated that the late captain, Pringle Stokes, stalked the decks at midnight. Jemmy's story was particularly significant, though, for it suggested to his overseers the possibility of a belief in the afterlife, of some form of hitherto unexpressed spirituality, and as the journey proceeded, it became clear that the three were indeed superstitious and that 'their ideas were not limited by the visible world'. Bad actions resulted in bad weather, brought about by a great black man who lived in the woods and who knew everything that was done, asserted York. When he witnessed Bynoe shooting ducks too young to fly, he chastised the surgeon: 'Oh, Mr Bynoe, very bad to shoot little duck – come wind – come rain – blow – very much blow.' York also told a story about his brother, who, he said, had murdered a man for stealing birds. He had immediately regretted it because

'rain come down – snow come down – hail come down – wind blow – blow – very much blow. Very bad to kill man. Big man in woods no like it, he angry.' At the word 'blow' York imitated the sound of a strong wind; and he told the whole story in a very low tone of voice and with a mysterious manner; considering it an extremely serious affair.

In tandem with these conversations, there were the frequent and inevitable questions on cannibalism. Mr Low, a sealer who came aboard the *Beagle* in Tierra del Fuego, told them that when hunger set in during the winter months, the Indians would kill the old women of their tribe and eat them. He had interviewed a Fuegian boy who had said that the women were suffocated in the smoke of a campfire. When asked why they did not eat their dogs, the boy had replied, 'Doggies catch otters, old women good for nothing: man very hungry.' As a joke the boy had imitated the sounds of a woman screaming. Jemmy had confirmed the truth of this story, and an appalled Darwin wrote in his *Journal*, 'Horrid as such a death by the hands of their friends and relatives must be, the fears of the old women, when hunger begins to press, are more painful to think of; we were told that they then often run away into the mountains, but that they are pursued by the men and brought back to the slaughter-house at their own fire-sides!'

However, the three Fuegians were uncomfortable talking about the subject, and when they did there were inconsistencies in their stories: they would not eat vultures because the birds might have fed on a human; they would not dump their dead in the sea because they might be eaten by fish, which might in turn be eaten by them. When cannibalism was talked about, Jemmy would refer to his people with shame and deny that he had ever eaten a human. He would prefer, he claimed, to 'eat his own hands . . .'

Chapter 11

On 4 December 1832 Robert FitzRoy wrote to his sister from Monte Video: 'I am again quitting the demi-civilised world and am returning to the barbarous regions of the south . . .' Less than two weeks later the *Beagle* entered Good Success Bay on the eastern coast of Tierra del Fuego. Along the way sightings of Indians had confirmed the captain's words, and underlined a change in the returning Fuegians. At Cape Penas a group of 'tall men' had been spotted with their dogs; both Jemmy and York called them 'Oens men' and said they were very bad. They demanded, without success, that the ship open fire on them.

At the same time they were, as FitzRoy wrote, 'very much elated at the certainty of being so near their own country; and the boy was never tired of telling us how excellent his land was – how glad his friends would be to see him – and how well they would treat us in return for our kindness to him'.

As the *Beagle* approached Good Success Bay, a band of local inhabitants who had been hiding on the forested heights that surround it leaped up, waved skins and lit a fire. This was Charles Darwin's first sighting of the natives of Tierra del Fuego in their natural state, and he later wrote to his old mentor John Stevens Henslow:

> The Fuegians are in a more miserable state of barbarism, than I had expected ever to have seen a human being . . . I shall never

forget . . . the yell with which a party received us. They were seated on a rocky point, surrounded by the dark forest of beech; as they threw their arms wildly round their heads and their long hair streaming they seemed the troubled spirits of another world.

After anchoring on 18 December, FitzRoy went ashore with a party that included Jemmy, Darwin and a new addition to the ship's company, Robert Hamond, who had joined the voyage in Monte Video and who would soon leave the Royal Navy because of an uncontrollable stammer. On the shore they found a small group of men decorated with red ochre, black charcoal and oil, the eldest with a splendid display of white feathers in his hair and two thick bars of white and red paint across his face. They wore shabby guanaco skins across their shoulders and all looked miserable, bearing little resemblance to the Fuegians on the ship 'except in colour and "class of feature"' – one of the four was even six foot tall. Hamond, for whom this was also the first sight of a native people, said, 'What a pity such fine fellows should be left in such a barbarous state!' They talked with a rapid nervous stutter, which suggested that they were afraid.

The ship's company responded by handing out strips of red cloth, which the Indians tied around their necks. The tension was broken; the Fuegians administered pats of welcome to their new friends. Darwin took a short stroll with an old man, who slapped him three times front and back simultaneously before offering his own chest for reciprocation. Darwin obliged and there were frenzied grunts of approval that sounded like the clucking of a chicken.

The Fuegians were quick to spot a difference between the ship's crew and Jemmy Button. The old man took him aside and assailed him with a long, loud harangue. Jemmy turned to his *Beagle* colleagues in shame: he had not understood a word and was embarrassed at the appearance of these poor creatures, whom Darwin would later describe as like 'the devils which come on the stage in such plays as *Der Freischutz*'. Be that as it may, both groups found an affinity with one another. The natives mimicked their new friends' every move: the sailors pulled faces, the natives pulled faces, the sailors squinted, the natives squinted, the sailors spoke, the natives repeated word for word. When the party began to sing sea shanties, the locals tried to join in. The tallest Indian, anxious to show off his height and good looks, stood back to back with the tallest crew member, then stood on tiptoe and shuffled up the sand to higher ground. He bared his teeth for examination and presented his face in profile for all to admire.

Later in the day, FitzRoy returned with another party. This time both Jemmy and York were present and, emboldened by each other's company, they ridiculed the natives, laughing at their appearance and their voices. The Indians responded by scolding York as they had earlier scolded Jemmy. They compared the colour of his skin with that of the sailors and told him he ought to shave, yet, commented Darwin in the *Narratives*, 'he had not 20 dwarf hairs on his face, whilst we all wore our untrimmed beards'. York burst out in uncontrollable laughter and, although both he and Jemmy claimed to be unable to understand the Indians, he reported to FitzRoy that the old man had said that he was dirty and should pull out his beard.

There was little unease this time. The native men had brought children with them, and the mood of playfulness soon returned. Despite the sailors' long, ragged beards, the Indians apparently believed that some of the shorter men were English women – one waltzed with an officer, as the ship's party gave an impromptu display of ballroom dancing. They joked and laughed with the younger members of the crew, and only when wrestling broke out did FitzRoy put an end to the fun. It would have been inappropriate, he felt, for one of his crew to lose a bout to an Indian. A note in Darwin's diary records, 'In the evening we parted very good friends, which I think was fortunate, for the dancing and "sky-larking" had occasionally bordered on a trial of strength.'

This first encounter with the Indians made a deep and lasting impression on the 'fly-catcher', or 'stone pounder', as Darwin was known. As he wrote to his sister Caroline,

An untamed savage is I really think one of the most extraordinary spectacles in the world. The difference between a domesticated and a wild animal is far more strikingly marked in Man: in the naked barbarian with his body coated with paint, whose very gestures, whether they may be peaceable or hostile are unintelligible, with difficulty we see a fellow creature. No drawing or description will at all explain the extreme interest which is created by the first sight of savages. It is an interest which almost repays one for a cruize in these latitudes and this I assure you is saying a good deal.

The *Beagle* pulled out of Good Success Bay at four in the morning of 21 December. The crew's new friends had disappeared after their first evening together, but had returned two days later in large numbers to beg for *cuchillas* – the Spanish for knives – and though relations had remained cordial, it was time for the ship to move on.

What followed was a nightmare journey of horrific seas, near escapes and negligible progress. The *Beagle* doubled Cape Horn in fine weather, but it was the last they saw for over three weeks. The little ship was battered from all sides by gigantic waves and terrifying gales. On 13 January 1833, despite all their best efforts to get to York and Fuegia's land, they had made only twenty miles from the Cape. That day the sea boiled over in one stunning final onslaught. At noon the *Beagle* was hit by three gargantuan rollers in quick succession. She shipped a sea that filled the decks and smashed one of the precious whale-boats. Another breaker would have sunk her. Confusion reigned. The shattered boat was cut free with an axe and, with the ship looking certain to go down, the ports were bashed open. The floodwater poured out and the *Beagle* bobbed up again. As the ship turned tail and headed back east, a shaken FitzRoy told Darwin that it was the worst storm he had ever weathered.

Two days later the ship came to a halt in the sanctuary of Goree Roads. They were now near to the eastern entrance of what was soon to become known as the Beagle Channel, significantly closer to Jemmy's land than that of York and Fuegia. As the ship lay in calm waters, York announced that he would rather stay in Jemmy's country than go home. The captain was delighted and mightily relieved. 'This was a complete change in his ideas, and I was very glad of it; because it might be far better that the three, York, Jemmy and Fuegia, should settle together. I little thought how deep a scheme Master York had in contemplation.'

At the time FitzRoy attributed York's change of heart to his realisation that the missionary Matthews, with his collection of gifts, was going with Jemmy Button. He wanted to make sure that he, too, had a share of the booty.

The next day a party put ashore at Goree Roads to scout out a possible site for a settlement. This was a strange action: to have left the Fuegians here would surely have been the worst of all worlds, for it would have meant that none had been returned to their own people. It is indicative that FitzRoy was making plans on the hoof. As it happened the area was singularly unsuitable. It was the only flat land that FitzRoy had seen in Tierra del Fuego, and he had hoped that it would make good farmland. A long walk soon put paid to that idea. It was a morass of boggy moss and peat that sank up to six feet deep. There was little sign of life, just a gaggle of wild geese, a few guanaco, and the remains of a still warm fire near which a man had recently slept and eaten limpets. York Minster said that such isolation indicated he was 'a very bad man', somebody who had been caught stealing. They determined to push on into Jemmy's country. The idea was to inch around the north-eastern coast of Navarin Island, into the Beagle Channel and on towards the Murray Narrows. Here they would deposit the Fuegians and Matthews at Wulaia Cove.

The next couple of days were spent putting together a small flotilla of whale-boats, yawl and gig. A temporary deck was built onto the yawl to carry the 'outfit' of equipment Matthews had brought from Walthamstow. In his diary Darwin vented his spleen: 'The choice of articles showed the most culpable folly and negligence . . . [and] shows how little was thought about the country where they were going to. The means absolutely wasted on such things would have purchased an immense stock of really useful articles.'

Among the gifts were five rabbits with which to populate the area, given to FitzRoy by a Tom Wood in England, and which, he told his sister, he 'had cherished religiously in spite of their knawing through every machine which could be contrived for their safety and further protection from numerous salt sea waves'.

At just before nine o'clock on the morning of 19 January, the four boats departed from the *Beagle*. With FitzRoy went the three Fuegians, Matthews, Darwin, Bynoe, Hamond, the mate Stewart, midshipman Johnson and twenty-four seamen. It was a party of formidable size, capable of towing the heavily laden yawl against contrary winds and tides.

For once the weather was glorious, and by early afternoon they had entered the channel, putting thirty miles between themselves and the *Beagle*. Not a native person had been seen, the sun shone, the water was smooth, the boughs of large trees hung across the passage and spectacular serrated mountains, iced in snow and cloaked with thick forests, decorated their route. It had been an ideal start. As darkness fell they pulled into a pleasant cove formed by a cluster of small islands. Darwin was evidently content: 'Nothing could look more comfortable than this scene. The glassy water of the little harbour, with the trees sending their branches over the rocky beach, the boats at anchor, the tents supported by the crossed oars, and the smoke curling up the wooded valley, formed a picture of quiet retirement.'

The fires they built that night were, FitzRoy said, big enough to roast elephants whole. Only one mishap shook their optimism: while hacking through a log, seaman Robinson's axe slipped and he all but severed two fingers. It was considered a bad omen. Hamond wrote in his diary: 'I turned into my tarpaulin bag but slept very little that night.' The idyllic enclave was named Cutfinger Cove.

At four the next morning they struck camp and, as the sun rose over the mountains, they paddled along the shore past several Indian canoes. They glided on over smooth water, past cliffs that narrowed the channel to just a mile. The new territory was more thickly populated: everywhere fires were lit to mark their passage — the Fuegian warning to others that strangers were on the way. A group of men on the shore ran for miles in pursuit of the boats. As they rounded one set of cliffs, three or four Fuegians leaped up yelling, flailing their arms, shaking sticks, their naked bodies and straggling windswept hair startling those below.

Still they continued, into a strong breeze, striving to maintain their momentum. In the shadow of the hills the temperature was bitterly cold. Jemmy told FitzRoy that these people were enemies and often warred with his people. York laughed at them, mocked them, and screamed, 'Monkeys – dirty – fools – not men,' from the safety of his boat. Fuegia buried her face from them, unable to bring herself to look at these people. FitzRoy noted in himself a mixture of surprise and pleasure: 'It was interesting to observe the change which three years only had made in their ideas, and to notice how completely they had forgotten the appearance and habits of their former associates; for it turned out that Jemmy's own tribe was as inferior in every way . . .'

At noon they came to rest near a native camp. The Fuegians stood and shouted, beckoning the sailors in, but though the gig and second whale-boat went closer, they did not land. FitzRoy bartered for fish from a little distance out. Meanwhile, the men rested on their oars and, after a short breathing space, moved off into a stiff, tiresome breeze. In two hours they made little progress, and took dinner near a group of Indians who kept their slings in their hands and who, for a while, looked decidedly threatening.

FitzRoy defused the situation by tying red tape around their heads and giving them gimlets, which they liked but not as much as if they had been given knives. These Indians, according to Hamond, were 'miserably thin in the arms and legs with large bodies', yet they were fussy over the food that was offered them, enjoying biscuit, but expressing outright disgust when handed a tin of preserved meat.

The afternoon dragged on. The wind slowed progress to a sluggish mile an hour, and as nightfall loomed, they found themselves being pursued by three canoes. FitzRoy dropped back to encourage them to leave them in peace, but without success. He fired a musket over the Fuegians' heads and then, when that did not work, he fired another through one of their canoes. They fell behind, but as the boat party began to put up their tents, canoes arrived and their occupants joined them on the beach.

Early next morning, the sailors awoke to find that the Fuegian numbers had swelled, and they now appeared to be looking for trouble. All of them carried slingshots, and had crossed a boundary line marked on the ground to keep them out. As they raised a terrible din, FitzRoy flourished a cutlass in warning, which inflamed them further. The women and children among the group backed off and one man picked up a large rock. FitzRoy stepped up to him with a bravura display of self-confidence, took the rock from his hand and patted him on the back. The Fuegian fell quiet and the sailors breakfasted as if nothing had happened.

As they set out to sea, one of the Indians stepped up to the water front and launched into a loud speech. York Minster warned those around him that this was 'very bad talk'. The rest of the day, though, was a largely uneventful row along the beautiful thoroughfare of the Beagle Channel. They were three days out from the ship, new explorers to a virgin territory, and were thankful for the quiet.

The following day, 22 January, began with a welcome fresh breeze that soon gave way to a blistering sun that stripped the skin off the sailors' backs and faces. As they pushed off at nine o'clock, Fuegia Basket almost capsized her boat by getting her dress stuck on the sheet hook. Hamond wrote in his diary, 'We took the precaution to shift her over upon each tack, for she was more like a bundle of dirty clothes, and much more in the way . . .' Nothing, though, dampened York's ardour, for he remained in love with her and deeply jealous. FitzRoy's entry for this day in his *Narratives* tells of the not always serious problems this was causing him:

> The attentions which York paid to his intended wife, Fuegia, afforded much amusement to our party. He had long shewn himself attached to her, and had gradually become excessively jealous of her good-will. If any one spoke to her, he watched every word; if he was not sitting by her side, he grumbled sulkily; but

if he was accidentally separated, and obliged to go in a different boat, his behaviour became sullen and morose. This evening he was quizzed so much about her that he became seriously angry, and I was obliged to interpose to prevent a quarrel between him and one of his steadiest friends.

In spite of the heat and long distance covered, the day's row was magnificent in scenery and low in native interference. Jemmy told FitzRoy that nobody lived here because it was dangerous territory, a 'land between bad people and his [Jemmy's] friends', a sort of buffer zone that was periodically transgressed by the Yamana's deadliest enemies, the Oens-men. He was afraid that they might stop there for the night, but they pulled on as far as Ponsonby Sound, and landed among the wigwams of a group in the same tribe as Jemmy.

There were three men and two women, and they had been so frightened at the sight of the flotilla that they had run away. On landing FitzRoy sent Jemmy and York to reassure them. The Fuegians rejoined the camp, but they brought sad news: Jemmy's father was dead. Jemmy turned to the coxswain James Bennet and reminded him of the dream that he had had out at sea. He was grave, but not distraught, uttered the words, 'Me no help it!' and left to collect green leaves, which he burned with a gloomy look on his face, 'after which he talked and laughed as usual,' FitzRoy noted, 'never once, of his own accord, recurring to the subject of his father's decease'.

That night the seamen made another of their blazing fires and sat around it with the polite, meek Fuegians, their faces like ghastly masks in the flickering wood fire. Jemmy narrated long stories about his life in the area and about the cruel and much feared Oens-men, who crossed the mountains at the time of 'red leaf' – April or May – to attack the people of the Yahgashaga and steal their women, children, dogs and weapons and to kill their men.

As everyone listened attentively to his tales, Darwin observed the Fuegians who had joined them: 'We were well clothed and though sitting close to the fire, were far from too warm; yet these naked savages, though further off, were observed to our great surprise, to be streaming with perspiration at undergoing such a roasting.' Yet they appeared content, and when the crew struck up a song they joined in the chorus as best they could, though Darwin added, 'The manner in which they were invariably a little behindhand was quite ludicrous.'

Late in the evening a couple of the Fuegians left in their canoes to spread the news of the return of the prodigal son, and the strange, singing friends with hairy faces he had brought with him.

Chapter 12

The morning of 23 January 1833 saw an extraordinary start to what became an extraordinary day. Not long after sunrise, as the sailors loaded their cooking utensils into the boats, they heard a distant yelling. Within minutes a large gang of Indians had arrived on the beach, running so quickly that their noses were bleeding, talking and shouting in such rapid-fire chatter that their mouths frothed with saliva. The faces of many were covered in white spots and their hair was smeared with clay; others had black and red stripes painted over their noses and cheeks, and all wore strings around their neck. The startled seamen thought they were facing demons returning from a battle, but there was no aggression and little trouble, other than a feeble attempt at pilfering – one man was caught with Hamond's axe under his arm, but when challenged he gave it up with a lack of shame bordering on nonchalance.

The weather was magnificent, a glorious day in which to begin the final, crucial stage of FitzRoy's long experiment. No sooner had the boats pushed off than Fuegian canoes started to fall in behind them. There were thirteen at first, but as each settlement was passed and each island circumnavigated, more canoes paddled out to greet them. FitzRoy described the scene in a fine passage of a letter to his sister:

The day of our arrival at Wullia was beautiful – the steep-sided snow-capped mountains glittered in the sun on one side while on the other they threw a deep darkness over the icy smooth dark blue water. Thirty or forty canoes followed our boats as we pursued a winding course amongst inlets and around projecting precipices. The deep voices of the natives, shouting with all their might, were echoing from height to height. From the fires in each canoe, small columns of blue smoke ascending added to the novelty and picturesqueness of the scene. It was not what one would expect in Tierra del Fuego, it was (except in the tops of the mountains) a scene of the South Sea Islands.

Over the next few hours the combination of hard rowing and a fortuitous breeze, which billowed their sails, meant that the boats stole a substantial march on their pursuers. They arrived at Wulaia Cove in the early evening with valuable time to evaluate the settlement and get organised. FitzRoy had never been here before – he had kidnapped Jemmy at sea, and had no idea of what to expect. What he found was a delight beyond all his hopes: gently inclined pastureland, with a good deep soil, well watered by a crystal clear stream, that promised fertility and augured well for the agricultural ambitions he had for the returning Fuegians. He was overjoyed at the prospects for a permanent settlement here and complimented the proud Jemmy on the quality of his home turf.

There was no time to waste: the crews may have rowed themselves beyond exhaustion over the last few days, but the Fuegian hordes would soon arrive. Already one family, happily living on Wulaia, had had to be placated with gifts and reassurances, and FitzRoy had no illusions about the difficulties that might lie ahead. A party was detailed to dig out a boundary trench around the planned settlement and sentries were placed at strategic points along it to prevent encroachment. One group pitched the tents for the boat party, another turned the topsoil near the brook for a garden and yet another was set to chopping down trees to use in the construction of three houses – one for Matthews, one for Jemmy and one for York and Fuegia, who, it was now agreed by all, were effectively married.

Even as the work parties were being detailed, canoes began to pour in. Leaving their women behind, Fuegian men and boys dashed across to the camp. Very soon a hundred indians crowded along the boundary, which was only enforceable with a combination of coercion, good humour, Jemmy's explanations, and presents of knives, scissors and gimlets. One by one the Fuegian men squatted on their haunches along the line. To Jemmy they directed a thousand questions and tirades. His temper was being tested to the limit when, at the height of his exasperation, there came a deep roar. He halted in his tracks and turned. The roar came again. A man was shouting from a canoe a mile out to sea. Jemmy dropped the bag of nails he was carrying. 'My brother!' he exclaimed, and climbed a rock to watch the canoe approach.

Aboard it were his four brothers – one man and three boys – two sisters, and his mother. As the boat arrived Jemmy descended from the rock to the water's edge. His mother, barely able to look at him, ran away to secure the canoe, then hid her possessions – a tatty basket of tinder, firestone, paint and fish. Jemmy's sisters went with her, leaving the four brothers staring at their returned sibling. A few seconds passed without a word, and then they walked up to him and around him, circling silently again and again.

'Strange dogs meeting in a street shew more anxiety and more animation than was manifested at this inhuman meeting of a lost child and his afflicted mother and relatives,' FitzRoy wrote later to his sister Fanny. Darwin, too, used an animal analogy: this first reunion, he said, was 'less interesting than that between a horse turned out into a field when he joins an old companion. There was no demonstration of affection; they simply stared for a short time at each other . . .'

Jemmy tried to communicate, but was stunned by his inability to use his own tongue. He attempted to converse with his eldest brother in English, and when he got no reply, asked repeatedly, 'No sabe? No sabe?' Darwin viewed the proceedings with sadness: 'I do not suppose any person exists with such a small stock of language as poor Jemmy,' he noted in his diary. 'His own language forgotten, and his English ornamented with a few Spanish words, almost unintelligible.'

The crew were also confused. They had expected great emotion, but had witnessed what seemed to be cruel indifference. It was another of those apparent instances of cold-heartedness that appeared to confirm their ideas of savagery. It is worth noting that later that evening, after York had spoken with Jemmy's mother, he disclosed that she had been inconsolable on the abduction of her son and had scoured the furthermost coasts of Tierra del Fuego for weeks on end in the hope that the ship had left him behind.

That same evening the three Fuegians spent time at the native encampment that had been built a short distance away. Their aim was to explain where they had been and what had gone on. Jemmy took his mother a carter's smock frock to cover her nakedness. To his eldest brother he gave a Guernsey frock, trousers and a Scottish cap. Both were delighted. At sunset those Fuegians who had not built wigwams went home, while Jemmy, York and Fuegia returned to their shipmates.

Over the next four days, Wulaia Cove was a hotbed of activity. Three large, spacious wigwams were built for Matthews and the Fuegians. Trees and branches from the nearby woods were chopped down and whittled into tapered poles. The thick ends of these were planted in a circle in the ground and the thinner ends brought together at the top. These structures were covered with several insulating layers of thatched boughs and grass. The one assigned to the missionary was provided with an upper floor made from boards carried from the ship, so that he could squirrel tools and provisions away from the eyes of the larcenous Indians. Around the wigwams a couple of smallholdings were dug and planted with potatoes, carrots, turnips, beans, peas, lettuce, onions, leeks and cabbages.

Every move was observed by the assembled Fuegians. For a couple of days, at least, relations remained amicable: some of the Indians carried wood for the wigwams or brought material for thatching. They bartered fish for trinkets and iron tools and were entertained by the antics of the sailors. One day the mate and the surgeon got the whole of the Fuegian gathering dancing, with the mate demonstrating the actions while Bynoe plucked away on a Jew's harp. At other times crew members led singing lessons, which the Indians adored, giving full vent to their powers of mimicry. However, the sight of white-skinned men washing themselves was, to the Fuegians, the greatest spectacle of all. As the crew removed their clothes and splashed around in a brook, a hundred pairs of eyes were on them. However, on their third day in the cove when a group of men were stripped to the waist by the stream, a large party of Fuegians turned up and used the sailors' preoccupation to steal whatever they could get their hands on: handkerchiefs, shoes, shirts and the like. Theft was a problem: the ship's hands had lost much property, and FitzRoy had witnessed one Fuegian distract Jemmy in conversation while another picked a knife from his back pocket. Even the ever cautious and somewhat daunting York Minster had lost out to the pilferers.

As time moved on, the numbers of Fuegians grew. At one point as many as 300 sat on the boundary line, and Jemmy warned FitzRoy of some unsavoury characters, including an uncle of his.

Things turned hostile on 26 January when there was a concerted attempt at theft during the sailors' ablutions, but more serious was an incident at the boundary marker. Here, two or three old men tried to break the camp's perimeter. When a sentry asked one to move back, the old man walked up to him and spat in his face. He then stepped back behind the trench and, over a sleeping Fuegian, acted out a scene in which he skinned the body, cut it up and ate it. The implication was clear.

Later that evening FitzRoy ordered a firearms practice to impress and warn the natives. The Fuegians watched and chattered as the balls hit their mark or splashed great distances out to sea. At sunset they left the camp as usual, but FitzRoy noticed they were 'looking grave, and talking earnestly'. An hour later one of the guards opened fire on an object scuffling around by the tents, thinking it was a wild animal. It was not. It was a man, who jumped up and ran off into the night.

The next morning a strange atmosphere hung over the encampment. At nine o'clock, as the final touches were put to both the wigwam thatches and the gardens, all the Fuegians but four men climbed into their canoes and left the cove. There were no explanations as to why they were leaving, or where they were going, not even for Jemmy and York, and speculation ran through the camp: had they been alarmed by the show of strength the night before, or were they planning an attack? FitzRoy feared the latter, as did most of the rest of the party. In the last day or two, the arrival of many strangers had diminished the influence of Jemmy and his family among the Fuegians. His friends and relatives might have suspected that fighting was about to break out, and FitzRoy was puzzled as to why they had not told Jemmy or York.

He decided on a plan of simultaneous retreat and advance. If 300 Fuegians were to attack, there would be no chance that his party of thirty could survive the onslaught. He thought it sensible to leave the settlement, set up a camp a little way off and let any violence that might erupt burn itself out. At the same time, this mini crisis offered an opportunity. He called Richard Matthews and asked him how he felt about spending his first night alone with the three Fuegians in the wigwams. The absence of Indians would give the crew the chance to unload the yawl away from their covetous eyes, and a night on their own in the wigwams would be a test of both Fuegian intentions and the missionary's mettle. The plan seemed tough on Matthews: on the one hand FitzRoy was saying that he suspected treachery and a major assault that thirty men would be unable to resist, and on the other he was suggesting that Matthews, Jemmy, York and Fuegia spend the night alone undefended.

Nevertheless, Matthews agreed. He was not held in high regard on the *Beagle* – Darwin said of him at this moment that he 'behaved with his usual quiet resolution: he is of an eccentric character and does not appear (which is strange) to possess much energy and I think it very doubtful how far he is qualified for so arduous an undertaking'. However, thus far he had yet to show any fear and any hesitation in the face of potential adversity, and he was not about to start now. Stores were brought across from the yawl and carried into Matthews's wigwam, where they were placed in the upper partition. A box of especially valuable items was buried, safe from Fuegians and from fire With the afternoon fading York and Fuegia went to their wigwam, Jemmy joined Matthews in his, and the boats sailed off, as if for good. Three miles away they pulled into a bay and pitched their tents in the dark.

At daybreak the crew headed back. In the boats anxiety built up as the men speculated on the fate of the missionary. Would he be dead? Would Jemmy have gone the same way? What would have happened to York? And Fuegia? The convoy rounded a point, the camp came into view and there was Richard Matthews, kettle in hand, relaxed and confident after a trouble-free night. Many Fuegians had returned, he said, but they could not have been friendlier. Jemmy agreed, adding that those Fuegians who were presently on Wulaia were friends of his and that all the bad men had gone back to their own country.

Encouraged, FitzRoy ordered the test to be taken a stage further. He directed the yawl and one whale-boat back to the *Beagle* and, with Hamond, Darwin and a contingent of sailors, he headed off to survey and explore the north-western arm of the Beagle Channel, with a promise to return in just over a week. Matthews was to be left alone with the Fuegians for an extended period; whatever happened while the boats were away would determine the feasibility of leaving him alone in Tierra del Fuego.

Nine days went by. The surveying boats went along the unexplored north-west arm of the Beagle Channel to Whaleboat Sound and Stewart Island and turned back.

On 5 February they encountered a large party of Fuegians opposite Shingle Point. This was a fair distance from Wulaia Cove, and on the way out Indians here had acted threateningly towards them. These were the same ones, but now they were fully dressed, their faces were smeared in red and white paint, their hair decorated with goose feathers. One woman was wearing a dress that had belonged to Fuegia Basket; ribbon and red cloth adorned the bodies of others. Worse still was their attitude, which gave little reason for optimism: there prevailed, commented FitzRoy, 'an air of almost defiance among these people, which looked as if they knew that harm had been done, and that they were ready to stand on the defensive if any such attack as they expected were put into execution'. His heart sank. With grave concern for the well-being of the missionary, Jemmy, Fuegia and York, the crew pulled on for as long as daylight would allow. The next day they began at dawn and, Hamond noted in his diary, that after they shot through the Murray Narrows and entered Ponsonby Sound,

> many canoes came out and we heard shouting as usual from every little valley and cove on the beach. Several canoes came close to us, but we left them astern; but I could not help observing a great many pieces of cloth etc, amongst others a man with a piece of Fuegia's gay plaid petticoat tied round his head. This foretold a tale . . .

The crews on the two boats fell quiet and, though conditions were favourable, it was not until midday that Wulaia came into sight. On the beach sat several canoes, and all around stood a great crowd of Fuegians, dressed in ripped shirts and scraps of cloth. They ran at the two boats as they landed, bellowing, barking and jumping about wildly. FitzRoy ordered his men to pick up their guns. From the back of the screaming mob there was a shout. Matthews, Jemmy and York pushed their way through: all three were well, and Fuegia was waiting in a wigwam.

The missionary appeared relieved to see them and climbed into FitzRoy's boat for a conference at sea. Jemmy got into the other boat, but York waited on the beach. All around him the Indians squatted down to watch the two boats like 'a pack of hounds waiting for a fox to be unearthed'. What Matthews told FitzRoy made for depressing listening. The departure of the two boats had been followed by a couple of days of relative peace and quiet, but the third brought canoe loads of more aggressive Fuegians. Resolved that the *Beagle*'s boats had gone for good, they began several days of looting. Matthews's life had been made a misery: the Fuegians stripped him of clothing, tools, crockery and food. They entered his wigwam and demanded presents, threatening him with violence, holding his head down to demonstrate their strength. One day when he asked an old man to get out of his way, the man fetched a large rock and threatened to smash it over his head. Another group encircled him and shoved him backwards and forwards, teasing him, pulling hideous faces and tearing the hair from his face. On another occasion a large party of men went after the missionary with stones and stakes. One of Jemmy's brothers, who witnessed this, burst out crying, though Matthews headed off his would-be assailants with gifts.

The nightmare was unceasing: his wigwam was constantly surrounded by groups of men who deprived him of sleep with ceaseless chatter throughout the night and doleful howling as the sun rose in the morning. The only escape was provided by the women, who treated him with compassion and gave him food and shelter in their wigwams. By the end of the week he could not even go there, so numerous were his attackers and so vigilant did he have to be with his possessions and his well-being.

When the boats returned he had lost almost everything. Jemmy, too, had been stripped of most of his property, though Fuegia and York had been left untouched. The gardens had been trampled underfoot, despite Jemmy's efforts to explain their purpose and their benefits. 'My people very bad; great fool; know nothing at all; very great fool,' he told FitzRoy when he had the chance to explain his version of events. Only Jemmy's family had behaved in a friendly fashion, although one brother had joined in the plunder.

It was clear that Matthews could not stay and carry out his work without putting himself in great jeopardy. FitzRoy agreed that he should go back with the boats to the *Beagle*. He detailed men to spread out among the natives to create the impression of strength and numbers, then ordered the remaining hands to clear what was left of Matthews's property – essentially the buried box – out of the wigwam as swiftly as possible. Hamond considered it a brave action: 'I certainly thought that we should not have got away without a breach of the peace, for the Indians were making a great noise, and some of the chiefs making menacing gestures. However, by being very much on our guard, we got away without a row . . .'

When the last man was safely aboard the boat, FitzRoy handed out axes, saws, knives, gimlets and nails to the Indians and said goodbye to Jemmy and York, promising to come back once more in a few days. The two returned Fuegians stood waving on the beach still clothed in their kid gloves and button boots, breeches and tunics. The sadness of the farewell touched many of those there, and Darwin wrote in his diary,

It was quite melancholy leaving our Fuegians amongst their barbarous countrymen. There was one comfort; they appeared to have no personal fears. But, in contradiction of what has often been stated, 3 years has been sufficient to change savages into as far as habits go, complete & voluntary Europæans. York, who was a full grown man & with a strong violent mind, will I am certain in every respect live, as far as his means go, like an Englishman. Poor Jemmy looked rather disconsolate & certainly would have liked to have returned with us; he said 'they were all very bad men, no "sabe" nothing'. Jemmy's own brother had been stealing from him; as Jemmy said, 'what fashion do you call that'. I am afraid whatever other ends this excursion to England produces, it will not be conducive to their happiness. They have far too much sense not to see the vast superiority of civilized over uncivilized habits, yet I am afraid to the latter they must return.

Despite the sadness of saying goodbye, there was a sense of release all round. Of the experience Darwin said, in a letter to his sister Caroline, he had felt 'quite a disgust at the very sound of the voices of these miserable savages'. Of Matthews, FitzRoy stated in the *Narratives* that he 'must have felt like a man reprieved, excepting that he enjoyed the feelings always sure to reward those who try to do their duty . . .'

Sadly for Richard Matthews, life did not improve for him. In 1835, when the *Beagle* eventually reached New Zealand he joined his brother and attempted once again to become a missionary. Unfortunately he was found wanting: he behaved improperly on many occasions, causing a deterioration in the fragile relations between missionaries and natives there. One Sunday he made a Maori boy shoot a dog that had been bothering his chickens, and when the dog's owners complained, he horse-whipped them. In 1840 he was at the heart of a financial scandal in Wanganui that involved the misappropriation of missionary funds. He and his pregnant wife and children were forced to sell their property and walk 400 miles across the heart of New Zealand to his brother's home in Kataia. In 1845, seeking to make amends for his misdeeds, he opened a native school eighty miles from 'civilisation', and was found writing to the Church Missionary Society, 'It hath pleased the Lord that I should lose the use of one eye and with a wife and four children I am at the present reduced to the greatest distress . . .'

As for FitzRoy, the return to Wulaia and the chaos and ruin he found were crushing blows. He could tell himself that he had made a change to the lives of three Fuegians, but he could not fool himself that his efforts had borne great fruit. Hamond observed in his diary, 'It was very mortifying to Captain FitzRoy who had taken so much trouble and in so disinterested a manner to better the conditions of these poor savages, to have all his plans frustrated at the very commencement.' In what was undoubtedly not meant as a metaphor, but serves the function perfectly, his next entry read: 'All the seeds that were sown had made their appearance above ground, but I am afraid it was too late in the season for them to come to maturity. We all went to bed very much out of temper with the conduct of the Indians.'

Eight days after he had last seen Jemmy, York and Fuegia, on 14 February 1833, FitzRoy paid them another visit at Wulaia. He found them well and in the company of a few local people, who were fishing. All three were smartly dressed and in good spirits. Nevertheless they had had an eventful week. Jemmy had continued to lose things to general thievery, most notably a looking-glass, but York and Fuegia had fared considerably better. A large canoe that York was building sat by his and Fuegia's wigwam.

Not long after FitzRoy and his party had gone, strangers had turned up, Jemmy told the captain. There had been 'very much jaw' and a lot of fighting with 'great many stone'. They had stolen two women and Jemmy's people had stolen one, but all was calm now and he believed the worst was over. In the gardens the beans, peas and corn were flourishing. Jemmy's mother came to meet the captain in the dress her son had given her. It was a fond farewell, which lifted FitzRoy's spirits. In his own mind, the project still had a chance of blossoming. Perhaps it was not yet time to abandon all hope. In a letter to his sister he wrote that he 'left them with some satisfaction . . . Things might have turned out worse, as well as better.'

Chapter 13

On a bright, breezy day in early March 1834, the *Beagle* dropped anchor off the shore of Wulaia Cove. It had been thirteen months since FitzRoy had said his last, optimistic goodbye. In the interim they had charted the eastern extremities of Tierra del Fuego, checked and rechecked the longitude of Patagonia, put in to Buenos Aires, Monte Video, and the Falkland Islands. Now, with the work on the Atlantic section of the survey near to completion, he took advantage of fair winds and blue skies to become the first captain to penetrate the Beagle Channel in a ship.

The Fuegians had not been forgotten, and in their quieter moments many a crew member's thoughts had turned to them – mostly with anxiety. On 3 December 1833 Darwin wrote, to his sister Susan, 'It will be very interesting, but I am afraid likewise painful to see poor Jemmy Button and the others – I expect to find them naked and half starved – if indeed they have not been devoured during the past winter.'

The *Beagle* had reached Port Famine on the Straits of Magellan in the first days of February. From here they beat westward across Nassau Bay, through Goree Roads and into the channel. Things were very quiet. In the final stretch, seven canoes followed them and, for a short while at Wulaia, threatened a fight. But they had been driven away and all that was left was silence. From the ship it could be seen that the cove was deserted.

As FitzRoy climbed into a boat to be rowed ashore, he steeled himself for bad news. His fears were justified: the wigwams were empty and long abandoned. Their structure was undamaged but they were just shells: all their fittings and furnishings had been removed. There were no signs of the Fuegians. He walked to the gardens and shuffled disconsolately around them. A clutch of healthy potatoes and turnips had pushed their way to the surface, but the rest was frustratingly neglected. The captain ordered that they be dug up and served at his table that night. He strode back to the boat and returned to the *Beagle*.

As the hours passed FitzRoy prowled the upper deck. Then, in the distance, three canoes – the foremost bearing a ragged flag – were spotted moving at speed from a small island. FitzRoy had difficulty making out the occupants through his telescope, but he could see that two were washing their faces. As they came nearer he recognised Jemmy's brother 'Tommy Button' but, as he wrote in a letter to his sister, 'could not make out another individual whom I was sure I knew well. At last he saw me and by the motion of his hand to his head (like a sailor touching his hat) I knew my poor little friend Jemmy – so altered . . .'

The young Fuegian was naked, save for a knot of cloth modestly covering his loins. He was emaciated, his hair long and matted, his eyes caked with the ash of woodsmoke. Where before he had been a stout, but neatly groomed boy, he was now a shadow of his former self. So ashamed was he of his appearance that as the canoe neared the ship Jemmy turned his back to it. Darwin noted, 'It was quite painful to behold him . . . When he left us he was very fat, and so particular about his clothes, that he was always afraid of even dirtying his shoes; scarcely ever without gloves and his hair neatly cut. I never saw so complete and grievous a change.' The effect was emotionally explosive. 'I could almost have cried,' wrote FitzRoy. 'I was not the only one who was disposed to play the woman's part for he was a great favourite and his altered appearance was enough to move harder people than sailors.'

Jemmy scampered aboard the *Beagle*, greeted his old companions affectionately and was rushed below deck to be scrubbed and clothed. Within half an hour he was dining at the captain's table 'using his knife and fork and behaving in every way as if he had only left us the preceding day'. His English, too, was as good as it had ever been; he remembered everyone and expressed pleasure at the reunion, singling out Benjamin Bynoe and James Bennet for particular attention. He handed out presents he had been keeping for them: two carefully preserved otter skins, one for FitzRoy, the other for Bennet; a bow and a quiver full of arrows for Mr Jenkins, the schoolmaster back in Walthamstow; and two spear-heads he had made for Darwin. FitzRoy was touched and made a special note in a letter to his sister Fanny, 'These things, from their clean appearance, had been, I am certain, laid by ready for our expected arrival. Whatever could the poor little fellow do more?'

But Jemmy was not seeking sympathy. Life was good, he proclaimed. Since leaving the *Beagle* he had not had a day's illness; to the contrary, he felt fitter than ever. 'I am hearty, sir, never better,' he told the captain, who from the Fuegian's appearance had surmised that he had been ill. His only complaint was that he had been eating far too much. 'Plenty fruits, plenty birdies, ten guanacoes in snow time, and too much fish,' he said, patting his malnourished stomach.

When urged to return to England with the ship, to take up where he had left off, he replied that he had no wish to return or to change his way of life. He would stay here, where he belonged. The refusal surprised those around him. Darwin wrote to his sister Catherine, 'He was quite contented; last year in the height of his indignation, he said "his country, people no sabe nothing; —

damned fools." Now they were very good people, with too much to eat and all the luxuries of life.'

In the days immediately following FitzRoy's departure the theft of property had continued and Jemmy had occupied his days with carving a canoe out of a large log and making daily inspections of the gardens for vegetables. The first frosts of winter had followed quickly in the wake of the departing boats. Within a month or two the returned Fuegians had found themselves chilled to the bone and isolated in their new, impractical homes, which had proved too large, too high and almost impossible to heat. They had moved back into the relative warmth of a Fuegian wigwam.

At the same time news of the encampment at Wulaia had spread to the furthest reaches of Tierra del Fuego – to the Oens-men. They crossed the Beagle Channel in stolen canoes and ran swiftly over the mountains, descending on Wulaia from the heights behind the cove. In the skirmish that followed, Jemmy killed one of the attackers before joining with his people in fleeing to the sanctuary of nearby islands. One might have expected him, as the most 'civilised' Fuegian, to have been particularly disturbed by the fighting, but it was York who had been most gravely unsettled: in the heat of battle he had stood at the door of his home with a raised spade, threatening to decapitate anybody who came near. Soon after the attack he persuaded Jemmy and his mother to go with him on a visit to his land in the west. By this time, Jemmy said, York had become a daunting figure, 'very much jaw . . . pick up big stones . . . all men afraid'. He had felt obliged to accompany him.

They left in four canoes heading west. At Devil Island, near the junction of the north-west and south-west arms of the Beagle Channel, they had met York's brother and a party of Alakaluf Fuegians. That night, the Alakalufs had robbed Jemmy of his clothes, his tools, everything they could get their hands on, except a large knife that hung round his neck. Fuegia was implicated in the treachery and helped York to 'catch his clothes during the night'. The last time Jemmy had seen her she had been smiling and laughing as usual and she and York had been well clothed. He had subsequently heard that, having passed through the Beagle Channel to Christmas Sound, they had reached their home territory safely.

Jemmy's abandonment yet again — for the second time in a matter of months — on a lonely shore, this time as naked as he had come into the world and with only his mother to help him, was the final straw. As York stripped him of his clothes — the crisp white shirt and the stiff breeches, the kid gloves and the button boots — he took from him the last vestiges of Englishness. Frightened, cold and lost, this was when Jemmy realised his isolation. He could choose to maintain the charade that he was something else, that he had a mission to achieve, a new way of life to pass on, or he could accept that he had been cast aside by all but those closest to him. Now, a Yamana Indian, he chose the only path that was open to him. He returned to his people.

After dinner, Jemmy and his brother went for a stroll along Wulaia with the surgeon Bynoe. He pointed out where the sailors' tents had sat in 1833, and where the boundary trench had been dug. Bynoe tried to persuade the Fuegian to return to London.

On the ship, FitzRoy was disenchanted. His grand scheme had been frittered away. Ever since the events of 1833 and the rescue of Matthews, he had feared an outcome like this. He had always been uneasy with York Minster. Where Jemmy had a gentle, light side, FitzRoy felt that York had always been a brute, except in his dealings with Fuegia. He had failed to capture the hearts of shipmates and home friends alike. FitzRoy saw what York had done as the fulfilment of a long-term, well-calculated strategy.

He wrote in the *Narratives* that when York decided he would rather go to Wulaia than to his own country, he had already made the plan:

> York's fine canoe was evidently not built for transporting himself alone; neither was the meeting with his brother accidental . . . He meditated taking a good opportunity of possessing himself of every thing; and that he thought, if he were left in his own country without Matthews, he would not have many things given to him, neither would he know where he might afterwards look for and plunder poor Jemmy.

Early that evening, with Jemmy still on the *Beagle*, a rumour reached FitzRoy's ears. A canoe had come alongside and in it sat a beautiful young woman, crying. She said she was Jemmy's wife. Jemmy had not mentioned her and, when asked about her, he denied knowing anything about her until an older Fuegian announced to the ship's company, 'Jemmy Button's wife, Jemmy Button's canoe and Jemmy's wife come!' Then he admitted it, sparking off a general celebration and gentle mirth. Handkerchiefs, shawls and a gold-laced cap were given to the woman as presents. She was 'decidedly the best-looking female in the company', commented Lieutenant Sulivan, but she was distressed: since her young husband had raced out to greet the ship she had feared that another attempt might be made to take him away. Her tears were only stemmed by his appearance on the deck.

Her arrival lightened FitzRoy's mood. Jemmy was married, he was happy. Here was the proof. He might not make a missionary, but at least he was reconciled to his people.

To his sister Catherine, back in England, Darwin wrote, 'The Captain offered to take him to England, but this to our surprise, he at once refused: in the evening his young wife came alongside and showed us the reason.'

One of the remarkable things about the day's visit was the language in which it had been conducted. When the *Beagle* had returned to Tierra del Fuego at the end of 1832, FitzRoy had been dismayed that Jemmy could no longer speak Yamana. As the Fuegian's family — his brothers and their wives — had walked around the ship this afternoon, it had become obvious that even now Jemmy had not fully recovered his mother tongue. He had, however, taught his friends some English. The two languages had coalesced into a variety of pidgin, shared now by those around him. 'Strange as it appears he had actually taught his family more English than they had taught him Fuegian,' wrote FitzRoy. 'Every word which we heard him use — either to them or to his wife — was broken English — and he told me that he could say very little in his own language — that he knew English better — and that his family understood him when he spoke in English.'

'Give me knife', 'canoe', 'come' echoed around the decks from Fuegian mouths. And he remained Jemmy Button: there had been no return to Orundellico, the name of his childhood. This was, perhaps, his most significant tribute to his time in England.

The next morning, 6 March 1834, broke on a warmer but dull day, an overcast sky threatening squally showers. FitzRoy was keen to be moving on, and greeted Jemmy for breakfast at first light.

Their discussion in the captain's cabin was lengthy and private. FitzRoy was keen to pump the young Fuegian for whatever information he had on York and Fuegia, and the threat of the Oens-men returning.

As FitzRoy listened to his former charge, he convinced himself that even if the grand scheme had fallen apart, the 'good effects' on Jemmy and his family, whom FitzRoy thought much more 'humanized' than the other 'savages' in the region, were unmistakable. He took comfort in crumbs:

> I cannot help still hoping that some benefit, however slight, may result from the intercourse of these people, Jemmy, York and Fuegia, with other natives of Tierra del Fuego. Perhaps a ship-wrecked seaman may hereafter receive help and kind treatment from Jemmy Button's children; prompted, as they can hardly fail to be, by the traditions they will have heard of men of other lands; and by an idea, however faint, of their duty to God as well as their neighbour.

When the conversation was over it was time for goodbyes to be said. As his family waited in canoes below, Jemmy and the crew exchanged a final sad farewell. Darwin noted in his diary: 'Every soul on board was as sorry to shake hands with poor Jemmy for the last time, as we were glad to have seen him. I hope and have little doubt he will be as happy as if he had never left his country; which is more than I formerly thought.'

If the Fuegians made a profound and lasting impression on anybody it was Charles Darwin. His writings show a man deeply affected by his contact with the primitive peoples of the Cape Horn region. He had first met Jemmy, York and Fuegia in Plymouth. They were the first natives he had ever come across and had been away from their homes for almost two years, but were well-mannered, politely spoken and neatly dressed. What he experienced in Tierra del Fuego was a shocking contrast. When he thought of how far Jemmy Button had come, he wrote, 'It seems yet wonderful to me when I think over all his many good qualities, that he should have been of the same race and doubtless partaken of the same character, with the miserable, degraded savages whom we first met here.'

Darwin did not mince his words on the Fuegian Indians: he believed that here on the tip of South America 'man exists in a lower state of improvement than in any other part of the world'. But in Jemmy, York and Fuegia he saw the possibility of change and adaptation. The native Fuegians, he said, were more base than even the Australian Aborigine, who could at least 'boast of his boomerang, his spear and throwing stick, his method of climbing trees, tracking animals, and scheme of hunting. Although thus superior in acquirements, it by no means follows that he should likewise be so in capabilities. Indeed, from what we saw of the Fuegians, who were taken to England, I should think the case was the reverse.' He concluded, 'Viewing such men, one can hardly make oneself believe that they are fellow creatures, and inhabitants of the same world.' Yet he saw them mirrored in FitzRoy's Fuegians. It was possible to change, to grow, to evolve. In his account of the voyage of the *Beagle*, Darwin wrote,

> Whilst beholding these savages, one asks, whence have they come? What could have tempted, or what change compelled a tribe of men to leave the fine regions of the north to travel down the Cordillera, or backbone of America, to invent and build canoes, and then to enter on one of the most inhospitable countries within the limits of the globe? Although such reflections must at first occupy one's mind, yet we may feel sure that many of them are quite erroneous. There is no reason to believe that the Fuegians decrease in number; therefore we must suppose that they enjoy a sufficient share of happiness (of whatever kind it may be) to render life worth having. Nature by making habit omnipotent and its effects hereditary, has fitted the Fuegian to the climate and the productions of his country.

In Tierra del Fuego the kernel of an idea was born in him that would come to dominate his life. Nevertheless he left the area for the last time feeling pessimistic about its future . . .

> until some chief shall arise with power sufficient to secure any acquired advantages, such as the domesticated animals or other valuable presents, it seems scarcely possible that the political state of the country can be improved. At present, even a piece of cloth is torn into shreds and distributed; and no one individual becomes richer than another. On the other hand, it is difficult to understand how a chief can arise till there is property of some sort by which he might manifest and still increase his authority.

Jemmy waited for the *Beagle* to leave. As the ship lurched forward, his wife in a canoe below shrieked with anguish, and his brother screamed, 'Jemmy Button – canoe – come!' Loaded with as much booty as he, his family and the three canoes could carry, Jemmy climbed out of the *Beagle* for the last time and paddled off to the safety of the island that he had informed the captain was his. The ship pulled away from Wulaia and, as it stood out in Ponsonby Sound, those who looked back observed a curling plume of smoke from Jemmy Button's farewell pyre.

PART FOUR

The Selfish Crotchet

Weep! weep for Patagonia!
In darkness, oh! how deep,
Her heathen children spend their days;
Ah, who can choose but weep?
The tidings of a saviour's love
Are all unheeded there,
And precious souls are perishing
In blackness of despair.

Plea for Patagonia,
Patagonian Missionary Society

Chapter 14

The Patagonian Missionary Society was born of the religious fervour and Protestant determination that gripped Britain in the nineteenth century. The haphazard, almost accidental, spread of the country's overseas power and influence in the late Georgian and early Victorian periods roused in the hearts of the pious a desire to carry the Gospels to newly opened territories. Missionaries were in the vanguard of empire. In Africa, Asia, the Pacific and Australasia the onward march of Christian soldiers cleared the path for colonial and imperial exploitation. And yet they were often more trouble than they were worth: British missionaries, driven by intense religious passions, led the empire up alleyways and down dead-ends in which it had little business and along which it should never have wandered.

It was up one of these alleyways that the Patagonian Missionary Society had been heading ever since its foundation. Its creator, Allen Gardiner, was a former naval officer possessed of remarkable energy, enviable charisma and an insatiable desire for adventure. Where Gardiner began and the Patagonian Missionary Society ended was impossible to tell: his beliefs, vigour and intellect informed the character of the venture and in him were embodied all the organisation's strengths and weaknesses: its flair, dash and courage, and the naïvety and fragility of thought that eventually brought calamity and tragedy.

Born in 1794, Gardiner had received his calling to Christ when

155

in his thirties. He responded with a fundamentalist fanaticism and devotion that plunged him, time and again, into horrifying situations. Just three months after his first wife had died in 1834, he entered Zululand intent on building a mission station on land controlled by the Zulu king Dingaan. At first rebuffed, for the King was more interested in guns than gods, Gardiner persevered, brokering a treaty between white traders and the Zulu people. This promised the forced repatriation of Zulu fugitives from Natal to Zululand in return for the guaranteed safety of the white residents of Port Natal. Dingaan was delighted, and granted the missionary land near kwaBulawayo.

Gardiner soon discovered the awful truth of the treaty he had helped bring about: under it his first duty was to transport seven runaways into the hands of Dingaan. These unfortunates, who included a woman and three children, were starved then executed. Then, in February 1838, Dingaan's Zulus slaughtered 283 Boers, ripping the heart and liver out of their leader Piet Retief for use in magic. Although Gardiner could not be held directly to blame for the massacre, it took place near one of his mission outposts, and had been caused principally by conditions he had helped foster in the area.

Zululand was a dispiriting experience, even for a man of such indomitable enthusiasm, so Gardiner moved on. Over the next twelve years he tried unsuccessfully to establish mission stations in New Guinea, Chile and Gran Chaco – an area at the heart of South America bordered by Bolivia, Argentina and Paraguay. He had no commission for such work, little support and even less financial backing. Conditions were frequently different from what he had been led to believe, and his difficulties were often exacerbated by local political feuds and what he saw as the scheming of small but powerful Catholic oligarchies.

Tierra del Fuego, Gardiner decided, would be different. It was virgin territory, beyond the pernicious tentacles of Rome. Most importantly, he had heard of a group of friendly Fuegian Indians who had been brought to England in 1830 by Captain FitzRoy and who not only understood the basic tenets of Protestant Christianity but also spoke English. If he could find Jemmy Button, success, he felt, was guaranteed.

After a visit to the Magellan Straits in 1841, in which he made friendly contact with a small tribe of Indians under Chief Wissale, Gardiner returned to Brighton and founded the Patagonian Missionary Society. He had plans to establish a foothold at Oazy Harbour on the northern shore of the straits, but when he returned there in 1845, with Robert Hunt, a school teacher, the locals had turned threatening. The two men fled to England, but Gardiner did not give up. Three years later he and five men hitched a lift to Tierra del Fuego, on board a ship taking coal to Peru. For a day or two things went to plan, and at Banner Cove they began to build an encampment, but news of their presence spread. Swarms of Fuegians descended on them, stealing everything they laid hands on. In exasperation the frustrated party climbed back onto the ship that had brought them and headed for Lima, whence they made a slow and expensive return to England. The mission had been years in the planning, and barely a week in existence.

The stage was set for what was, for some, Gardiner's greatest triumph and for others his greatest débâcle. With hindsight it might appear that by the late 1840s his actions were tinged with madness. Most people would have returned from Banner Cove vanquished and demoralised, but Gardiner demanded a redoubling of effort. Success, he believed, was within his grasp, but he needed a floating mission station, a ship that could be anchored off Tierra del Fuego, small enough to enable contact with the native people but large enough to withstand their unwanted attentions and the possibility of attack. In England he launched a campaign to fund an 120-ton schooner. He gave lectures, spoke at rallies, and made stirring pleas; most significantly he became friendly with another man of strong character, the Reverend George Packenham Despard, who became the Society's secretary. But, at the end of it all, public interest was not there, and neither was the money. A well-wisher from Cheltenham donated £1,000, but that aside the coffers remained disappointingly empty.

Now, against the wishes of the committee of his own society, Gardiner amended his plans. Rather than a schooner he would take two 26-foot metal launches, the *Speedwell* and the *Pioneer*, along with two dinghies to Banner Cove. Accompanying him was a crew of six men: three Cornish fishermen, John Pearce, John Badcock and John Bryant; a Staffordshire surgeon, Richard Williams; John Maidment, a waiter and Sunday school teacher; and a ship's carpenter, Joseph Erwin, who had accompanied Gardiner on previous missions and who had declared that being with him 'was like heaven on earth'. This might have been so, but within days of their arrival in Tierra del Fuego, in December 1850, it must have seemed like hell too.

The party was carried to the islands by the *Ocean Queen*, a barque headed for San Francisco. Once she had departed, native aggression forced the group out to sea, and on a rough passage to Bloomfield Harbour both dinghies were lost. It was a tough beginning, but it was not long before things deteriorated further: a few days later they found that the *Ocean Queen* had left with the powder and shot for their guns. Fish were scarcer than they had previously believed, and now hunting too would be difficult. In the coming days both launches were badly damaged on Lennox Island. After the group had repaired them and sailed forty miles to Spaniard Harbour, the *Pioneer* was smashed in half.

The remains of the shattered launch were brought ashore and used for shelter by Gardiner and Maidment. A mile and a half away, rocking at anchor in the Cook River, the other five stayed on the surviving boat. By March 1851 Badcock and Williams had scurvy. In June their fishing net was ripped to shreds by ice. In the grip of delusions brought on by illness and religious fervour Williams wrote in his diary: 'Ah, I am happy day and night. Asleep or awake, hour by hour, I am happy beyond the poor compass of language to tell . . .' The hunger was cruel: mussels became a staple, mice a luxury. On 28 June John Badcock succumbed. In late August Erwin and Bryant died of scurvy and starvation. They were soon followed by Williams, Maidment and Gardiner. When a rescue ship under William Smyley arrived from Monte Video, in October, the wreck of the *Speedwell* was found with one body still lodged inside, an unexplained scar across its head and neck. Two more bodies were lying on the beach with papers, clothes and tools around them. Smyley was forced to leave in the face of a storm. Three months later HMS *Dido* arrived and found the remains of Gardiner, Maidment and the others. Next to the expedition leader they discovered his diary and a largely intact fragment of a letter to the already dead surgeon informing him of the demise of Maidment:

My dear Mr Williams,

The Lord has seen fit to call home another of our little company. Our dear departed brother left the boat on Tuesday afternoon, and has not since returned. Doubtless he is in the presence of his Redeemer, whom he served faithfully. Yet a little while, and though . . . the Almighty to sing the praises . . . throne. I neither hunger nor thirst, though . . . days without food . . . Maidment's kindness to me . . . heaven.

Your affectionate brother in . . .
ALLEN F. GARDINER
September 6, 1851

A funeral service was held, and the bodies were buried. The *Dido*'s colours and those of her boat were struck half-mast and three volleys of musketry were fired over the graves.

The endeavour had been naïve. Despite the problems that had beset his earlier attempts, Gardiner had arrived without his floating mission station and less well prepared than ever. Failure rarely came more complete than this. No contact had been made with Jemmy Button, and nothing had been achieved, yet seven men had given up their lives. *The Times* reported the tragedy on 29 April 1852 and used its leader column to pillory the venture:

> Neither reverence for the cause in which they were engaged nor admiration of the lofty qualities of the leader of the party, can blind our eyes to the unutterable folly of the enterprise as it was conducted, or smother the expression of natural indignation against those who could wantonly risk so many valuable lives on so hopeless an expedition . . . Let us hear no more of Patagonian missions! The promoters of the scheme have already incurred a responsibility which should give them subject for poignant regret, to cease only with their lives.

But the newspaper was out of tune with its readership, which liked nothing more than an emotional tale of derring-do, another example of British bravado, the ultimate act of selflessness. The slow death of Gardiner and his comrades on a far-off beach was a boon for the Patagonian Mission Society. For the first time funds rolled in, and once-empty coffers overflowed. Under the ruthless and opportunistic stewardship of George Packenham Despard, support was mobilised around an idea of using the Falkland Islands as a mission station, to which Fuegian Indians could be brought for education then return to civilise their people. Gardiner himself had expressed the idea to one of the islands' earliest colonisers and Society committee member, Bartholomew Sulivan, former lieutenant of the *Beagle*, to whom it must have had a familiar ring. At packed meetings and rallies the idea received warm support. Robert FitzRoy's backing was sought, and on 6 December 1852 he wrote,

> I have given the subject . . . my best consideration.
>
> It appears to me that your present plan is practicable and comparatively safe: that it offers a fairer prospect of success than most missionary enterprizes at their commencement, and that it would be difficult to suggest one less objectionable.

Demands grew for an appropriate monument to Gardiner: a statue, a plaque in Westminster Abbey. By March 1854 these had crystallised into the call for a ship to be built and named after him. 'What more suitable [memorial] can be devised than what we are now raising – a vessel bearing the Christian sailor's name, and a chief instrument in furthering the object for which that Christian sailor died?' asked the Patagonian Missionary Society's magazine, the *Voice of Pity*. 'If the good Lord prosper our efforts for the conversion of these savages, in a few years, the approach of this vessel to these shores will be hailed with delight, and her name, teaching His name, will come to be a household word for Christian philanthropy.'

High ambitions indeed, but at a punishing cost. In a blatant call for cash that presaged the TV evangelists of a later age, the Society launched an emotional appeal, exalting its members to use self-denial, social influence, and prayer to bring in funds:

> We want £2,300 . . . We want it at once. The exigencies of the heathen cannot brook delay. Souls are in misery; sinners

are dying; hell is filling; Satan triumphs . . . Give pounds if you can; give shillings if you cannot give pounds; give pence if you cannot give shillings; give a postage stamp if you cannot give pence . . .

The *Voice of Pity* reported that energetic ladies in Scotland were going from house to house with appeal leaflets. An association in Maidstone had bought a boat for the ship. A chronometer had been donated, and a dress made for a Patagonian chieftain. For those with doubts it painted an idyllic picture of its aims, a vision of a future Tierra del Fuego, civilised and Christian. With a ship, hard work and God's help, the Society would stud the archipelago's inhospitable shores with

gardens, and farms and industrious villages . . . The church-going bell may awaken these silent forests; and round its cheerful hearth and kind teachers, the Sunday school may assemble the now joyless children of Navarin Island. The mariner may run his battered ship into Lennox Harbour, and leave her to the care of Fuegian caulkers and carpenters; and after rambling through the streets of a thriving sea port town, he may turn aside to read the papers in the Gardiner Institution, or may step into the week-evening service in the Richard Williams chapel.

By August 1854 the *Allen Gardiner* was afloat on the river Dart, and two months later it sailed out of Bristol, bound for the Falklands. In command was William Parker Snow, and with him went his wife, a catechist named Garland Phillips, a surgeon called James Ellis, Richard Dayas, a carpenter, and John Webber, a mason.

Gardiner's mission had been rejuvenated, but at its heart was a shambles, characterised by a lack of clear and realistic goals, far-fetched expectations and little understanding of the area that the ship was visiting. Channels of communication, which were extraordinarily complex under the best of circumstances, had not been clarified. Methods of payment were uncertain, lines of authority flawed. Events had moved so quickly that the Society had not even been able to find a mission superintendent to take control of the station, whenever and wherever it was established. In the *Voice of Pity*, the Society rarely reflected the troubles it was experiencing at home and abroad — but, try as it might to hide it, there can be no doubt that by the time their ship reached its destination there were deep-rooted problems.

Much of the trouble revolved around the turbulent temperament of the captain of the *Allen Gardiner*, William Parker Snow. He had come to his present position after replying to an advertisement in *The Times* in August 1854. The thirty-seven-year-old son of a naval lieutenant who had fought at the battle of Trafalgar, Snow had been at sea off and on for twenty-five years. His had been an up and down career, high in incident, low in achievement. At the age of sixteen he had left the Royal Navy and emigrated to Australia, where he had wandered into the bush and taken up a wild life that had verged on criminality. In 1836 he returned to England, but fell into bad company and destitution. To escape his debts he joined another ship, but was punished for desertion soon after. He finally won his discharge after rescuing a shipmate from the jaws of a shark off the coast of Africa. A short career in writing followed, but as success beckoned he was robbed of all of his money and went blind for a time. Then he ran a hotel in Melbourne with his wife, but illness forced them back to England, where he became amanuensis for Thomas Macaulay, transcribing the first two volumes of his *History of England*. After a dream in which he learned the 'true' location of the Franklin expedition — Sir John Franklin and 128 officers and crew had gone missing while searching the Arctic for the north-west passage in 1848 – he joined an unsuccessful rescue mission that left for polar waters in 1850.

The triumphs and adversities of Snow's life had shaped his outlook. He was a liberal humanist, with a keen interest in the world around him and a special concern for the well-being of native peoples, whether they were in Australia, Africa, the Arctic Circle or South America. However, the batterings and setbacks of his life had made him cynical of authority and to some he was a whinger, one of life's more dogged complainers, forever predicting disaster or crying foul play. He was a nineteenth-century Cassandra and, like Cassandra, was rarely believed by anyone, which was a pity for he was frequently right.

When he applied for the job with the Patagonian Missionary Society he offered to work for free. They snapped him up, but although they insisted on paying him a wage, he had immediate regrets: the ship, though brand new, was uncomfortable and leaky, its decks were strewn with planks to be transported to the Falklands and his colleagues left much to be desired. Garland Phillips, the catechist, was arrogant and zealous to the point of subversion, the crew – so hard to come by because of the ongoing Crimean war and the insistence of the Society that they were religious men – were insolent and verging on the fanatical. By the time the ship left England, Snow had already tendered his resignation three times.

Snow believed that Phillips, with his teachings of the 'elect', religious ascendancy and the supremacy of God, was instilling both insolence and insubordination in the crew. He felt that the man had been waging war with him ever since they had left Bristol. 'The strange mode of religious teaching that was adopted, against my repeated warnings and remonstrances,' wrote Snow, 'was enough to bring the best disciplined ship into disorder.' It had resulted in 'constant jealousy, opposition, and evil-mindedness, masked under a demure and humble countenance'. On one occasion Snow was punched to the ground and kicked in the ribs by a crew member. Another time, in Monte Video, the captain announced that, due to the pressure of work, there would be one religious service a day, not two as before. Next day the ship's two mates refused to work until the second service was restored. Their truculence was sufficient to warrant a call for the help of a passing French man-of-war. The two were discharged, and deposited unpunished in Monte Video, where they wished to go about 'converting the wretched sailors and bigoted papists'. The first voyage of the *Allen Gardiner* was not a happy one.

On 28 January 1855, after skirting round West Falkland in bad weather, the *Allen Gardiner* took shelter off Keppel Island, to the north of the small archipelago. An inspection the next day showed it to be an ideal location with good soil, water and a plentiful supply of wildlife. It looked like the north of Devon and Wales, wrote the surgeon, Ellis, in his journal, though there was 'nothing picturesque about the land, all being monotonous and unvarying, but regarding it with the eye of a Missionary settler, rather than that of a tourist, I thought more of its capabilities than of its external beauty . . .' Snow and he agreed that this should be the place for the mission station.

After a few days' scouting the island and examining other locations, the mission party went ashore to claim the island for the Society. The ship was dressed in its full colours, the men instructed to wear their smartest kit and to stand attentively as Captain Snow declared,

We give to this place the name of 'Cranmer', in honour of our martyred Archbishop, and zealous reformer of the Church of

165

England, and to the house about to be erected here, we give the
name of 'Sulivan House', in honour of Captain B. Sulivan, RN,
one of the Committee, and a most efficient helper in the Mission.
The bay before us we call 'Committee Bay', and this particular
spot of ground 'Despard Plains' for obvious reasons . . .

Snow declared a holiday, and within two hours somebody had
set fire to the island. A blaze half a mile wide burned out of
control. The newly declared mission station was saved only by
hard work and a fortuitous change of wind. A few days later the
inferno threatened once more. Flames cascaded down the hills,
engulfing the *Allen Gardiner* in smoke. Again the wind swept back
the fire. It smouldered in the hills for another month, growing to
more than a mile wide, the glowing embers lighting up the night
sky. Nevertheless the danger had passed, and the arduous work of
unloading the ship and building temporary accommodation could
begin. On 10 February foundations for a house were laid; a week
later the building was habitable.

By 5 March Snow felt ready to go with Ellis to Port Stanley,
the capital of the Falklands, 150 miles away. When he looked
back on this period of his work, Snow did so with great bitterness.
His sense of being undermined at every step by Garland Phillips
had been exacerbated to breaking point. The fire, which he was
convinced had been started deliberately, flabbergasted him. The
pace at which his colleagues worked, and what he perceived as
their unsuitability for both the task and the conditions ahead of
them, startled him. As tensions mounted, tempers frayed. Just
before Snow left for Stanley there was a major argument, resulting
in mutual contempt between himself and those he left behind.

The Falkland Islands were one of the British Empire's most
isolated and grim colonies. Over the course of three centuries,
since their discovery by John Davis in 1592, there had been

a succession of minor squabbles between countries claiming jurisdiction over them. England, France and Spain had at various times believed the islands belonged to them, but eventually all three had decided that the islands had no material value. In 1774 an English colony was withdrawn from Port Egmont, because it was felt that it was not worth defending. Spain kept a small garrison on East Falkland until 1809, and in the 1820s Argentina began to make its case for ownership. In 1833 HMS *Clio* rehoisted the flag and the Falklands became British, but not with any great enthusiasm. These were bleak windswept islands of no obvious virtue other than as a stopping-off point for ships rounding the Horn and for the sealers who trawled the area. One British officer described Port Stanley in less than encouraging terms:

> The colonists are about 200 in number, living in wooden huts on one side of the harbour, in three long rows one above the other. This is one of the most dreary and miserable places I have set my foot in. A moorish land, it is one of the last spots in the world you could suppose any government in their senses would induce people to emigrate to . . . The majority of the settlers are pensioners and Irishmen, who were induced to come here by the promise of 100 acres of land for pasture, and 10 more with a house, besides a cow and a pig. They arrive here and to their dismay the 100 acres are found to be bog and heath, about eight miles from the settlement, with a cow and pig as wild as 'March hares,' which no one dare approach, and a house of wood, through which the wind howls most piteously. Everything except beef, is 300% higher than in England. All seem dissatisfied with the place, and as soon as they collect a little money, go off to the old country again, or some more congenial clime.

Snow shared this opinion, saying that Port Stanley was 'one of the dullest and most miserable places I can imagine in the world. A sort of mental miasma seems to hang over it . . .' His purpose in going there was to pay George Rennie, the governor, an embarrassing courtesy visit: he had to inform the Queen's representative that the Society had claimed land without first seeking his permission.

When he and Ellis arrived, Snow found that Rennie had been expecting them, and was waiting to pass on a few home truths. He said he was startled that the Society had seen fit to take possession of an island under his government. Nevertheless, though he thought they had been discourteous, and notwithstanding that he had severe reservations about their plans, which he called imprudent, he was not about to throw obstacles in their way – so long as they understood that he was the power in the land. He told them he had been forewarned by the colonial secretary in London, Sir George Grey, that a Society ship was on its way. Grey, too, had not been impressed with their proposals, but had instructed Rennie not to get in the missionaries' way. Rennie granted the Society the right of occupation, at a nominal rent of £1 a year. (This was changed soon after when he allowed the mission to buy 160 acres outright, and lease all of the island, except for a small government reserve, for twenty years at £10 a year.)

The meeting was cordial but cool and there were shocks in store for Snow and Ellis. Rennie told them they had a good deal of fence-mending to do. He read a letter that George Packenham Despard had written to Sir George Grey in which he said that the Society desired a location 'away from the depraved, low, and immoral colonists of Stanley'. Local people had taken offence, Rennie said, and were not necessarily going to treat them with the charity that such an enterprise might normally expect.

The governor then explained a legal difficulty that the Society must overcome. When he had arrived at the Falklands in the winter of 1848, Rennie had found a number of starving South

American gauchos in a terrible state of destitution. They had been brought to the islands in the summer by beef farmers to capture the wild cattle that roamed the island. When winter came the gauchos had been sacked, not given a passage home and left without employment, food or shelter. In a letter to *The Times* in 1859, Rennie wrote that he thought that some had died from cold and want before he could do anything. He had been obliged to open up colonial funds for the survivors, but had then pushed through the Falklands Legislative Council an Alien Ordinance which stated, 'That no shipmaster or settler would be allowed to land or leave on the islands any alien without entering into a bond or security to the amount of 20*l*, that the alien should be re-exported or maintained free of charge on the colony.'

This ordinance would apply to Fuegian Indians brought to Keppel Island, Rennie pointed out, and if any harm came to them the master of the ship that transported them would be held responsible. Twenty-pound bonds would be required for Fuegians before they would be allowed onto the Falklands and, in the case of any deaths among them, the captain of the ship that brought them might be charged with manslaughter. Snow was horrified, but Rennie had not finished. How were they intending to obtain their natives? he asked. There was an awkward silence, before Ellis offered, 'I suppose we must buy them from the chiefs.' It appeared to be the first time the question had crossed their minds, and Rennie warned that such actions might lead to charges of kidnapping. He would consider it his duty, 'if they brought any of those miserable savages to the Falkland Islands, to make strict inquiry whether they had come voluntarily and with lawful contracts as far as could be intelligible to their limited intellects'. It also verged on slavery, he added, and that, he reminded them, was illegal in the British Empire.

If Snow had felt that the whole enterprise had been ill conceived and ill prepared so far, it must now have appeared to be coming apart at the seams: the tattered relationships, the governor's disapproval, the Alien Ordinance, the disgruntled locals. Could the situation get worse? Waiting for him in Stanley was proof that it could. As he killed time in the port, he found Ellis trying to buy 130 cattle at £3 a head and proposing 'going shares with us in a different kind of speculation . . .'. Snow was outraged: here was something completely outside his remit, 'so very different to what we were supposed to be engaged upon . . . that I determinedly opposed it, and wrote home to say so, and also to state that it was not a part of my agreement . . .'

In a gesture of goodwill, the governor had asked Snow whether he would deliver and collect the Falklands mail to and from Monte Video. It was a potentially valuable source of income for the Society — Rennie would pay Snow between £85 and £100 each time — it kept Snow away from his despised colleagues, and it gave him periodic opportunities to check whether the mission superintendent they were awaiting had arrived. He accepted the offer, and in the course of the next six months he flitted to and from mainland South America, stopping briefly at Keppel Island to pass on provisions and observe the health and progress of the land party.

On 19 August 1855 he arrived at Monte Video half expecting to find the sorely needed missionary waiting for him. Instead he received the mystifying news from a Liverpool skipper that the intended missionary had been arrested just days before he was due to leave England. Snow was astonished: where would all this end? He returned to the Falklands ill-humoured and impatient. They had been away almost a year but contact with the Fuegians appeared just as remote as it had on the day the ship slipped its mooring in Bristol. Snow decided it was time to break ranks. He wrote to Garland Phillips on Keppel Island inviting him to join a trip to Tierra del Fuego. After a short hesitation, the catechist accepted. Snow laid down the law: he was in charge on the ship, which must be subject to rules, discipline 'and no more of that extraordinary hallucination of mind evinced on the passage out . . .'. Phillips accepted. On Sunday 14 October 1855 the *Allen Gardiner* left Committee Bay. On board were the antagonists, Mrs Snow and a troublesome crew.

Chapter 15

In early November 1855, the *Allen Gardiner* sailed through the Murray Narrows and into the Yahgashaga. Nearly twenty-two years had passed since Jemmy Button had last been seen and not a word had been heard of him. The evening sun was warm, the scenery stunning, and Snow was impressed by the immensity of the beauty he found there. 'The whole neighbourhood strikingly reminded me of the high peaks of Greenland . . .' he wrote in his account of his time working for the Society.

> Some of the steeple-like mountains directly in front of us, at the extreme limit of our view, seemed like so many cathedrals with their lofty spires; those on our right were in many places bare, like the denuded crown of a man's head, but with verdure above and below such spots. On our left were the Codrington Mountains of Navarin Island, dark and sometimes frowning, with four or five singular peaks like sugar-loaves appearing at the back between two other mountains, and over a level snowy ridge. Many of the brown summits of these mountains, free from snow, darted upwards, in several other places, not unlike whales' teeth, while the lower parts of the hills, down to the water's edge, were covered with a mantle of green.

Wulaia Cove was only five miles away, but he noticed the smoke and sparks of many fires on nearby Button Island. It was five o'clock in the afternoon and all the men, with the exception of the

173

helmsman and a lookout, were down below taking tea. Acting on a hunch he unfurled a British Ensign and ran it up the flagstaff. As the breeze caught it, two canoes shot out from the shore. Snow cried out, 'Jemmy Button? Jemmy Button?' Then, 'To my amazement and joy — almost rendering me for a moment speechless — an answer came from one of the four men in the canoe, "Yes, yes; Jam-mes Button, Jam-mes Button!" at the same time pointing to the second canoe, which had nearly got alongside.'

He was overcome with surprise, and in a confused moment called for the sail to be shortened and all hands on deck. Mrs Snow, the catechist and the two mates rushed to the ship's side and watched as a portly 'shaggy-looking man' stood up and shouted, 'Jam-mes Button, me; where's the ladder?' A rope was found and thrown over the side, and the Fuegian was hauled aboard. There were handshakes and stutterings in broken English. The Fuegian touched his forehead in respect. 'What is your name?' he asked Snow.

The crew could not believe it. Here was a fat little Indian, dirty and naked, speaking understandable phrases of their own language. Seaman C—, who held the Fuegians in contempt, was aghast:

'Well, I'm blowed! What a queer thing! This beats me out and out! There's that blear-eyed, dirty-looking, naked, savage, speaking as clearly to the skipper as one of us; and I be hanged, too, if he isn't as perlite as if he'd been brought up in a parlour, instead of born in this outlandish place! — Well it is queer, and so is all the whole affair. — I can't make it out. — Fair winds, — never any harm, — lots of wild barbarians civil to us, — and now one of 'em talking as plain a'most as ourselves! It knocks me down quite!'

Snow had to find a mooring for the night, and as soon as the initial introductions were over, he asked Jemmy for a good place to anchor. The Fuegian spluttered an answer, and Snow ordered the ship to follow a route into a small, rocky cove.

By now, sixty or seventy people were floating in canoes around the ship, and the captain, worried that they would be overrun, gave orders that nobody should be allowed on board except Jemmy, an uncle, two brothers and a man about to be married to Jemmy's daughter. For the time being the shifting crowd below remained calm, but Jemmy advised Snow that there were one or two bad men in the canoes, men 'not of his country', and said that the captain should stay on his guard.

As soon as he discovered that there was an 'Ingliss lady' on the ship, the Fuegian demanded clothes. Snow fetched a pair of his own trousers and a shirt and handed them to Jemmy who, although only five foot three, was so fat that they were too small. Snow, insultingly and out of character, commented that in his clothes Jemmy looked like 'some huge baboon dressed up for the occasion'. Jemmy said, 'Want braces,' and, after a pair was brought, he began to relax.

It quickly became clear that for somebody who had not spoken the language for over twenty years his English was remarkable. He found fluency of speech difficult but managed 'broken sentences, abrupt and pithy. Short inquiries, and sometimes painful efforts to explain himself were made, with, however, an evident pleasure in being able to converse with some one in the "Ingliss talk".'

Jemmy was taken to the captain's cabin, where he met Mrs Snow, and was offered food and tea. He sat at the table, took a knife in hand and asked for meat, but when it arrived the moment overwhelmed him, and he was unable to eat. Snow, who had also lost his appetite, tried to engage Jemmy in conversation, to question him on his life, what he remembered of the *Beagle* and England. The answers came back thick and fast, disjointed, confused and sometimes barely intelligible. 'Yes: me know — Ingliss conetree: vary good,' he said. 'You flag, me know; yes: much good — all good in Ingliss conetree — long way — me sick in hammock — vary bad — big water sea — me know Capen Fitzoy — Byno — Bennet — Walamstow — Mit Wilson — Ingliss lady you wife?' Snow's wife had a 'lovely colour' and 'vary good looks', said Jemmy. 'Ah! Ingliss ladies vary pretty! vary pretty!'

Jemmy had two wives, and was father to several children. Snow met three of Jemmy's grown up offspring and one young child. His eldest son was married and his eldest daughter, who was 'mild and gentle in her manner', was betrothed to a much older man despite being no older than fourteen. He had put on a great deal of weight, but was otherwise as FitzRoy had found him on their last visit, with long, matted hair and eyes impeded by the sting of woodsmoke. He confirmed that he had never lived again on Wulaia after the initial invasion by Oens-men, but added that, yes, the gardens were fertile. There had been no ships in the area since the departure of the *Beagle*, he said, and when Snow expressed disbelief he replied, 'No: — no ship — Capen Fitzoy — you.'

As they talked Snow tested FitzRoy's vocabulary of Fuegian words, published in the appendix to the *Narratives of the Voyage of the Beagle*, and found them accurate. He showed Jemmy the two portraits of himself that had also been included in the *Narratives*, one of the civilised young man of English cultivation, another drawn after his return to the wild. Jemmy laughed, then looked sad as he thought back over his life, asking himself, Snow reckoned, 'which, after all, was the best — the prim and starch, or the rough and shaggy? Which he thought, he did not choose to say; but which I inferred he thought was gathered from his refusal to go anywhere again with us.'

Over the course of their conversation, Snow spoke of the mission station being built in the Falklands, and how important Jemmy might be to its work. Would he, asked the captain, consider returning to the Falklands with him? Jemmy said no. Snow persevered. 'I expressly put the question in every possible and attractive form . . . but a decided and positive negative was the reply . . .'

The evening was getting on, daylight was fading, and Snow was anxious to secure the ship. Out on a canoe Jemmy's wife was calling, 'Jamus, Jamus.' Before they parted for the night, Snow gave him a short tour of the ship, showing him his library, the ship's instruments, guns, photographs, ladies' fancy articles and perfumes. Jemmy was delighted, putting names to many of the objects. He asked Snow to fire his guns, but the captain demurred, fearing it might alarm the other Fuegians. When he requested a book, Snow handed over a set of religious tracts and a copy of the *Voice of Pity*. 'A fine musical box gave him intense pleasure; and when I played a Harmonium . . . he stood beside me as if entranced. He said it was "Oh! vary good – all Ingliss vary good!"'

Snow led Jemmy onto the main deck and told him it was time for him to leave but that in the morning he would hand out clothes and presents. Jemmy assured him that there would be no problems during the night, that the people around here were good, and with that he and his brothers climbed over the side of the ship and into their canoes.

It was a quiet night, the stillness broken only by the distant yapping of dogs, and at four in the morning Snow arose to prepare presents that he had brought from Bristol. As soon as the sun appeared on the horizon, the Yamana came to the ship, this time as many as a hundred, their canoes 'covering the water like wherry-boats round an important launch at home'. It was not long before Jemmy and his brothers, in the company of some other men, had scrambled on board. Their mood seemed to have changed: they were more aggressive, more demanding, and not a little intimidating. Jemmy looked 'more hideous and deplorable' than Snow could have previously imagined, for despite returning in the clothes he had been given the night before he had obviously been sleeping on the ground and he was covered in red mud.

Nevertheless, Snow welcomed him and suggested he bring his wife and daughter on board to meet Mrs Snow. Jemmy shouted for them to come up and, after a show of reluctance, they climbed up the side of the ship and were taken to the captain's cabin where they were dressed by Mrs Snow in cast-off clothes. To Jemmy, Snow gave a small mountain of gifts, including a clasp knife, an axe, blankets and shirts, and the Fuegian's mood seemed to mellow, but as they all chatted on deck the atmosphere changed again. Captain Snow had sent a party of men in a boat to tow the ship out of the cove and was giving the order to raise the second anchor, when four or five Fuegians, including two of Jemmy's brothers, set upon him, pushing and pulling him. They grabbed at his jacket and tore at his waistcoat, crying, 'Ingliss come – Ingliss give – Ingliss plenty.' More Indians scrambled up the ship's side. From the middle of the mêlée, Snow shouted again for the second anchor to be lifted, but the mate with 'the worst feeling of obstinacy' ignored his instructions. In the boat the men strained to pull the anchored ship away. Snow called on Jemmy for help but found that 'he could not or would not prevent his brothers' and companions' rudeness'. Forestalling any further danger, and gambling that if the Fuegians felt they were about to be carried away they would flee, Snow shouted for the sails to be loosed. They billowed in the light draught and the ship lurched forward. 'One and all, but Jemmy first . . . after an affecting farewell, scrambled back over the ship's side as they saw her slowly moving, while a Babel of tongues and cries resounded everywhere about us,' wrote Snow. With the ship moving, he looked back towards Button Island and saw Jemmy and wife struggling with an overloaded canoe and the unwelcome attentions of fellow Fuegians. Snow raised his cap one last time and waved it.

Chapter 16

The trip to Tierra del Fuego did little to ease relations among the mission party, despite its success in finding Jemmy Button. Phillips, who had attempted to persuade the Fuegian's wife to give up her young daughter to the mission, felt that Snow should have tried harder to encourage the Fuegians to join them in the Falklands. For his part Snow argued that he had done all he could – and, besides, he still had the governor's admonitions on kidnapping and liability ringing in his ears. At some point, whether because of the governor's warning, or because of unease brought on by his distrustful relations with the mission's personnel, Snow began to question the tenets of his work. He would later write:

Jemmy Button had tasted the sweets, or, as they might be to him, the bitters of high civilization: he at all events knew what it was, and all about going away; yet what was his answer, when I and the catechist asked him if he, or any of his boys, would accompany us only a little way? Why, a positive negative! and, therefore, if I were to hear of 10 or 50 Fuegian boys as being at the mission station in the Falklands, I would never believe, until I knew that the Fuegians had learned our language, that those poor lads had gone there as only a religious society ought to let them go, namely, with a full and perfect knowledge of what it was for. Evil must not be done that good may perchance, and only perchance, come.

Moreover, he argued, conditions at Cranmer were nowhere near ready to accept an influx, no matter how small, of Fuegian Indians. Despite reports in the Society's journals to the contrary, it was clear to those who saw the station that the work had not been done. The main house was unfinished, there were no cottages for workmen, no corrals for cattle, and just one little storehouse. Work had yet to begin on a road connecting the settlement with the sea and no landing place or pier had been finished. Conditions were made worse in January 1856 when the carpenter and the mason announced that they could no longer tolerate the behaviour of Ellis and demanded to be taken away from Keppel Island.

In England things were proceeding far from smoothly for the Patagonian Missionary Society. Contradictory messages coming from the Falklands, the time delay built into the mail system, and the need to get a positive message out to the Society's burgeoning membership, which now had thirty-one associate branches, all created new perceptions, expectations and pressures. Impatience was creeping in here too: members and officers alike of the Society, oblivious to the problems of its advance party at Cranmer, craved news of contact with the Fuegians and could not understand what was delaying such a meeting (the story of the discovery of Jemmy Button did not appear in *Voice of Pity* until 1856).

In May 1855, two days before the ship bearing the intended missionary Mr Verity had been due to sail, police boarded it and arrested him as an accomplice in a breach of bankruptcy law. Chaos reigned, and the search for a missionary had to begin all over again. On 9 October the Society chairman wrote to Snow, 'No clergyman has as yet appeared suitable . . . Reports have reached me from respectable sources showing that Mr Verity would have entirely ruined the Society had he been permitted to be connected with it . . .' In a letter of 7 December 1855, George Packenham Despard, the organisation's secretary, offered his services:

Mr Verity failed us – and so did advertising – to bring the suitable head for our stations. It came from many quarters; the Mission is tottering, the interest is waning; your work is becoming frustrate. A voice within said, you are a suitable person in some respects; at all events you have the confidence of people at home – witness £6,400 gathered through you in almost only three years, and you have the affection of Snow and others abroad . . .

The matter was agreed, the Society could breathe a sigh of relief. Despard was to be the first mission superintendent in the Falkland Islands and Tierra del Fuego. In January 1856 a young German called Schmidt, who had lived in Despard's home for a year, was sent to the Falklands to act as the Society's linguist, responsible for compiling a new vocabulary of the Fuegian tongue. The Reverend John Ogle volunteered to go as assistant missionary, and Allen Gardiner, son of the martyred captain, put his name down as an unpaid catechist. Charles Turpin, another lay preacher, was added to the party, which, by the time it left Plymouth on the *Hydaspes* in June 1856, had grown to seventeen persons:

Rev. G.P. Despard, missionary
Rev. John Furniss Ogle, missionary
Frances Margaret Despard, stepmother of Despard children:
    Emily, about 12
    Bertha, 11
    Florence, 9

Harriet, 8
E. Packenham, 7
Despard's two adopted boys:
Thomas Bridges, 13
Frank Jones, 10
A.W. Gardiner and Charles Turpin, catechists
Miss Louise Hanlon, governess
Margaret, servant
William Bartlett, herdsman
Emma Bartlett
Mr Foster, carpenter

They took with them 80 tons of goods, which Snow later complained were mainly personal effects for Despard himself – a pianoforte, furniture and books – and a cow that died on arrival at Port Stanley.

By now Snow was spending most of his time in Port Stanley, seeking the advice of the new governor, Thomas Moore, refitting the *Allen Gardiner* and awaiting news about the arrival of the missionary. Only Phillips and Ellis remained at Cranmer. Snow checked on them occasionally and offered them a passage away, which they steadfastly refused, claiming to be content in what had effectively become a hermitage.

In April 1856 Schmidt arrived. His presence did little to shake Snow out of his growing depression. In *A two years' cruise off Tierra del Fuego, the Falkland Islands, Patagonia and in the River Plate: a narrative of life in the southern seas*, Snow's account of his work in the South Atlantic, he painted a picture of Schmidt as a feeble sycophant, a timid but sneaky place-man sent by Despard to snoop on the mission party and even to open the private mail of the governor and the colonial chaplain. Snow mocked him from the moment they met in a Port Stanley lodging house; it was 'like having a baby to deal with', he wrote. Far from being a linguist, Schmidt could not even speak English and Snow was 'so amazed and disappointed at beholding the gentleman who had come under that high-sounding title that I could hardly speak to him'.

Snow also claimed that Schmidt was unaware of the line of work he had come to, and that when he found he was to live on Keppel Island with Despard his distress was shocking. According to Snow, the cook of the *Allen Gardiner* found him 'in the cabin on his knees, praying for some one to come and help him, – to save him! and, with bitter cries and tears streaming down his face, extravagantly regretting that he had not taken the advice of his parents and remained at home'.

The *Hydaspes* arrived at Port Stanley on 30 August 1856. On the way over Emma Bartlett had given birth to a baby girl, and Frank Jones and Miss Hanlon, the governess, had suffered badly from sea-sickness, but all in all it had been a good passage. At just after 5 p.m. Snow came on board and shook hands with Despard. They met with a warmth that betrayed little of the tension that lay just below the surface. The arriving preacher noted in his journal, 'Seldom have I shaken the hands of man with more hearty good-will than his. He had been expecting us about four weeks . . . and was on the eve of a start to look for us stranded and shattered on some one of the many dangerous points in these parts.'

Despard and his family were given a house in Port Stanley and the next few days were spent in unloading the *Hydaspes*. The young Allen Gardiner remembered the chaos at the quayside:

Perhaps the most amusing incident that I can remember was the landing of the livestock – Mr Turpin and I borrowed a boat . . . The pigs were put in the bows, the sheep in the centre and the goats I had in the stern so that I could look after them — Then came the geese, ducks, goats and hens till the boat looked all alive — As soon as we pushed off with this our last load the crew on board gave us three cheers which we returned and soon reached the shore safely . . . The poor cow died the day we anchored so her house was sent on shore and converted into a temporary shelter for the poultry. The Governor kindly allowed us to put the sheep and goats into his paddock. The goats followed me very nicely . . . The pigs were most horrible fellows to manage. It took us an age to get them up into the sty which was at a little distance.

Dockside goings-on aside, under the surface the mission was continuing to fray. If Snow had held out any hope that the arrival of Despard would herald a new clarity and unity, then he was sadly mistaken. Besides, his months of pent-up frustration and seething anger meant that Snow was spoiling for a fight.

Two days after the *Hydaspes* arrived, he received an unexpected visitor. John Furniss Ogle had paid £500 towards his own passage, but now he was looking for a sympathetic ear to bend. In a state of uncontrolled agitation he told Snow how Despard had verbally abused him during the passage: '"A shoe-black would be better than he." "He was not fit to preach to pigs," and many other similar expressions did the "Missionary Superintendent" apply to him.' Furthermore, Despard had stolen part of a wooden house Ogle had brought for himself, and had decreed that when the party went to Cranmer, Ogle must stay at Port Stanley where food was scarce and prices were rocketing.

What followed was a fit of pique on Snow's part, an act of suicidal petulance. Despard requested a lift in the *Allen Gardiner* to Keppel Island. He was naturally anxious to see what had been achieved there and to check on the well-being of his colleagues. Snow refused to take him. Giving Despard a literal interpretation of the Alien Ordinance, Snow said that to take him to Cranmer would leave him responsible for his safety and, should anything go awry, he might be hauled up on a charge as serious as manslaughter. Besides, he added, the crew was due to be paid off, and some had a guaranteed passage back to England.

Despard was furious. On 18 September he chartered a ship, the *Victoria*, and set sail for Keppel Island. A day later Snow made the *Allen Gardiner* ready to sail. He said later that he was simply intending to follow the *Victoria* and make sure that, in the dangerous conditions that prevailed, the missionary arrived safely at his destination. The Patagonian Missionary Society insisted that Snow was about to abscond to England in the mission ship. However, before the ship could go anywhere the port authorities impounded her, under threat of being fired on by guns now pointing at her from Port Stanley's fortress. Snow ordered the crew to stop hauling the anchor and to stand down.

Ten days passed before Despard returned. On his arrival he delivered a letter to the *Allen Gardiner*, giving the captain three hours to get off the ship. Snow protested that he had all his effects on board and would need longer. Despard granted him three days. Snow asked for compensation – money for lodgings and a passage home for him and his wife. Despard refused.

This was harsh treatment indeed. Port Stanley was facing famine, there was no cheap accommodation, and no ship bound for England. Standing on the quayside Mrs Snow started what eventually became a full-scale nervous breakdown. Nearly destitute, Snow bargained with Despard for whatever he could get: he bought two old mattresses, pillows and blankets for £2, thirty pounds of hard biscuit for 10 shillings, and eight pounds of ship's pork for a further four shillings. With his wife's health deteriorating, he rented a house from the Falkland Islands Company for £2 10 shillings. In order to pay for it he sold off books and instruments at knockdown prices. Four weeks later he obtained a passage for them both on a ship bound for England at a cost of £47. On 30 December 1856 he arrived at Ramsgate.

Next month the *Voice of Pity* announced, 'The peculiarly distressing duty devolves to us of announcing to the friends of the Patagonian Mission, that Captain Snow and the Reverend J.F. Ogle are no longer connected to the Society.' Snow, it declared, had expressed views on the way that the mission should be run that were at variance with those adopted by the organisation. All they could now do was offer him their prayers. In respect of Ogle they were vicious: 'Indeed some strange hallucination of mind seems to have seized him, almost from the moment of the arrival of the Missionary party at Stanley, to be accounted for only on the ground of ill health, or some sinister representations made to him by certain parties there.' It was part of a new ruthlessness that characterised the Society over the coming years.

Chapter 17

The clash between William Parker Snow and the Society had become a highly personal, spiteful affair in which it was difficult to establish who was right. In his more coherent moments, though, Snow had challenged the fundamental philosophy and operation of the endeavour. He came to realise that it was immoral to transport uncomprehending Fuegians several hundred miles from their homeland to a new way of life. In his account, published in 1857, he wrote that missionary work should be about good deeds, poor relief, spreading knowledge and understanding, and taking God to the heathen. It should not be about going among the natives to 'plant an idol in their hearts — disturb the economy of their nature by sudden change; by an irruption of mystic ideas, which they can only understand as you may choose to make them understood, and which is done by various methods not always the most straightforward and truthful'.

However, Despard, the missionary, was now free to assess the achievements of the project and take the enterprise into a period of much-needed consolidation. Over the next two years much lost time needed to be made up. Mrs Despard remained with the children at Port Stanley while her husband transplanted the rest of the mission party to Cranmer. Homes, storehouses and roads had to be built; cattle, sheep and pigs had to be purchased, timber fetched, and short exploratory trips made to Patagonia and the fringes of Tierra del Fuego, where the graves of the original Allen Gardiner expedition were visited.

Conditions at Cranmer became cramped. James Ellis and Garland Phillips, who had spent eight months living alone on the island, had to adjust to a new overcrowding. The Bartletts with their baby, Annie Jemima, took over Phillips's room in Mission House, while he moved into a small room with Despard's two adopted sons, Thomas Bridges and Frank Jones. Schmidt, Ellis and Turpin occupied the large room in the house, the new carpenter lived above them and Despard spent most of his time on the *Allen Gardiner*.

They quickly fell into a routine. Schmidt, Phillips and Jones handled most of the indoor activities, cooking and cleaning, while the rest of the party dealt with the larger construction tasks of building a settlement. The day's work began at six thirty in the morning, with breakfast at eight, prayers at nine and then, after another three and a half hours' work, it was time for dinner. By two in the afternoon they were beginning their third work session, taking tea at half past five and evening prayers at seven. On Thursdays the week's supplies were fetched up from the storehouse. Friday was spent cooking for Sunday, Saturday was a half-holiday, set aside for bathing, walking and shooting, and Sunday was a day of prayers, hymns, readings and conversation. The accommodation was cold and the food bland, consisting of vegetables, penguin eggs, anything that had been hunted or fished and, once every three months, a piece of beef.

Despard spent much of his time away at sea. Between June 1856 and December 1857, he made twenty-five voyages in the ship, commuting between the mission station at Keppel Island, his family at Port Stanley and mainland South America, where he went to raise funds and collect provisions. In Rio de Janeiro in 1857, he learned that HMS *Madagascar* was in port and that Benjamin Bynoe, former surgeon of the *Beagle*, was on board. In his journal Despard recorded that he went on board the ship 'and saw and had long and interesting conversation with Mr B, who was surgeon in the *Beagle* on both surveys; and was well acquainted with our three Fuegian hopefuls. He says Boat Memory, who died at Plymouth, was far the best of them.'

Despard comes across as an abrasive character, who would not tolerate fools or anybody else. He was forty-five and had been acclimatised to the bleak colonial life by a childhood spent in Nova Scotia. For the last sixteen years he had been chaplain of the Clifton Poor Law Union in Bristol and the master of a successful private school for the sons of rich gentlemen. Snow clearly detested him, and claimed that others – Ogle and Schmidt, for example – shared his opinion. To Snow, Despard was a megalomaniac, a tyrant bent on a course of self-advancement clad in the garb of a missionary. A sense of this emerges in the *Voice of Pity*: he is seen admonishing a workman for swearing, or found threatening others for not working hard enough. One Sunday he learned that the crew of the *Allen Gardiner* were not intending to attend church because they were going to wash their clothes. 'Not on Sunday in this vessel,' he roared. 'It has been built, launched and sailed in God's service, and His holy day is not to be profaned in it with impunity. If you wash it will be at your cost . . . The time is coming when you must repent, but it may be too late . . .' The crew were then ordered ashore with their jackets and told they had to stay off the ship for the whole day. 'Sailors are like children; the better they are treated, the more they want . . .' he concluded.

In November 1857, Garland Phillips set off for England. He had been away from home for over three years and wanted to press his case for ordination. What he found on his arrival two months later was a besieged Society, taking a battering from the wrath of their vengeful former captain, William Parker Snow.

In 1857 Snow had released a sixpenny pamphlet entitled *The Patagonian Missionary Society and some truths associated with it*, which asserted that 'a mission to Tierra del Fuego could be carried on for an eighth of what it is costing you now. What is it you are doing now? Merely establishing a colony at Keppel Island for monks and hermits . . .' Later that year his two-volume account of his time as captain of the missionary schooner was published to great critical acclaim and public interest. He had also relentlessly lobbied the Secretary of State for the Colonies and launched a major lawsuit against the Society. The charges were largely familiar, though there were a few extra thrown in for good measure. He claimed that the Patagonian Missionary Society had unfairly dismissed him, leaving him and his wife impoverished thousands of miles from home. He had never been paid and the Snows had been forced to find their own way home. He further alleged that the Society was, in fact, a cover for cattle ranching and financial speculation, that it was proposing to kidnap natives and drag them off to Keppel Island where they would be used to tend the cattle. This, he added, was slavery. His attacks did not finish there. Others, too, felt the lash of his tongue: the authorities on the Falklands were corrupt and the local agent for the shipbrokers Lloyd's was profiting from the deliberate wrecking of ships. Unless something was done, Snow warned, there was grave trouble ahead.

The Society attempted to counter Snow's accusations in *A brief reply to certain charges made against the Patagonian Missionary Society, or South American Missionary Society, by William Parker Snow*, but the captain had stolen a march on them. The arrival of Garland Phillips in England was, therefore, a godsend to them, for they were able to publish first-hand accounts of their achievements, progress and hopes for the future. Phillips said he had thought that he would have carried out more missionary work than he had in his first two years, but there had been a great deal more to do than had been initially realised. Everything was working now, he was pleased to report: the road had been macadamised, stone buildings were going up and visits had been made to Tierra del Fuego and Patagonia. A big hope was that 'two or three of the Mission party will, for a short time, make a trial of remaining among the natives and endeavour by all means to persuade some to return with them to Keppel'.

At the same time the Society was able to announce that, after a series of temporary and none too successful appointments, they had, on the recommendation of the incumbent of St Paul's, Whitechapel, employed a capable and religious captain to replace William Parker Snow and take command of the missionary schooner. Robert Fell had already left for the Falklands. This was the sort of good news the Society needed to boast about and, in early 1858, Despard felt ready to give them more. On 20 April he boarded the missionary ship, with catechists Turpin and Gardiner, and set a course for Wulaia Cove. It was time to reel in Jemmy Button.

A harsh wind cut across the *Allen Gardiner*'s bow: winter was beginning to draw in. When they arrived at Wulaia Cove, on the night of 9 June, snow covered the decks and drifted into the sails and rigging; the moon lit the islands like 'spectres rising out of the water . . .' Two canoes welcomed them and a Fuegian screeched, 'Hillo! Hoy, hoy, hoy.' When Despard shouted down for Jemmy Button the man stood up and pointed across the water to Button Island.

Next day as the missionary walked around the cove, identifying the scene from sketches in FitzRoy's *Narratives*, five more canoes pulled in, one carrying Jemmy's eighteen-year-old daughter.

Despard asked her if she would fetch her father, but he was not here, he understood her to say. 'I gave them all a few things; but kept shewing them far better ones, and saying "Jemmy Button". At last it had the desired effect, for the daughter started back for the island again, saying, "Jemmy Button."'

Nothing more occurred that day, and Despard began to wonder whether he had understood the young woman or whether she had tricked him. The next morning broke with a glorious sun skimming off the frosty ground. At just after nine, four canoes paddled around the northern tip of Button Island. As they approached a man shouted. The people in the canoes on the cove looked across at Despard: it was Jemmy Button, they said.

The Fuegian climbed on board the *Allen Gardiner* and was given clothes, a box of carpenter's tools sent by Benjamin Bynoe, and coffee, bread and butter in the captain's cabin. His daughter, Jemmy explained, had been rowing for a long time to find him and they had set off early this morning to be here. He asked Despard if he would like to see the locations of the old wigwams built by FitzRoy and the crew of the *Beagle*.

The missionary expressed great enthusiasm and climbed down with Jemmy into one of the native canoes. Together they strolled the shoreline. 'Here his canvas houses were placed,' Despard later wrote. 'There he made a garden, and its earth fence and surrounding trench still remained. Across the brook, in a nook of the thicket, was the missionary's wigwam; here, near by, was Jem's; there, York's . . .' As they walked, the Fuegians built their own wigwams for the night and Jemmy pulled out an old axe that he said FitzRoy had given him; it was worn to a sliver. He, too, began to build a small hut: 'Tomorrow make very big wigwam,' he promised, as if the occasion demanded that he impress his visitor.

In June the days pass quickly in Tierra del Fuego, and the sun sets shortly after three. As light leaked away, Despard asked to be returned to the ship and Jemmy called to his children, who were sitting out to sea in his canoe, 'Come way, wigwam-sleep.' They paddled ashore, unloaded their baskets of mussels and limpets and carried them to their home. Jemmy's wife took over the canoe and rowed it to a promontory, where Despard and the others boarded without getting wet. She then delivered them all back to the *Allen Gardiner*, manoeuvring the craft skilfully through a flotilla of canoes that clogged the cove's entrance.

As Despard sat in the boat he could feel pleased at having made contact with FitzRoy's Fuegian, but there was one frustration. Having established friendly relations he had asked Jemmy to go back with him to Cranmer – he could bring his family, he could bring his canoe, he could leave whenever he wanted. The missionary cajoled, bribed, spoke of Jemmy's duty to God, calling on old 'obligations', but he got nowhere. He decided to set Turpin and Gardiner to work on him.

Not long after breakfast on 24 June 1858, a shout echoed through Mission House and across the Cranmer settlement: 'The *Allen Gardiner*, the *Allen Gardiner* is coming in.' Mrs Despard, her children, Ellis and the Bartletts ran down to Committee Bay and waved the ship in. Very soon the news reached them that it carried five Fuegians and a shout of joy rippled through the welcoming party.

'Rejoice with me, and again, I say, rejoice,' Mrs Despard wrote in a letter. 'For the Lord hath seen fit to give an answer to the daily prayers addressed to Him, the Sovereign Disposer of all hearts, that He would be pleased to put it into the mind of some of those poor benighted Fuegians, to trust themselves to our hands, and come over to us here . . .'

Jemmy had agreed to come. After eight days of browbeating

and gentle encouragement from Turpin and Gardiner Jemmy had said he would confer with his people, and finally he had succumbed once more to British pressure. With him he brought his stout elder wife Lassaweea, whom the mission party would call Jamesina, his inquisitive twelve-year-old son Wammestriggins (henceforth known as Threeboys), his daughter Passawullacuds, a lively eight-year-old now designated Fuegia, and the fifteen-month-old baby Annasplonis, who quickly became Anthony Button.

There was general delight, both on ship and on shore, but as yet no place had been prepared for long-term visitors. In the two years that Despard had been in the Falklands the settlement had grown into something more deserving of the title. A new central meeting-house, the Cenobium, had been built, the Bartletts had constructed their own home, and sixteen months after arriving in Port Stanley Mrs Despard and children had moved into Sulivan House. Jemmy had agreed to come for 'five moons' and was kept on the *Allen Gardiner* while the settlement's brick store was converted into a residence. It would be a small home, barely ten foot square, and its location near the sea would help the Buttons feel at home and grant them easy access to plentiful supplies of mussels, limpets and fish. It had a well-boarded floor, a watertight roof and a calico window. A bed was brought in, with a pile of clean blankets, and a fireplace and chimney were built. The family would be warm and able to cook.

As they waited to disembark, Despard engaged the Buttons in conversation, instructing his two catechists to listen out for, and make lists of, Fuegian words. He found Jemmy's English comprehensible, though lacking in vocabulary, and long sentences were nearly impossible. Still, his memory was good: he talked of meeting King William and could name most of the important characters from his days on the *Beagle*, including FitzRoy, Bennet,

Bynoe and Sulivan, and said of his first trip to England, 'He look much Monte Video — Boat Memory die — he not cry, York cry much.'

Two days after the ship pulled into Committee Bay, the house was ready and the Buttons were taken ashore. Despard remembered that Jemmy's 'appearance in sou'-wester, red comforter, p-jacket and heavy boots, was that very much of the skipper of a Dutch lugger; and his wife, in colour, features, and dress, looked like a middle-aged gypsy woman . . .'. Mrs Despard had a more vivid recollection:

Yesterday, when Mrs Button came on shore, I walked down to receive her; she appeared pleased to see me, and smiled kindly when I patted her on the shoulder, and noticed her children; she repeated all my words, but of course without understanding their meaning; she had on the clothes I gave Mr Turpin to take to her, while on board and before she landed, and the overcoat that fitted her best was one, among many others, sent me by kind Miss Harvey, from York. Jemmy is sometimes very funny in his manner of expressing himself. When Mr Despard introduced me to him, he bowed in a most orthodox manner, at the same time pulling off his cap, a red flannel one, given him by Mr Gardiner, and much admired by its present owner. He said, pointing to me, 'Dat your wife? vary good gal; vary fine gal.' The same expressions of admiration were bestowed on the children; he seemed quite astonished to see such a party, and so did his wife! I sent for little baby Bartlett, to show her to the squaw, who looked at and viewed the dear little thing, with eyes which did manage to express some wonderment at the sight of Annie's rosy cheeks and fair skin!

The Buttons were introduced to the whole mission party and taken to what was to be their home for the next five months.

Accounts of the Fuegians' stay on Keppel Island are slender. The only real source of information on the Button family's months there are the reports, journals and letters sent home to the Patagonian Missionary Society and reprinted in the *Voice of Pity*.

William Parker Snow was to complain that this publication was little more than a publicity sheet, with the Reverend Despard as its arch-propagandist. Communications from abroad, he alleged, were rewritten, successes emphasised and problems omitted. In fairness, it was unlikely that the Society would admit in its journal to any difficulties or setback and the arrival of Jemmy at Cranmer was a huge boost to its credibility, an indication that its intents were serious and achievable. In its reports on the Buttons' progress the *Voice of Pity* placed particular emphasis on those stories that its publishers knew would impress the readers at home. There was a focus on Button's manners: the number of times he said please and thank you, how he wiped his boots before entering a house, the way he passed a knife, handle first.

The delivery of Jemmy Button to Keppel Island was a feather in Despard's cap. It heightened the morale of the mission in the Falklands and raised his stock with a British public desperate for news of progress. Even with Despard's reinvigorated mission it had been over two years since the *Hydaspes* had left British shores. With the prospect of William Parker Snow's potentially damaging court case due any day, the success with Jemmy must have seemed long overdue to the committee of the Patagonian Missionary Society. Now that the Fuegian family was actually at Cranmer, work had to begin in earnest. Language was a priority, and while it was important that Jemmy's English improved, Despard was desperate to learn as much Yamana as possible. At the same time it was crucial that Jemmy was reinculcated with Christian values and reintroduced to the rituals and beliefs of the Church of England. Finally Despard held high hopes of using him as a conduit for the future success of their project.

Whenever possible Despard or Turpin talked with Jemmy (Allen Gardiner had gone back to England shortly after the Button family arrived). They found him a sensitive, always courteous man, affectionate but rather slow of comprehension. Conversations would often be about the Bible and Creation. 'Jemmy Button came to visit me in the storehouse,' the missionary wrote on 16 July.

    — Who made sun Jem?
    — God.
    — Moon?
    — God.
    — World?
    — God.
    — You?
    — English God.
    — God?
    — God.

When asked what happened after death, Jemmy replied, 'Good man go to Ever, bad men to the ground.' He could name the days of the week and recalled his time in Walthamstow: in the village, he said, there had been a 'great church-house, two churchmen, one white gown, one black . . .' and music from an 'organ; much noise'. One day the missionary tried without success to teach him to read. Instead they fell into conversation about his former colleagues: 'York go home to his country — his brother come and cheek away very much — say, where my son? [Boat Memory] York say, your son dead. Brother say, very sarry.' If it was true, then this was the first, and only, suggestion that York and Boat had been uncle and nephew. He recalled many other things: on seeing a portrait of Queen Victoria he said he had met the King's wife. He spoke of conversations with the Reverend Wilson about dying, and when Despard pushed him, he added, 'Yes, me die in my country; you die in England; your wife die in England. Me old, die; you old, die. Me got benty children, all same as you; bye and bye die . . . Me go to heaven; no eat there, no drink, no sleep, but sing; Ellis (English) sing.' Despard pressed Jemmy about cannibalism too, but the Fuegian used this as an opportunity to attack York Minster's people who, he said, decapitated the marooned crews of shipwrecks. York's land was, he said, 'Man eat country; eat head; eat arm; eat foot; eat all. Cut throat and eat.'

From the start the Buttons attended the daily religious services at four o'clock in the afternoon, Jemmy trying to keep up with hymns by moving his lips to the words, and gradually progressing to the point where he was confident enough to give short talks at the ceremonies. One Sunday he missed a service because he said his son had eaten too much. He was cautioned by Despard, who reminded him that Christ had suffered on the cross for the sinners. 'Yes, sir, I know Son of God came down to die,' replied the Fuegian.

Jemmy, it seems, settled quickly into his old, well-mannered self. The missionary's reports on him were full of knowing winks to Victorian etiquette, the benchmark against which were measured the possibilities that the Fuegians represented. When offered cake Jemmy took the smallest piece on the plate; he never wanted to eat too much, for fear of being thought greedy, but liked a second cup of tea. He always knocked on doors before entering, held gates open for the missionary, and touched his forelock when addressing Mr or Mrs Despard saying, 'Yes, sar' or 'Yes, mam'.

He appears to have been as conceited as ever too. He washed every day and insisted that his wife washed the children. He brushed his clothes incessantly, and washed his red cap so often that its black border turned brown and it shrank beyond a point where it would fit on his head. One Saturday afternoon while he watched the governess, Louise Hanlon, making a pudding, a sprinkling of flour spilled onto his jacket. He was mortified and, having vigorously brushed it off, departed the kitchen immediately in case the accident recurred.

A picture began to emerge in the *Voice of Pity* of domestic behaviour and contentment that any middle-class British family could appreciate. Despard gave Jemmy a new broom and the Fuegian was meticulous in his daily sweeping of the house. Tin utensils for cooking and eating were polished until they shone. In July the missionary superintendent visited what had become known as Button Villa, where he had recently installed a stove, and commented, 'What was my surprise and delight to see the worthy fellow sitting, denuded of his jacket, sewing very neatly, with thimble on finger, a strip of calico, to make braces for himself?'

At other times Mrs Button was found plucking a duck for dinner, taking needlecraft lessons, or doing the ironing. She liked to indulge herself with sugar plums and raisins, which she piled into her mouth as quickly as her hands could be filled. In a letter to a friend in Ireland Mrs Despard told of how Jamesina would stand in the kitchen and watch everything – cooking, baking, washing – then rush back to her house to copy it. Every day she, Threeboys and Fuegia would attend lessons in English in the mission house, and her children got along famously with the Despard children. Fuegia loved to be tickled by the slightly older Bertha, and offered her cheek to Louise Hanlon for a kiss. The first words of baby Annasplonis, or Anthony, were 'Button, butt—.'

Yet behind the idyllic reports there was a creeping sense of frustration among those at the mission at their lack of progress with the Fuegian language. Charles Turpin would give a daily report at breakfast to Despard of the new words he had picked up. By the end of July he had begun to translate the Lord's Prayer into Fuegian, but he was coming across some fundamental problems: he could not uncover the words for kingdom or heaven, and found it nigh on impossible to explain to the Fuegians the idea of the third person singular. In September he claimed to have completed the task, but when Despard tried to read out the Yamana version of the prayer at church on the first Sunday of the month he had to stop at the beginning. According to Jemmy, what Turpin had written translated as 'Dead Father, who art in . . .'

The missionaries undoubtedly succeeded in obtaining some words from the Buttons – Despard claimed by November to have a list of 400 – but no matter how much they boasted, this was a disappointing return. They argued that it was Jemmy's fault: 'It has been difficult to get words from Jemmy Button from the difficulty he felt in understanding even a simple sentence in English . . .' wrote Despard. 'He seems never to have tried to turn English into Firelandic, but rather to make his people understand about England in English.' It may have been more interesting than that: very early on Mrs Despard recorded that when her husband demonstrated the extent of his Yamana vocabulary and told the Fuegians the words he knew, 'Jemmy seemed quite surprised at his knowing so many. The other day, he said laughingly, "You know too much my language; no good, no good."' Could it have been that Jemmy was deliberately concealing his language from his British hosts? It is certainly clear from the *Voice of Pity* that some suspected he was unwilling to pass on Yamana: every time one of the mission party approached him while he was talking to his family, he would shift from his own language into English. Perhaps, as Jemmy said, it was 'no good' for Despard to know his language. Or perhaps he did not like the missionary and was not happy at Cranmer. It is possible that he valued the privacy and secrecy that he and his family maintained by being able to talk in a language that others could not understand, and the kudos it gave him when he acted as go-between for the missionaries and his people. Just possibly he understood the power of language, and the dangers that might result from open dialogue between his people and the foreigners.

Whatever the reason, Despard and Turpin turned their attention away from Jemmy to his son. Threeboys was a bright lad, quick to learn, hardworking and keen to pick up the words and grammar of English. Short and stout, he had his father's eyes and the 'rosy-brunette' complexion of his mother. The missionaries found him a delight: not only was he intelligent, he was always anxious to lend a hand with the heavy construction work at the settlement. Early on, Despard realised the boy's potential; in July he reported:

> Threeboys has begun to learn the English alphabet. He gets on fast in learning our names of things. He looked yesterday at Captain Gardiner's portrait, and said, 'Appanna,' – dead. Then he looked at a portrait of a lady, and said, 'Keepa,' – woman; showing thus that he at least understands the meaning of pictures.

Threeboys became the apple of their eye. He said, 'Pank you,' and was always first to give a cheery 'Good morning' or 'Good afternoon'. He went to religious service most days, and by August he was able to put an English name to virtually any object that Turpin presented to him and, more importantly, was willing to give its Fuegian equivalent. Despard was anxious to hold on to him: 'I do hope this boy . . . may be the first native evangelist to Fuegia. James is too old to expect much from in this way.'

Meanwhile Jemmy Button was continuing much as before. He spent his days in idle leisure, wandering from the carpenter to the doctor to the kitchen to the quarry. He busied himself with small tasks like making arrows for Despard and Turpin, or spearing fish in the brook, and affected concern over the health of Mrs Despard – she had a bad eye for a short while – making sure to ask after it every day and occasionally taking her flowers he had picked from the garden.

Behind this veneer of politeness, however, discontent was rising on both sides. For Jemmy and his family five months away from home was a long time. As much as the missionaries tried to disguise it, it is evident that the Buttons were not happy with the new regime and that they were homesick. At first small niggles and later larger strains emerged. On one occasion, the wife of one of the workmen shooed the Buttons out of her house. She had apparently not come to terms with the 'savages' in their midst and was terrified at the Fuegians wandering into her home. Jemmy was affronted and refused to go there again. When he was found in Despard's house he was given a telling-off, which upset him so much he was moved to tears. 'Gentleman very angry; say not come to church,' he later commented.

In August there was a complaint against Mrs Button for taking wooden fence palings for use as fuel. Jemmy was indignant: 'People here think me and my family steal; I no steal; my wife not steal; I not stay Kebbel Island; I go way when schooner comes. No, me not steal.' As it happened, the wood had been cut for the Buttons' fire and their accuser was wrong. When on another occasion he was asked how one says steal in Yamana, Jemmy replied with vehemence 'No say, I steal; I not steal . . .'

Jemmy was also concerned about the immediate future. There seemed to be no plans for returning him and his family to Tierra del Fuego. At the end of June the *Allen Gardiner* sailed for Monte

Video. (It was away until October when it brought with it the returning Garland Phillips and his wife.) Jemmy was afraid of Despard's plans: the missionary obviously coveted Threeboys, and Despard's wife doted on Fuegia and spent much time carrying the baby Anthony in her arms. In the middle of August, Despard noted in his diary that his wife 'has an inclination to bring up the little girl'. In a short assessment of Jemmy's character the missionary included the following revealing reference. The Fuegian was

> . . . affectionate; fond of his children; fidgeting very much to go away, after I had asked him to leave Passanulla [another version of the name Passawullacuds] to my wife, to be brought up in our family, as a daughter; from the idea I wanted to take her by force; and only quieted when he got me to confirm Mr T's assurance, they would all go back together.

So, contrary to almost everything else that was written on the Fuegians' stay at Keppel, there was clear contemporary evidence that they were 'fidgeting' to get away.

Their desire was not all one-sided. The mission party had realised the limits of Jemmy's co-operation and were tiring of him. Frequent references to his laziness litter the journals, and there is unmistakable disappointment at his failure to help with the general work of the settlement. His self-importance and unwillingness to indulge in heavy labour earned him the nickname the Admiral, though to some extent this might have been attributable to a cultural misunderstanding on the value of work: in September when Turpin was cutting wood for the Button household he 'called the "Admiral" out of his mansion, where he was at leisure, and bade him give the required aid. He did so readily. I think if he were only told to work, he would . . .'

At other times the irritation simmered just below the surface.

Mrs Despard commented in a letter that the Fuegians were very lazy, that they would not fetch wood for their own fire even when it was placed just yards from their door. She found the only way to get a reaction was to tell Jemmy that God did not love idle men.

Towards the end of September two weeks of peat cutting began, 'Mr Button, the only gentleman of leisure in the place. He paid me a visit; remarked my work to be wet and dirty, but certainly made no effort to help. Jemmy Button employed his time in looking at a large book of pictures.' The next day when he played on a toy trumpet Despard reproved him: 'Jemmy, everyone work here; you no work.' Only when Turpin was busy cutting peat could Despard report that 'Mr Button condescends to cut and split his own fuel.'

As the time approached for the return of the Fuegians to Tierra del Fuego, questions were raised about the mission's future and Jemmy's part in it. The missionaries were not entirely happy with the success of their work with the older Fuegian, but in the children they saw distinct possibilities. If they could reach young Fuegians they could exert an important influence at a tender age. But Jemmy was crucial to them. Would he help to ensure that other Fuegians came to Cranmer? Would he allow his own children to return without their parents? Jemmy was coy. When Despard asked him whether he would come back, he answered, 'Me old man now – I go long way England, come here, twice go away. My brother come next time!'

On another occasion Mrs Despard asked, 'Jemmy, will you come back to us?' but the Fuegian would make no promises and replied, 'Perhaps, by and by, me no tell now! People say in my country, no God; I go tell my people God in my country; made me and them, trees, moon.'

Nevertheless, the mission could take some heart: Jemmy said he would 'go home my country; I say, Mr Despard, Keppel Island; very good; churchman. My brother come; by and by, I come. Keppel Island very short; England very long.'

Chapter 18

Captain Robert Fell had arrived at Keppel Island in the last week of June 1858, around the same time as the *Allen Gardiner* came in from Tierra del Fuego bearing Jemmy Button and his family. The new captain had a Master's Certificate from the Board of Trade, but had spent the last five years in England doing missionary work among seamen. The work had been exhausting, and ill-health had forced him to give it up on the advice of a doctor, who told him he needed to feel a sea breeze on his face.

Fell was ideal for the command of the missionary schooner. As well as his seafaring experience, his piety and disdain for alcohol, smoking, swearing, theatres and houses of entertainment — whether innocent or otherwise — qualified him for an enterprise of this stamp. He was a fervent rough-and-tumble Baptist, for whom life was one long crusade, an extended opportunity to inform the heathen and stem the monstrous tide of Catholicism. As he had sailed up the Tagus on his way to the Falklands he had written of Portugal, 'How this country has been wasted and ruined by the superstitions and dominion of the Roman Church — how the iron grasp of Popery has tyrannised over its inhabitants, kept from their view the word and lamp of life for so many centuries . . .'

At every port of call he had handed out tracts to sailors on the dockside and locals in the market-places. Quarantine laws at Madeira prevented him stepping on land, so he threw bundles of religious propaganda, translated into Portuguese, to traders who came to the ship's side. At the Cape Verde Islands he boarded an English ship and, in the absence of its captain, rounded up the crew and took a religious service. The sight of slaves hauling coal in Bahia provoked him to go ashore to enlighten the locals, always keeping an eye open for any bigoted priest who might object. The first thing he did when he arrived at Cranmer was to assemble the crew of the *Allen Gardiner* and warn them, 'If you want to disgrace the vessel, and cause me a good deal of pain, you have only to get drunk, and you will accomplish your task, if that is any satisfaction to you. But if you do not want to do so, keep sober.' In Robert Fell, the Patagonian Missionary Society surely had the man they had so long craved.

There was little time for the new captain to acquaint himself with the arriving Fuegians. The young catechist Allen Gardiner needed to be in Monte Video to meet a ship and, having dropped him off, the captain spent the next few months between there and Buenos Aires, paying off the old crew, employing new men, giving fund-raising lectures, collecting unwanted clothes for the Fuegians and finally waiting for the arrival from England of Garland Phillips and his wife. By the time the ship pulled into Committee Bay, Jemmy Button was ready to go home to Tierra del Fuego.

He and his family departed on 20 November and, after a rough passage, anchored at Banner Cove six days later. Within minutes, four canoes bearing twenty Indians approached the ship. That morning Jemmy had been tonsured and both he and his family were anxious to impress their countrymen: as quickly as they could they put on all their clothes, Passawullacuds wearing two frocks over the dress she had been travelling in. The Indians asked Jemmy for the clasped knife that hung around his neck, and though he refused this, he handed out small gifts of buttons, needles, a fork and another knife from his own property. Three men boarded the ship and were given shirts, ties and trousers. But while Jemmy was behaving kindly, his wife was less forthcoming. Lassaweea apparently felt herself above all of this now and looked down on her fellow people with a glower of derision that suggested she thought them rather vulgar people. One of them called her Pallil-keepa, Englishwoman. She handed a man a necklace of beads in return for a piece of whale-gut, but snatched it back and walked off in a sulk when the man refused to give her the meat.

Despard called on Jemmy to interpret for them, but whether from ignorance, exhibitionism or an unwillingness to speak Yamana in front of the missionary, he talked to the visitors in English. They responded in Fuegian with 'What, countryman, you there in English ship?' Jemmy added, 'I come from far-way-off land.' Nonplussed, the Indians asked, in Spanish, '*Que?*' The missionary noted, 'We tried to impress upon him the absurdity of speaking to them in English which we ourselves could do better than he . . .' but without success.

On 27 November, while the ship was anchored near the Beagle Channel more canoes arrived, one of them carrying friends of Jemmy. As Despard gave out gifts, Jemmy and Lassaweea bought baskets to send back to Cranmer for Mrs Despard and Louise Hanlon. One Fuegian climbed on board the *Allen Gardiner* and started to dance and sing, holding both his fists up to his chin. Fell gave him a white shirt, which he did not know how to put on, and said to him, 'You are a very fine fellow.' The native replied, 'You are a very fine fellow.' When he was shown his reflection in a mirror he was frightened and ran to the side of the ship. Fell put down the mirror, ripped some old shirts into strips and called the remaining Yamana on board so he could tie cloth bandannas around their heads.

The next day was a Sunday and Despard banned all trading. As it was a warm, sunny day, he also agreed to hold morning service on the main deck. Jemmy looked over at the Fuegians in their canoes and addressed them solemnly from the gangway, 'What for you no go away your own country? go away – go ashore; no want noise now.' It had no effect, and he became annoyed, unaware once more that he had been speaking English. When the crew laughed at him, he pushed his hands into his jacket pockets and wandered off in a huff. The ship's bell was struck and the Yamana shouted out in surprise, but a few minutes later they joined in the hymn singing.

That day another friend of Jemmy arrived. Tish-pinnay was a peculiar-looking Fuegian, with a nose so aristocratic that FitzRoy had nicknamed him the Duke of Wellington. He had lost an eye in an accident, though Jemmy had a far more colourful explanation: 'Man die, here ashore, he very sorry, cry very much, eye ran away in water all over cheek; yes, sir!' When he came back from talking with his friend he was slightly disturbed for he thought he had caught whispers of a plot against him among the canoe Indians: 'They say, leave canoe other side, walk, walk, walk down to my country. Come night, take away my clothes and knife. I keep quiet on island.'

Two days later, strong winds whipped up the seas as the *Allen Gardiner* drew close to Wulaia Cove. Native canoes were unable to keep pace with her and, not wishing to stop for them, Robert Fell floated presents back to them in the vessel's slipstream. However, as they entered the Murray Narrows the storm cracked the topsail halyards and the main sail crashed down. Mrs Button screamed in terror. The captain turned the ship and headed back to the shelter of Wellfound Bay, from where they had set out that morning. Jemmy was furious, Fell noted.

No sooner was the ship running back than Mr and Mrs Button, having their expectations blighted in getting home, began to show themselves. 'I say, what do you call that? no go to my country that way. Go back to England.' Both Jem and his wife were quite put out about it, not understanding the difficulties in which we were placed . . . the seas were fit to sink the vessel, or sweep her decks. Mrs Button in the difficulty could shout with fear, but complained when we ran for safety . . .

Jemmy feared that he had been duped and was now being taken back to Keppel Island or, worse still, England. When a flotilla of canoes came alongside the next day with news that his son Queerentze was about to be killed, he announced that he was getting off the ship and would make his own way home. The missionaries, he proclaimed, could sail on to Wulaia with his possessions and he would meet them there. Then, with his wife and children following at a distance, he went ashore, to where a council of Fuegians sat around a small pyramid of mussel shells. He walked round and round them, then sat at a slight distance with his family.

A few minutes went by, and then a deputation of Fuegians went over to him, an argument broke out and Jemmy stood up and waved frantically at the *Allen Gardiner*. The missionaries ignored him – Despard claimed he thought that Jemmy wanted to borrow a canoe, but from the dismissive remark in Garland Phillips's journal, 'He hailed us, but no notice was taken . . .' it seems that Jemmy was being taught a lesson. Eventually the Fuegian removed his waistcoat and traded it for a ride back to the ship in a canoe. As he clambered on board he told Despard, 'Bad men wanted me to cooshie [sleep]; wanted to steal all my close. Not take to my country. Tried to cut great piece off my wife's shawl. All story about my son. I stay, very well, sir; go up country with you.'

As the *Allen Gardiner* sailed on to Wulaia Cove, the journals kept by the missionary party and published in the *Voice of Pity* became increasingly dismissive of the Buttons. Captain Fell, who barely knew the Fuegians or their people, wrote, 'James Button, although kind and good natured, seems to be one of the dullest of his race.' Despard added his condemnation:

> Poor Jem is very stupid as interpreter – he understands neither them nor us – and when we tell him to say something to them, persists in using his broken English. His wife even tries this plan. This morning she was calling out to a canoe, 'Basketta,' for a basket (*kay-jan* is the word). Of course she got no answer till one of us used the proper word.

The missionaries also seemed more willing to report Jemmy's tantrums. He had been upset at the ship turning tail in the face of a storm that threatened to tear it apart, and when they arrived in the Yahgashaga he was reportedly annoyed that the *Allen Gardiner* went to Wulaia rather than Button Island where he lived and where he could unload his accumulated treasure with more ease. It seems that now they had accepted that Jemmy's usefulness had run its course, the mission party could be more honest about their feelings towards him. He had only one function left, as far as they were concerned, and that was to persuade another party to go to Cranmer. After that he could be disregarded.

They anchored off Wulaia on 4 December, and after dinner Jemmy took a party ashore to explore what Fell anticipated from his reading of FitzRoy's *Narratives* would have been 'the celebrated city of Woollya'. The captain was not impressed, though: 'We were at first greatly disappointed, nor could we help conveying to each other's mind the impression by our looks.' He added that as they walked along the beach and into the cove Jemmy appeared ashamed and the look on his face seemed to say, 'Neither myself nor my countrymen were worth the trouble which Captain

FitzRoy took with our garden, as we have allowed it all to go to waste.'

That night, Macooallan, Jemmy's brother, was the first of many visitors to the *Allen Gardiner*. He was a *yacomosh* – responsible for looking after both physical ailments and weather conditions. On board the ship, he and Jemmy were brusque with one another, avoiding eye-contact, Macooallan preferring instead to stare at Despard and repeat his every word. Jemmy put his hand on his brother's shoulder and indicated the missionary superintendent: 'This Mr Despard,' he said.

His brother repeated, 'Dis Mr Despard.'

Jemmy turned to Fell: 'This Captain FitzRoy . . .' and then correcting himself, 'Captain Fell, Captain Fell.'

'Dis captain Fell.'

And so the conversation continued.

'This Mr Phillips.'

'Dis Mr Flips.'

'This Mr Turpin.'

'Dis Mr Turpan.'

Soon, others had joined the party: another of Jemmy's brothers, Waymeschoones, Jemmy's son Queerentze and his son-in-law Loole, his daughters Coolakayenche and Macooallkippin, his other wife and her infant daughter, the mother of both wives and his daughter-in-law Lookalke, and two men, Schwaiamugunjiz and his brother Tellon. It was quite a party and all were given biscuits, but this was not enough. Jemmy knew that there was a large store of clothes in the hold and demanded that his friends and relatives be given them. Both Fell and Despard refused, saying that it was getting late. Jemmy turned to Charles Turpin: 'What for Captain Fell no give my countrymen clothing? What do you call that? Captain Fell give nother man clothes, and no give my countryman clothes, what do you call that?'

Turpin replied that it was late, but that all Jemmy's people would be given plenty of clothes if they would wait. Jemmy seemed satisfied and bowed, touching his forehead, but Fell might have overheard the conversation and, thinking it best to keep up the good relations, relented. The clothes were fetched up and the visitors were helped into their new dress.

This first meeting with Jemmy's Fuegians left the mission party feeling optimistic about their chances for success. Despard had ambitions for Wulaia. He wanted to gather together a new party of Fuegians to take back to Cranmer and to build a small house of worship on the cove, which in time would become a mission outpost and a place where members of his team could live for short periods among the native people. They were to spend four weeks in the area, dividing their time between constructing the new building, learning snippets of language and developing a rapport with the Fuegians. They attempted now to introduce an extra dimension into their relationship with the Fuegians: the work ethic and payment for labour.

This new approach was evident almost immediately. On 6 December, as Jemmy prepared to leave the ship, he demanded breakfast. Fell explained the changed thinking: 'Well, Jemmy, you know muscles very good in your country. Suppose you work, we give you biscuit; suppose you no work, we can no give biscuit.' Later that morning work began on digging the foundations for the manse and cutting down trees for its walls. It was an exhausting task for the ship's small crew, but Jemmy, one of his sons, a son-in-law and a Fuegian called Silagalesh agreed to help for a biscuit each. A system of payment was quickly established and on the first day Jemmy earned ten biscuits, his colleagues only five. The missionaries offered to pay the Indians for cutting and fetching bark, and as more helped in the construction work Despard found that paying them at the close of the day was unproductive: the

Fuegians lost motivation. He tried paying them at the end of every job and watched as the work rate climbed. Interestingly, the labourers soon developed an awareness of their industrial strength: by the time work began on the roof they were refusing to carry shoulder loads of timber up the ladder for just one biscuit.

Fell noted in his journal that now the Fuegians were paid they were breaking out of 'lazy habits, such as sitting by fires in the different wigwams all day, not moving hand or foot until hunger necessitates them to go on the beach for muscles [sic]'. He offered clothes from mainland South America in return for chopping down trees; they were he noted the 'worst portions' of clothes, but nevertheless the offer had the desired effect: the Fuegians took to their axes with enthusiasm. Soon Tish-pinnay – 'the Duke of Wellington' – earned a black frock coat, over which he wore a lady's petticoat. Another man wore just a petticoat.

> Great was the mirth at the masquerade. Here was a man trying to force himself into a pair of small boy's unmentionables; there a coat put over a bit of blanket, then a waistcoat outside of that; in another, a head was seen thrust through the armhole of a vest, and the rest of the integument hanging gracefully over the left shoulder. One lady had a long amply flounced black-muslin dress given to her; she put her arms through its sleeves, and let the tail and flounces follow in train. This droll figure excited a shout of laughter. I think there is now scarce an individual, out of 170 here, who has not a garment of some kind . . .

In the meantime relations with the Fuegians had reached a plateau. While not overly warm, dealings between the two parties were amiable and rarely threatening. Jemmy Button had isolated gripes, such as on 10 December when he informed the mission party that the women were complaining they were not receiving enough presents. Despard sent him back with the message that if they made baskets he would pay them.

An element of the beauty contest pervaded these relationships: as work progressed on the house, the four leading members of the missionary party – Despard, Fell, Phillips and Turpin – kept an eye open for what they considered the best Fuegians, the most intelligent and the most industrious, hoping to persuade them to return to Keppel Island.

Shortly after their arrival at Wulaia a most promising candidate had presented himself. Ookokowenche was a good-looking boy aged about sixteen. When Despard invited him on board the *Allen Gardiner* he fairly bounced up the gangway and submitted, without objection, to a haircut and a good scrubbing down. His reward was a meal of pork, biscuit and coffee (which he found repulsive and called bad water).

During the course of the next few days he made himself at home, eating and drinking all he could lay his hands on, admiring his reflection in a skylight and turning his hand to the occasional task. He was, he told Despard, not from Wulaia, but from a long way away and he had no objection to going to Cranmer. His mother was a widow, he explained, who had come to these parts.

Three days after he went on board the missionaries met her. On 7 December she arrived in a canoe, screeching at the enforced detention of her son and demanding he be released immediately. Despard said that he could leave, so long as he returned all the clothes he had been given as part of the bargain for agreeing to go to Keppel Island. The woman grabbed her son and dragged him off to the shore, berating him all the way for his misbehaviour.

Poor weather held up work on the house. On 13 December, with the rain pouring down, Macooallan – by now known as Tommy Button – came onto the *Allen Gardiner* to say he was happy to go to the mission station. His face was painted white and Despard called him unclean. The Fuegian 'pointed, and objected to, my beard, as dirty' wrote Despard. Another Fuegian, the nineteen-year-old Congorenches, declared his interest in joining the mission party with his wife, and still they had not given up on Ookokowenche. By Christmas it was time to make their selection public and find out whether they could take their plans any further.

Christmas Day fell on a Saturday and, with rain teeming down, the crew joined fifty-one Fuegians in the recently finished house. Despard and Fell ranked all the men down one side of the building, the women down the other. On a table in the middle were placed four huge plum puddings and a can of treacle. The chief missionary opened the proceedings with a prayer for the Fuegians then led the hymn 'His Praise Who Is Our God'. When that was over, Fell took out a knife and divided up the puddings, giving everyone a piece. Some were unable to finish their portions, others came back for a second, one or two even managed a third.

When the food was gone, buckets of water were brought in so that all could wash their hands and faces. The moment of selection had arrived. Despard read out a list of names the mission party had compiled and Jemmy shouted, 'Oh-he Keppel Island?' which meant, 'Will you go to Keppel Island?' Everyone named replied, 'Ow-a' – yes. Despard had his party of Fuegians. Delighted, he told the chosen ones to board the ship on Monday morning when they would be 'purified and dressed'.

The preceding events and those that were about to happen are crucial to defining and understanding the nature of Anglo-Fuegian relations and their deterioration. In 1860 and 1861 accusations flew around Port Stanley, and even reached London, that the Patagonian Missionary Society, under the stewardship of the Reverend Despard, had kidnapped Fuegians from Wulaia and taken them against their will to Keppel Island. Was this true? It is unlikely that the missionaries could have abducted them by force – there were simply not enough of them: it had been reported that as many as 170 Fuegians were encamped at Wulaia, there were probably no more than ten of the missionary party on board the ship and they had few firearms to back them up.

A more likely proposition is that the Fuegians who agreed to go to Keppel did so without fully understanding what this meant. Events over the next few days point to confusion between the Indians and the ship. They do not wholly exonerate the Yamana, and neither do they entirely damn the missionaries, but they do show that when Despard stood in the house and announced that on Monday he would be purifying and dressing his elect Fuegians, he had not grasped the complete picture.

Relations remained cordial the next day, Sunday 26 December, when just after ten o'clock in the morning, two canoes bearing those who were going to Keppel Island and a few of their friends arrived alongside the *Allen Gardiner*. The wind had shifted earlier that morning and Fell had moved the ship. Despard was unable to work out why they had come, but thought it was because they had feared the *Allen Gardiner* was leaving. Tellon made a long, earnest speech, and Macooallan seconded it with a shorter calmer address. They were each given food and told not to return until Monday.

Early on 27 December the 'Firelanders elect' boarded the *Allen Gardiner* and, as promised, were washed and dressed. The wives were missing, so shortly after lunch Fell took the ship's gig to find them. As he stepped off the boat, Lassaweea, Mrs Button, assailed him with abuse, and Macooallan jumped on him, ripping open his vest to his shirt, and shouted that he had expected better presents and, in particular, better clothes. Jemmy Button joined in: Captain FitzRoy had been generous to a fault, but Captain Fell? 'What do you call this?' he shouted, tugging at the clothes he had been given. Fell talked gently, promised them more biscuits, more clothes, and gave Macooallan a blanket. A potentially explosive situation was defused. Fell returned to the ship with the women, and where decent had them washed by one of the ship's crew and where not by their husbands.

Soon after, a canoe came alongside and, quick as a flash, Congorenches jumped into it from the ship wearing the fine clothes he had been given for his journey to Keppel Island. Luccaenches shouted after him that he was a bad man, and Schwaiamugunjiz hurled abuse from the stern of the ship. It was not over yet, though. After prayers Lucca's father, Tellon, paddled up to the ship and without a moment's hesitation Lucca, too, was over the side and away. Despard was exasperated. When Threeboys tried to come on board he was instructed to get off the ship. Then, under cover of darkness, one of Jemmy Button's daughters paddled stealthily to the *Allen Gardiner*. She made no noise, but was spotted by Charles Turpin who raised the alarm, whereupon the crew found the whole Fuegian party preparing to make their escape, complete with blankets, clothes and a handful of the ship's tools. Despard ordered that they all be arrested, detained and stripped of everything they carried. One by one Macooallan, Schwaiamugunjiz, their two wives and Ookokowenche were released naked into the night, the message resounding in their ears that they could only have the clothes if they agreed to go to Keppel Island. As Despard wrote in his journal,

This business has *disappointed our expectations very much* and makes us fear that this trip we shall return to Cranmer without any visitors, God knows best, what is best. Some think JB on the dog in the manger principle is at the bottom of this, others that Threeboys has been the inventor of the plot, others again that

Dr Button is the inventor – it is certain Satan will interpose every obstacle he *can* in the way of delivering these poor people from their degradation.

Two days later Lucca and Tellon returned to the ship as if nothing had happened. Tellon had had a terrible row with a brother and was worried for his safety; they had been forced to bivouac in an old wigwam nearby. That evening Macooallan, Threeboys and Schwaiamugunjiz climbed on board. It was getting late, they were unexpected and many things were lying about. Despard demanded they leave the ship, but they refused, saying they were going to sleep on board. Schwaiamugunjiz made a very angry speech and having signed that the missionaries were 'no good' he climbed over the side of the ship. Threeboys followed, promising never to come again, and finally Macooallan left after being bribed with biscuits by the captain.

It was against this backdrop that 30 December brought surprising news. Jemmy Button breakfasted with Despard and told him that, so long as he agreed to bring them back as he had been brought back, the original party was still willing to go to Keppel Island – not only that, but his other brother Macalwense and wife were willing to join them too. Next day he delivered on his promise.

The final party, when complete, consisted of nine Fuegians:

Macooallan aged 36
Wendoogyappa, wife of Macooallan
Macalwense aged 32
Wyeenagowlkippin, wife of Macalwense
Schwaiamugunjiz aged 24
Wyruggelkeepa, wife of Schwaiamugunjiz and their 2 year
    old daughter Kyattegattemowlkeepa
Ookokowenche aged 16
Luccaenche aged 12

On New Year's Day 1859 a large gathering of Yamana assembled on the beach at Wulaia to see off the *Allen Gardiner*. Despard handed out clothing, tools, beads, biscuits and sugar. Jemmy Button was given a barrel of biscuits, a few pieces of pork and twelve pounds of sugar for himself. He shouted, 'Goodbye, Mr Despard; goodbye, Mr Phillips; goodbye, Mr Turpin, goodbye, Captain.'

When the *Allen Gardiner* was well out of Wulaia, Garland Phillips arranged the washing and dressing of all the native guests, and afterwards fed them with as much biscuit and pork as they could consume. The weather closed in on the little ship and a storm crashed waves over its bow. Even the Fuegians became seasick.

From his point of view Despard's first visit to Wulaia had finished as nothing short of a success. Five Fuegians had been taken back to their homes safely; a house of worship had been built; and now, most importantly of all, he was returning to Cranmer with nine Fuegians on board. Not that his attitude towards them had changed: 'These people are self-willed and capricious as grown spoiled children, and require, to manage them, great patience and firmness, as well as undaunted spirit,' he noted in his journal. What was more the missionaries had spent four weeks among the Yamana, and had 'gone in and out among them without fear or hesitation, we have gone singly into their woods, have left our boat upon their shores – have left our vessel for hours with only one man on board, and have never had reason to regret our confidence. I need hardly say, that we never took any weapon with us ashore for defence.'

Chapter 19

The *Allen Gardiner* arrived in Committee Bay on the morning of 5 January 1859 and by the afternoon the Fuegians had been billeted in the house that had formerly played home to Jemmy and family, each couple receiving a corner to themselves. They had never before seen anything like the settlement at Cranmer or even a house, with the exception of the manse recently built on Wulaia Cove, so during those first days there was great adjustment and no little misunderstanding. On 6 January, while the Fuegian women were washed and dressed by the ladies of the settlement, their men were shown the livestock. Cows, horses, pigs and goats were all greeted with a lick of the lips and a declaration that here there was good food. Later that same day the native men discovered the mission's carefully nurtured penguin eggery and slaughtered more than a dozen of the birds.

There were fundamental differences between this party and the previous visitors to Cranmer. Not one of the Fuegians on board the returning *Allen Gardiner* had ever been to England – not one, in fact, had ever strayed further than the Yahgashaga. They had no understanding of British expectations, sensibilities or culture, they had little knowledge of English, even less affinity with their hosts, and no sense of the allegiance or obligation that, for whatever reason, Jemmy Button had felt. It was also a bigger party, more diverse than the Buttons. Whereas Jemmy had had some authority over those who came with him, this group consisted of separate families, adults, teenagers and children. If things went badly, an 'us against them' attitude might develop. Dealing with them otherwise might prove equally difficult, owing to the variety of opinions, tempers and characters.

The Fuegians came on the understanding that they would be back home for the start of 'wild bird egg season', one of the most important dates in their calendar when the harvesting of eggs from the cliffs and shores around the Yahgashaga heralded a period of general feasting and celebration. The season began in September, which meant that they would be on Keppel Island for nine months, significantly longer than the Buttons had spent there and sufficient time for the mission party to carry out the next stage of its work.

Five days after their arrival a large fire was seen spreading swiftly across the island. Memories flashed back to the near disaster of 1855, and those who had been there then recalled how quickly the flames had flared up. Then the settlement had been new – there were no buildings and little livestock. A blaze on the same scale now would have far more damaging consequences: all hands were put to digging a trench and into damping down the fire. Within a few hot and anxious hours the crisis was past, the fire dwindling.

When the danger was over, the cause was sought and, a little way off, just beyond a group of lakes that speckled the island, the Fuegians were found cooking mollimauks over an open campfire. Despard berated them for their lack of caution. 'In their own country they are not at all particular in lighting fires wherever they encamp,' he later wrote. 'Their practice there is to carry a lighted stick with them . . . they were clearly made to understand that they must not carry fire about with them, and the great injury it would do to the island.'

The warning, however, had little effect: just three days later

Garland Phillips, concerned at the early-morning disappearance of Schwaiamugunjiz and Luccaenches, climbed on a horse and went with Ookoko and Macalwense in search of them. They found them a little way off, sitting round an open fire on which seal flesh was 'hissing and browning'. Phillips ordered them back to Cranmer and doused the fire.

More consternation arose when, in their first week at Cranmer, Ookoko and Macooallan wandered into the mission house and rummaged around. The English ladies who were there at the time were troubled and frightened by the sudden appearance of the two Fuegians, and Despard was called. He instructed them to leave. The time was not yet right for such intrusion: 'Their habits as yet are too gross to allow of their coming in and out, ad libitum, as Jemmy Button and his family did.'

It was imperative to the success of this second stage in Fuegian-missionary relations that a routine was quickly established. It was also crucial that a pattern of work and education, aimed at knocking out the habits of a lifetime, was firmly imposed. Within ten days of the party arriving, Garland Phillips could happily describe such a daily routine. At seven each morning he went to the Fuegian house, woke its occupants and detailed one man to sweep the house clean. The Fuegians, who had been taught how to use soap for washing and had also learned to comb their hair, would perform their ablutions. At eight o'clock the breakfast bell rang and each was given ship's biscuits and a dab of treacle. Jemmy Button had been given more than this but, the argument went, he knew how to eat pork and bread and butter. Besides, it was thought advisable 'for their own diversion and amusement, that they should seek the bulk of their living in the mode usual in Tierra del Fuego'. That is, they should gather shellfish off the beach and could kill as many of the abundant supply of birds on the island as they wanted. This had the added advantage that they were not 'a heavy expense to the Mission'.

After breakfast Phillips said a prayer, wherever possible using Fuegian words, then led a hymn. At half past nine Mrs Phillips took away the wives and children, a signal to the men that it was time for work. At eleven o'clock there was break for biscuits and treacle.

Despite claims to the contrary, it seems that the men were worked hard. They were not natural labourers and there are many comments in the documents of the Patagonian Missionary Society about laziness, the ease with which fatigue overcame them and their tendency to wander away from jobs. Nevertheless, over the next nine months the mission had little reason to complain. The Fuegian men riddled and dug peat for fuel, painted window-frames, carried paving slabs. They tended the gardens and dug trenches, built bridges across streams, carried poles from the beach and took rudimentary lessons in carpentry. The women made baskets and table mats, and helped with chores around the house. If this was not the slavery that William Parker Snow was alleging back in Britain, then it was moderately gruelling labour, carried out by a workforce that had not signed up for such exertions and who were unable to leave of their own accord. When they downed tools and relaxed on the grass saying, 'Enough work done for money,' as they did from time to time, it is easy to sympathise with them.

Their presence on Keppel Island had an immediate impact on the missionaries' grasp of Yamana. The fact that it was a larger, less well-integrated group than the Buttons' meant that Despard, Turpin and Phillips heard far more conversation in raw Fuegian than they ever had before. Cranmer was filled with the constant chatter of Fuegians, both young and old. 'When Jemmy Button was here he would talk his English to his wife and his children when we were by, and they spoke to each other in such low tones that we could not catch their words,' wrote Despard. 'Now the eight natives at present on the island are incessantly talking Fuegian, and loud enough for any one to hear . . .'

Formal education of a party of this size was probably difficult for the missionaries to organise. Much work remained to be done around the burgeoning settlement and, despite his best intentions, Despard was still spending a good deal of time at sea. Instead, for the Fuegians the experience of being on Keppel Island had to substitute for education: the work regimentation of the men in the field, the domestic duties of the women and attendance at church were lessons that would, it was hoped, lead to a brighter future for Tierra del Fuego.

There were, however, two exceptions. The missionaries quickly became enamoured of the Fuegian boys, Ookokowenche and Luccaenches. Ookoko was the elder of the two, a good-humoured, inquisitive boy in his mid to late teens who took to work in the fields and in the classroom with enthusiasm and a great beaming smile. His ability in English and his readiness to exchange Yamana words cheered the missionaries greatly. Most pleasing of all, they believed, was his diligence when it came to cleanliness. He was, wrote Despard, so 'ambitious to become white that he washes very often, in the hope of washing the brown out of his complexion'.

Lucca was younger, and where Ookoko was good-looking, he was rather plain, with deep, sunken eyes and a somewhat sullen expression. He was extraordinarily bright, even quicker at grasping English and other concepts than Ookoko, but he had neither the playfulness nor the gregariousness of his fellow Fuegian and could be quite sulky. Nevertheless he had a strong sense of the ridiculous and was excellent at caricaturing those around him. In spite of his moods he was a friendly soul and as his English improved he would take Mrs Phillips by the hand and ask her questions about England and life there.

Despard noted the potential of the two and took them aside for special hour-long lessons in the meeting-house, the Cenobium. The sessions began with Despard giving them a box of phonetic letters. He then placed together letters to spell out a Fuegian word he knew, usually the name of an object in the room. Turpin, Schmidt or Phillips would say the word whole, then break it down into its syllable components. The letters were then mixed up and the boys were asked to re-create the word. Despard described an early lesson in the *Voice of Pity*: 'I place Lucca at my side, and range u-s-h-c-a before him. Mr Schmidt reads ushca. Then I point to Lucca and say, "Comodo shia?" What do you call it? "Ushca." "Quay?" – and he points to his coat. Then I take each letter and give it its sound, and jumble the word up and make him pick out the letters again.' For an hour this process was repeated. It was tortuous, but seemingly successful. By the time Despard set sail for Patagonia, where he was taking Schmidt, on 4 February, he felt so convinced of the boys' worth that he even took Ookoko with him as a sailor and travelling companion.

When he returned the experiment was extended. By May both boys had moved out of the Fuegian house and gone to live with Charles Turpin, Garland Phillips and his wife. Ookoko was renamed Robert, Lucca became James. Great amounts of energy and time were dedicated to their progress: every night they were given reading lessons and over the next months, unlike their Fuegian colleagues, they were socialised by the missionaries and seem to have been forever taking tea in the Cenobium or the mission house. The Despard children spent time teaching them the five vowels. In May the chief missionary rejoiced at eventually discovering the word for 'wc' (it was, he said, *macatoo*). Another time Ookoko was overheard praying to 'God for Jesus Christ's sake, to make him a good boy,' and Phillips's journal records with satisfaction that they prayed every night by their bedside. When Ookoko turned up for food at the catechists' home one night, he stood over the table and, of his own accord, said, 'Pray God, bless this!' It was, said Turpin, 'the first prayer offered by a Firelander and in English'.

The increased emphasis on education led Ookoko and Lucca to develop aspirations of their own. Garland Phillips wrote, in a letter home, 'The two boys . . . are living in my house . . . they are both much attached to me and Mrs P . . . we regard them with much affection . . .' They were, he added, better behaved, more docile and obedient than their English counterparts. Both loved drawing and Ookoko wanted to be a flautist after an evening spent blowing and toying with Phillips's flute.

Inevitably the special treatment the boys received created tension among the native party. In July the Fuegian women complained that Ookoko and Lucca took tea with the mission party every Sunday, while they and their husbands were rarely invited. In the fields, too, there was some evidence of ill-feeling between Ookoko and Macooallan, which Garland Phillips speculated was because 'the lazy is jealous of the hard worker, inasmuch as the latter fares better than the former, and enjoys more of the confidence of the white man'.

For the Fuegians, however, life was not all work and education. they played games with Despard's children and the women made the occasional visit in their best clothes to Sulivan House for tea and plum cake. In February Charles Turpin gave a moonlight concert on his flute, the climax of which was a stirring rendition of 'God Save The Queen' to which the Yamana attempted the chorus. British rituals also had to be observed. On 12 March James Ellis became the second member of the mission party to die at Keppel — Despard's adopted son Frank Jones had died almost exactly a year earlier – and the doctor's funeral and subsequent burial must have been the first the Fuegians had seen. Early in May Alfred Coles, the *Allen Gardiner*'s cook, rounded up all of the Fuegians, armed them with pieces of wood, rakes and brooms and marched them in single file around the settlement like some rag-tag army. The Fuegians reportedly enjoyed it and the missionaries found it amusing, but it might have been preparation for what was to come two weeks later. May 24 was Queen Victoria's birthday and Despard declared a general holiday and a lively celebration.

> At 10 mustered all the fencibles of the place, including seven Firelanders; rigged up banners, royal standard, and union jacks; Firelanders and children bore them. Self and E [Emily, his daughter] were at head of procession, and proceeded round the bounds of our township; at each of five corners of which we set up new posts (of coast wood) made for the occasion, with three cheers for the Queen. Sang the national anthem with full chorus at the last, in spite of wind striving, with borean prowess, to blow it back again down our throats. Firelanders highly pleased, Ookokko on the lead. He had assisted Bartlett yesterday digging holes, carrying poles, and knew the way. We were home from our walk by 12.

At five that evening the Fuegians were invited to join the missionaries and Captain Fell for tea and a spread of meat, fruit, pies and cake. Twenty-one people were crammed into a tiny room, though Schwaiamugunjiz had trouble using a fork and left early. After refreshments were over, they all sang the national anthem then followed Mrs Despard into another room to hear her play the piano. The evening culminated with a magic-lantern show that charmed and vastly impressed the Indians.

On 27 May Despard set sail for Port Stanley, with Macooallan and Schwaiamugunjiz on board. The missionary had business to transact in the Falklands' capital, but it would seem that the trip also bore the mark of a public-relations exercise. The islands were desolate and remote, and even though Port Stanley was only separated from Keppel Island by 150 miles, communications were difficult. It was inevitable that people would start asking questions about the mission and its activities with the Fuegians. The visit provided an opportunity for Despard to exhibit his happy charges and allay any fears that might exist.

The *Allen Gardiner* reached Port Stanley on 30 May, but the city, with its natural harbour and three miles of docks, its piers and jetties, its rows of pensioners' white cottages, ramshackle homes and slightly unworthy, rather humdrum government buildings, failed to impress the two Fuegians, who remained as little surprised as if they had been taken back to the Yahgashaga.

On their first full day in port, the party went ashore and visited Mrs Phillips, the catechist's wife, who was spending time in the town. The people of the town were reportedly curious about the Yamana presence, and on 1 June Despard dressed them in blue and red uniforms, like American sailors, and marched them through the streets. As they passed, locals came out to see them and commented that the two men were 'Nothing savage; nothing unpleasant; nothing un-English in form or face, only in complexion.' They walked on to the town's guard house where the soldiers found them highly amusing:

The sergeant gave Macooallan a musket to handle, and put him through part of the manual exercise. Afterwards I took them to see Mr H and his family. The natives sat down and behaved like gentlemen. Mrs H played for them, and Macooallan sang for her, and then Miss H sang a duet with her father, with which they were much pleased. Dr H gave them a handkerchief a piece, and Mrs H two coloured prints of English life.

At some point the Fuegians were taken to see what they believed were horses having their throats cut to make beef, and that night Despard took them to a meeting of the Port Stanley Temperance Society, where he gave a short address. Word of their presence had reached the Falkland Islands' governor, Thomas Moore, who arranged a meeting at which he compared them with the Eskimos he had seen while on Ross's Antarctic expedition. He gave each a sailor's knife on a short lanyard for hanging around their necks, and his daughter gave each a penknife.

It was almost time to leave. Whatever business Despard had there was completed. On Sunday they went to church twice and the following day, 6 May, sailed for Cranmer, where they arrived to an emotional greeting six days later. The women had been upset by the departure of their loved ones and had cried their hearts out. On the day after their husbands left, they had painted sad black lines across their faces and asked continuously for news of the schooner and when it was coming back.

Three days after the men arrived back at Keppel Island, a Fuegian delegation visited Despard. 'They came to beg me neither to send them nor to go myself any more to Stanley,' the missionary superintendent remembered. 'When I acceded to their wishes, they patted me on the shoulder, and called me "tagacollo-kyemah owa cow-shoo" (friend, good man, excellent fellow!).'

Once again the Patagonian Missionary Society painted a rosy picture of its operations on Keppel Island. After all, they were having a tough time at home. William Parker Snow's campaign against the Society had been stepped up over the course of 1858: a whole file of letters and representations between him, the colonial secretary, the governor of the Falklands and the Society's secretary had been lodged in the House of Commons library in May. In September 1858, the former captain wrote a vociferous warning to the Secretary of State for the Colonies, Bulwer Lytton:

> Is there no one to see to it, Sir? Will not Government ask how they were brought there, and have it proved? or must there be an indifference shown towards the subject because I name it, until some fearful massacre of a ship's crew on the Fuegian or Patagonian coast awakens the people of England to the folly and evil of deporting natives by any and every means, just to carry out some selfish crotchet emanating from the brain of a shrewd speculator or idealist?

Snow's legal case against the Society was adjourned in December 1858 to enable him to obtain documents from the Falkland Islands government. With its former captain winning the propaganda war, it was essential that the Society gave their supporters good news. This they did with stories of domestic satisfaction, successful contact with native peoples and proof of progress from savage to civilian. So it is that we learn that the women Wyeenagowlkippin and Wendoogyappa loved to dress neatly, the former wearing her hair neatly parted, tied in front with two coloured ribbons and behind with lace, the latter though short and broad being good looking 'even to English eye'. We learn that they were keen when it came to working around the house, that they liked needlework and basketry, came and went as they pleased, and were affectionate towards the mission children.

In June Despard recorded that his wife loaned Wyeenagowlkippin a saucepan and demonstrated how to use it for cooking a meal; the next day the woman brought back the pan cleaner than it had been when she borrowed it. Mrs Despard, too, noted changes in the women: 'They are gradually becoming modest in their ways,' she wrote in a letter home, 'and no longer uncover themselves, and squat down as they used to do upon their arrival here.' There was amusement too: the *Voice of Pity* informed the Society's members that Wendoogyappa was the best-humoured and favourite of the women. She would run into a room, sit down, make some remark, get up, run to another room then come back to the first.

As evidence of their domestic contentment, Fuegian men could be found sitting around the fire in their home, repairing their clothes with a needle and thread. On 6 February there was general astonishment when Garland Phillips produced a set of daguerreotypes and photographs of himself and his family. The Fuegians were fascinated and asked questions as to where the people in the pictures were and was it a long way away. They noticed the similarities between Mrs Phillips and her sister and laughed at a picture of the catechist without a beard.

In the mission's terms there were indeed a number of successes to boast of: all nine Fuegians attended church, moved their lips in time with prayers and said, 'Amen.' They were polite, they shook hands and said, 'Good morning, Mr Despard.' The women kissed the missionary women when they met them in the morning. There were hints, too, that the Fuegians had started to understand their keepers' idea of morality: when Wyeenagowl's daughter stole from the dining room her mother chastised her; when Macooallan found a turn-buckle he took it back to the carpenter.

The women in particular were singled out for praise. Their time at Cranmer had turned them from lethargic sloths into energetic, industrious labourers, who had 'learned to work at their needle, though in a rough way, to wash some of their clothes, to keep them and their persons clean, and also to perform many household duties'. And there were also, of course, the educational achievements of young Ookoko and Lucca to be proud of. Descriptions of the two told of them sitting at desks drawing and writing with pens, saying, 'God bless this food,' over dinner, and dressed in their best clothes for tea in the mission house. Late in their stay Lucca even wrote the following letter to a Mr Scott of Dublin, honorary secretary of the Patagonian Missionary Society in Ireland. It was written in phonetic Fuegian, the translation of which read,

My Friend
I am glad to saw much; to plane much. By and bye I shall be a carpenter.
I shall visit England; and you will give me a hatchet, a chisel, and a bradawl; and I shall say, thank you.
Luccaenche Tellon.

When Despard looked back on these months, he did do so with no small satisfaction. He claimed to have built his Fuegian vocabulary up to more than 800 words and felt the need to comment, 'We were sorry to part with Jemmy Button and his party, but we shall really grieve much to part with our present friends, and shall miss them very much, they have behaved so very well.' He also wrote, 'Jemmy Button could never have been what Ookoko is now – a really smart, good-looking, intelligent lad, full of cheerfulness, and perpetually coruscating in smiles . . .'

There was another side to this story, not formally recorded by the missionaries, but surprisingly easy to find amid the tales of good deeds and heartwarming progress. As early as 20 January 1859, just three weeks after the Fuegians' arrival, Phillips had had a serious run-in with the most volatile of the group, Schwaiamugunjiz. His wife Wyruggelkeepa had been passing time with the wives of the mission in Sulivan House, but after having been left on her own for a few minutes she was accused by Mrs Despard of stealing a piece from a chess set. Phillips went to the Fuegians' house, rummaged through Wyruggelkeepa's possessions and found a pawn in one of her bags. The catechist hectored the woman. It was bad to steal, they had been good to her, how could she do this? 'She seemed rather ashamed of herself,' Phillips noted in his journal.

The Fuegian men had been away collecting mussels and limpets and when they returned Phillips visited them to wish them goodnight. What he found waiting for him there was an incensed Schwaiamugunjiz, barely able to contain his anger. The Fuegian shouted and screamed at Phillips, who remembered,

He was in a terrible rage about his wife being accused of stealing (shraena). His manner was so fierce, and his bearing so threatening, that I felt for the moment fearful. I well knew, however, that it would not do to appear timid, and immediately went in, and shut the door upon the whole party, and then and there talked him down – explaining fully the whole circumstance, and giving him and others well to understand that although we should be very kind to them, and, if they worked a little every day, we would reward them accordingly, yet no stealing would be allowed; and, moreover, that they always would be found out. We parted for the night excellent friends, and they had from me the assurance which they eagerly desired, that I was their 'Tagacollo' (friend). I had evening prayer with them ere I left.

At times Phillips and the others were seen to be treating their Fuegian guests with disrespect and disdain. Even Ookoko was not immune. After a day's hunting with the catechist, in which many wild geese were shot, the boy was rewarded with a less tasty alternative. Phillips admitted, with disarming honesty, 'I intended paying him in victuals for his labour, but had not the remotest idea of giving him five geese, when loggerhead ducks would please his palate as well.' Ookoko was furious, but despite a vociferous argument and his refusal to accept the duck, Phillips eventually won the day.

Schwaiamugunjiz, though, was the most bellicose of the Fuegians. A small, but passionate man, with an extraordinary indentation on his forehead, he went by the nickname Squire Muggins, or just the Squire, and was described by Despard as the 'most light-fingered of the lot . . . his approach is the signal for gathering up and placing in safety any articles lying around'. When his wife stole it was said that she did so either 'by command or example of her Indian lord'. On 25 April, as Ookoko helped Bartlett pile turnips into the storehouse, Schwaiamugunjiz tried to snaffle a few vegetables for himself. Despard strode over and ordered him to stop, 'whereat he flew into a great passion, flourished his arms, and uttered a wild cry. I ordered him peremptorily out of the store; he obeyed but gesticulated fiercely, and looked daggers. I gave him look for look, and then he calmed down, and began to talk calmly about some other thing.'

A week later a comb disappeared, and Despard asked Schwaiamugunjiz if he knew anything about it. Wyruggelkeepa, or his wife, exploded with rage and, as Despard ignored her and ordered a search of her corner of the house, she seized furniture, clothes, anything she could get hold of and threw it on the roof. Equally crazed, Schwaiamugunjiz joined in, flinging his property out of the door, yelling in Yamana that he was 'as innocent as the babe unborn'.

Despard stood and watched, incredulous but affecting unconcern. When the noise died down, and the Fuegians' wrath had run its course, he walked up to Schwaiamugunjiz and said arrogantly, 'Quellala shrayena, pallill cowshoo bab shrayena' — bad man steals; English good man does not steal. With that he walked out. Soon after Ookoko called the missionary and pointed to the comb at the foot of the steps in the mission house. He claimed to have seen the Squire drop it there. Despard was sceptical and realised that

Schwaiamugunjiz had probably been telling the truth; Ookoko was the more likely perpetrator. To give him credit he noted, 'Schwy is a sort of a peg to hang all sorts of naughty things on.'

On 1 July Garland Phillips wrote to Charles Turpin, who had recently quit the mission and gone to live in Port Stanley, that Macooallan and Schwaiamugunjiz had attempted to break into the storehouse and 'when accused of it they denied it in toto and said the rats had been eating the wood away'.

The trivial nature of the thefts and the missionaries' overbearing responses to them beggar belief. The removal of a few turnips, a chess pawn and a comb hardly amounted to felony, yet the mission's officers repeatedly threatened their whole enterprise, risking the confidence and support of the Fuegians in whom they had placed so much hope in an effort to punish and teach them a lesson. There is no doubt that they saw theft as a serious crime, that the Fuegians had a reputation for thievery and that they believed such behaviour needed to be stamped out. At times, though, the accusations were ill-founded, clearly offensive and possibly ill-judged. The Saturday after the comb incident, Schwaiamugunjiz arrived at morning prayers, despite having announced that he would no longer be attending. He walked up to Despard and offered the hand of friendship. The missionary had neither admitted his mistake nor practised forgiveness. It is ironic that in this act the 'savage' was articulating the virtues and magnanimity espoused by the man with whom he was effecting a reconciliation.

The Fuegians were never as settled on Keppel Island as the missionaries led their backers to believe. As early as April, with six months of their sojourn still ahead of them, they were said to be growing restless and homesick. Even Despard recorded their disquiet in his journal: 'They begin to talk a good deal of going home to see parents and friends, wives and children and to get good "push-aki" fire wood.' In late June a meeting in the Cenobium raised the question of when they would be allowed to go home, and soon afterwards Macooallan, who had another wife and children in Tierra del Fuego, became fidgety. In September Garland Phillips wrote, 'Our present guests are very desirous of returning to their own people.' Despard remembered later that the Fuegians 'often asked when the schooner was coming back, but were satisfied when we told them soon'.

The *Allen Gardiner* was away on the South American mainland fetching the captain's wife, his son and brother John Fell, who would be the ship's chief officer. When it arrived back on 17 September it was two weeks ahead of schedule. As the next day was a Sunday all the Fells and four of the crew came ashore for morning service. Despard noted that they were

looking so nice in their Guernseys, with the words 'Mission Yacht' on their breasts. The new crew are certainly the finest, nicest-looking set of men we have had yet in the schooner. Three of them are fine young Swedes. One is old H McD, who was the ship's sportsman last year – a dead shot, an acute fisherman, an Arctic voyager, a veteran tar, and a capital seaman. The cook is Ookoko's 'cookoman' come back again, who says he won't leave the *Allen Gardiner* as long as there is a berth to be had in her, for he had never been in a better sea-boat.

The time to take the Fuegians home was fast approaching.

Chapter 20

At just after eleven o'clock on the morning of Wednesday 28 September 1859, Captain Fell sent Despard a message: the tide and winds were good, the ship was ready, it was time to get the Fuegians on board in preparation for their return. The start of 'wild bird egg' season was just a week away – on 4 October – and they were showing increasing signs of anxiety to get home.

Despard rounded up Phillips and three of the station's labourers, and headed for the jetty on Committee Bay. Here they waited as their departing guests arrived with odd-looking bundles and bags. The missionary stopped them in their tracks, and ordered his men to begin a thorough and uncompromising search. The Fuegians were outraged at the implication that they were thieves, and as the party opened the bags of Wyeenagowlkippin, her husband Macalwense roared at the top of his voice. At the same time Macooallan tried, without success, to pass his goods into the waiting boat, and when he failed he flung the lot, a bundle of biscuits and a box of gifts, into the sea. A furious Schwaiamugunjiz raised his fist at Despard's back, took his jacket off and threw it, too, into the water. A box that Despard had had made for his small articles and gifts followed. The women ripped off their clothes and flung them onto the jetty.

In the midst of the uproar Despard and his men continued the search, although according to some unconfirmed sources the catechist Phillips voiced strong objections. Nevertheless they turned up an axe, two chisels, a smoothing plane, a carpenter's line, an oil stone, Captain Fell's leggings, a long line belonging to the missionary's net, a new hammer, a mason's hammer, a gimlet, several pieces of iron band, rags, and various odds and ends including the necks of geese and animal entrails, pots and canisters of biscuits. It was, doubtless, an impressive haul and Despard would have been pleased with his initiative, though disappointed that his visitors had still to learn to refrain from pilfering. Yet one wonders at the wisdom of his actions. The Fuegians had just given up more than nine months of their lives on Keppel Island with little tangible reward. Despard was aware of how seriously they took the accusations of larceny, how deeply such allegations cut. He even recognised that the results of the search were

> highly illustrative of that dislike of being found out, which prevails, as it seems, beyond the precincts of civilised society. To do wrong is one thing; to be found out is quite another. And to many the latter is by far the more painful of the two. The Fuegians are very jealous of their character for honesty; the more so, perhaps, as it stands sometimes in peril.

He knew therefore from experience that, no matter how conclusive the evidence was, such accusations caused deep hurt to the Fuegians. However, at the risk of destroying any remaining vestiges of goodwill, Despard felt the need to drum home the message one last time that theft was a sin and thieves did not prosper.

The situation calmed, the Fuegians went to the ship and once on board Schwaiamugunjiz demanded the box that he had thrown into the sea. Despard gave each a blanket to keep them warm in their homeland. Now, however, having got seven of the party on board – Ookoko and Lucca were to be kept on shore until the last minute – it appears that the opportunity for sailing was lost. Heavy winds, whipped up across the Falkland plains, made it impossible for the ship to pull out of Committee Bay. After three days of sitting around the Fuegians became increasingly frustrated at the delay and anxious to get home. Indignation at the search still ran high, hours spent idle saw grumbles foment into groans and then into strident complaints. On Saturday their seething discontent boiled over: Schwaiamugunjiz and Macalwense jumped on the unsuspecting ship's cook, Alfred Coles, and in the ensuing fracas dragged him across the deck. Macooallan intervened and pulled them apart. Coles recovered his composure and punched Schwaiamugunjiz down into the hold.

In the meantime, back on shore, Despard was giving Garland Phillips his instructions for the journey ahead in a letter.

Dear Mr Phillips . . .
Should there be a friendly spirit in Woollyah, I would try and spend two or three days there on shore, in the house erected during my last visit there, and get a hand from the vessel to stop with you. The captain will furnish you with biscuits etc for encouragement to the natives; and I recommend you to cause a garden to be dug and seeds to be sown, etc.

Spend every day with the natives rather than go into the woods to fell wood, or other purposes. Keep your note book and pencil going. Spell in phonetic. Try them much with singing . . . I would advise, when the weather allows, that you should have a Sabbath morning and evening service on shore, that the natives may attend, and be aroused to inquiry. You will take presents with you for the boys' relatives, and I hope you will treat them (the relatives) with distinguished favour . . .

On 5 October Ookoko and Lucca went on board the *Allen*

Gardiner with presents of clothes for their mothers. Next morning, nine days after the main body of Fuegians had been searched on the jetty and shunted onto the ship, the schooner got under weigh. A gale was blowing from the south-west, but with caution she broke her ground and by three in the afternoon the *Allen Gardiner* had passed the Eddystone rock. By seven the next morning it had arrived at Port Stanley.

Relations between the Fuegians and the missionaries were now shaky. The former were still smarting from the search, still bruised from the set-to with Coles. They had demanded to be taken straight home but instead, against a tidal wave of objections, the schooner had slipped into Port Stanley where it was to sit for the next six days while coal for Cranmer was loaded into the hold. They were angry and their complaints warranted more attention than they received.

There are two distinct versions of this visit to the Falklands' capital, and while they are not contradictory they sit uncomfortably together. First, there was the mission's side of the the story, which conveyed the impression of a productive, enjoyable time, where business was done and the Fuegians captured the hearts and settled the minds of the townspeople. Captain Fell's diary told of a brisk stay dotted with meetings and church services:

Friday, October 7, – Having come to at 7 am, we did not land then, it being too early for the people on shore. The natives thought this a fair place. Mr Phillips soon took the two boys on shore. Having paid a visit to the Colonial Secretary, I called upon a few friends, and afterwards, with Mr Phillips, dined with Captain Packe.

Saturday, October 8, – Yesterday an American got Mr Havers to sketch the natives in the cabin in a group. Called to see a few friends, and arranged a meeting for Mr Phillips tomorrow night.

Sunday, October 9, – In the morning went to our Meeting, at the cottage. Mr Phillips preached.

Monday, October 10, – Mr Havers at the sketch in the cabin. In the afternoon the natives went on shore, and received many presents from the inhabitants of Stanley.

Tuesday, October 11, – Took the natives on shore (the young ones) to have their likenesses taken.

Wednesday, October 12, – The wind being about W.N.W., got under weigh . . .

Garland Phillips's account put more flesh on the bones. He told of how on 8 October he had taken Ookoko and Lucca ashore to show them Despard's store, then to see the governor, and finally Captain Packe, where the housekeeper was very kind. At the same time Mr Havers was on board the *Allen Gardiner* drawing the remaining Fuegians. During the course of the next day many of the residents at Stanley apparently let it be known that they would love to see the Fuegian women and the young child. Accordingly, on 10 October, the whole party was washed and dressed in their Sunday best – Phillips had bought the young girl Kitty a pair of gaiters the day before, but when she put them on she found them difficult to walk in so she left them off – and together they stepped ashore to be met by Mrs Sweeny and the American consul's wife Mrs Smiley. The two women gave the child more gaiters, a woollen coat, and a couple of handfuls of sweets.

The party went on a tour of the town: at the Sibbalds' the lady of the house handed out gingerbread nuts; up the hill, near the poorer cottages, men, women and children flocked to see them, handing out trinkets and little presents, 'all evidences of the kindly feeling entertained towards them'. Captain Molony had said he wanted to see them, but he was out boating so they moved on to two more houses before again meeting Mrs Smiley, who 'begged me to take them on to her house, as she had some more clothes for them. Poor creatures, they were evidently well pleased with Stanley and its people, and kept talking one to another about their gifts and the givers. It came on to blow very hard, so I got them on board again as quickly as possible . . .' Next day, as the ship moved out of Port Stanley, Garland Phillips wrote in his journal, 'It is very clear that the natives thought very highly of their "lionizing," yesterday, for, to-day, they have frequently told me and others that they do not want to go to Tierra del Fuego, but to England. "Tierra del no good; bar Tierra del."'

The second version of this stopover in Port Stanley is more sinister. Two of the most important figures in the capital saw things differently from the missionary party. Superficially what Phillips and Fell were reporting was true, but the governor and the colonial chaplain had noticed disturbing friction between the Fuegians and their missionary hosts: a despatch from the governor to the colonial secretary back in London noted, 'The *Allen Gardiner* put into Stanley on her way. The temper of the natives was known here and the Captain and Mr Phillips were warned by several friends to be on their guard.'

The chaplain, Charles Bull, backed him up. In a letter to the *Guardian* newspaper he wrote that after the ship had arrived at Port Stanley, to 'those who were fully acquainted with the native character, it became evident that there was a good deal of mischief brewing. The natives who had been searched previously to their leaving Keppel, had expressed a good deal of indignation at this proceeding.'

The *Allen Gardiner* crawled back to Wulaia with no sense of haste. A journey that could be completed in good conditions in three days took over three weeks. Along the way they pulled in at Sparrow Cove, Mare Harbour, Ship Harbour and several of the islands of the Fuegian archipelago. Time was set aside for collecting eggs, fishing and refilling the ship's water tanks from the many freshwater streams to be found in the area. Ferocious winds got up, pitching the ship, tossing and turning her like a piece of flotsam. On Thursday 20 October – ten days after leaving the Falklands' capital – land was spotted, but found to be the mountains around Port Stanley. Fell was disappointed, but so too were the Fuegians, who complained vociferously, Macooallan claiming that Jemmy Button had told him the crossing was easy and swift.

As the journey became rougher, the passage slower and the entire ship's company sicker, it became clear that it was not just the Fuegians who were unhappy with the administration of the venture. Robert Fell began to compose a letter to the committee of the Patagonian Missionary Society in Bristol. He told them he had come to the realisation that the maintenance of a mission station on Keppel Island was not viable if the enterprise was to be a success. The passage between Keppel and Tierra del Fuego could be tough, time-consuming and even dangerous. Progress with the natives was deadly slow because the sporadic visits to their homeland were not enough to provide continuity or understanding, and taking away a few natives at a time was not having the desired effect. He concluded that the only real chance of progress lay with the establishment of a station among the natives, on Tierra del Fuego, and urged the committee to consider it.

On 2 November the ship arrived at Wulaia and the captain prepared to demonstrate once again that if there was one truly great failing intrinsic to the Patagonian Missionary Society it was the inability of its personnel to learn from past mistakes. It might have been over a month since the departure from Keppel Island, and the search on the jetty might have been a distant, insignificant memory for the crew and captain of the *Allen Gardiner*, but those who had been subjected to it were still indignant.

As the ship dropped anchor that Wednesday noon, Jemmy Button came alongside, and Fell recorded in his diary,

Wednesday November 2, – A canoe came off, and we saw poor Jemmy Button naked, and as wild-looking as ever. It was almost too trying to behold him. It seemed to prove that all our labours with him had been thrown away. Something entirely different to what has been already done will have to be taken in hand, before the natives will be benefited.

The bedraggled Jemmy climbed on board and was not long in expressing his dissatisfaction at the shortage of presents that awaited him. In the meantime the returning Fuegians prepared to disembark, but as they did so Fell, who had been advised that some of the crew's possessions were missing, ordered another search of their bundles. Schwaiamugunjiz and Macalwense were enraged. As the captain attempted to open his bundle Schwaiamugunjiz grabbed him by the throat and pinned him against the wall. The captain lashed out, punching the Fuegian away. The incensed Yamana dropped their bundles, or left them where they lay, and climbed into the canoes waiting below. Only Macooallan, his wife and the two boys Ookoko and Lucca remained behind, startled by what they had witnessed. With the antagonists gone their bundles were opened. Amid their clothes were found a harpoon, a silk handkerchief, a knife and a steel.

That evening Fell took ashore Macooallan and his wife in the ship's boat, along with the bundles left behind by the disgraced Fuegians. That same night Jemmy Button was encouraged back onto the ship where he was given clothes and some presents that had been sent for him from Cranmer. Over the next days the crew went ashore unmolested, completed work on the house and began to dig a garden for it. Some Fuegians even worked for them, and Ookoko stayed on board, going ashore with the ship party to cut down trees, work on the house, and return at the end of each day to sleep on the *Allen Gardiner*. If any trouble was brewing, he either had not heard of it or was not going to tell. Things were changing, though, perhaps imperceptibly to the crew, but the atmosphere on shore was darkening. There had been few Fuegians at Wulaia on the Wednesday of the ship's arrival, but by Saturday seventy more canoes had arrived, swelling their numbers to over 300. On the Friday night Jemmy Button came on board once again for one of his unpleasant conversations with the captain, an exchange of views that the captain would probably have put down to Jemmy being 'one of the dullest of his race' and greedy with it.

In the final four days of Fell's Wulaia diary there are few clues to the deteriorating relations that the crew was experiencing with the Indians, but they are there:

Thursday November 3, – Crew cutting wood, and Mr Phillips and his boys at the garden. The natives went on shore, and Schwya-Muggins got his clothes in the evening.

Friday November 4, – Crew at the wood. Our natives too lazy to get their house covered in.

Saturday November 5, – Crew at the wood. Natives rather troublesome alongside.

Sunday November 6, –

The blank space after Sunday is ominous. Wishing to comply with the instructions given to Phillips by Despard, and hoping to set a good example to the assembled Fuegians, it was agreed that a service should be conducted in the nearly completed house. A longboat was lowered into the water and all the ship's crew, with the exception of the cook, Coles, climbed on board and rowed the 300 yards to the shore.

There were eight men in the boat, each dressed in their smart jumpers with 'Mission Yacht' emblazoned across the front. As they arrived on the beach the Fuegians eyed them idly, but did not stir from behind the small fires that speckled the cove. The boat was pulled out of the water and onto the beach, then the men walked to the house and arranged themselves for divine worship. A moment passed before hymn singing began.

Out on the ship, Alfred Coles looked up from the galley where he was preparing lunch, and saw the Yamana rise. 'They are up to mischief,' he said to himself. A group of naked men approached the unguarded boat, removed its oars and carried them off to a wigwam. The hymn singing stopped, and a dreadful noise pierced the air. Coles turned his gaze to the house. A large group of Indians were attacking it, smashing down the door, flooding inside. Hugh McDowall, the veteran sailor and one-time Arctic explorer, was clubbed to the ground. Seven unarmed men pushed their way out of the house, only to find a huge mob waiting. Wooden clubs carved from the branches of beech trees whipped down, cracking skulls, a rain of stones darkened the sky and thudded against the heads of the fleeing crew. The two Fell brothers, snared by a circle of Fuegians, fought and dropped, back to back; boulders continued to batter their lifeless bodies. The carpenter and two men fell under the dull bludgeoning of clubs. Along the beach Ookoko ran up and down crying, hands held out in front of him, imploring the assassins to stop.

From out of the crowd burst the Swedish sailor, August Petersen, and the screaming catechist, Garland Phillips. At the water's edge a boulder flattened the Scandinavian. Phillips plunged into the sea, black hair flapping in the wind, mouth contorted in anguish. He tried to launch a canoe, but as he pushed desperately, up to his knees in water, Macalwense, the Fuegian known to the missionaries as Billy Button, threw a stone that crashed against his temple. His head lolled to one side, then to the other, and finally his legs buckled under him as the life drained from him, his coat tails rising on the ebb of a reddening sea.

There were eight men dead on Wulaia Cove:

Garland Phillips – Catechist
Robert Fell – Captain
John Fell – Mate
John Johnstone – Carpenter and second mate
Hugh McDowall – Able bodied seaman
John Johnston – Able bodied seaman
John Brown – Able bodied seaman
August Petersen – Ordinary seaman

On the *Allen Gardiner*, Alfred Coles remained calm. He went below, collected a gun and three loaves of bread. He threw them into a gig hanging in the davits, cut the boat free, letting her drop to the water, picked a paddle from the scuppers, jumped over the side and rowed away from the slaughter.

PART FIVE

This Studied Concealment . . .

Chapter 21

Back in England the new year 1860 began optimistically for the Patagonian Missionary Society. Over the previous couple of years its missionaries at Keppel Island had received two groups of Fuegian Indians and, as far as they knew, were at that very moment shipping a third party back to Cranmer. More importantly, the case brought against them by their former employee, William Parker Snow, had been brought to a triumphant conclusion for the Society, after four years in which he had waged an unremitting war of attrition.

Snow's action had first reached the courts on 18 December 1858 when the Chief Justice of the Court of Common Pleas had agreed an adjournment to allow several crucial documents to be obtained from the Falkland Islands. Snow lobbied the Colonial Office relentlessly, but the civil servants and ministers there were convinced he 'was not completely in his right mind' and was of a rather 'excitable character'. These views were confirmed when the case resumed on 8 December 1859 and lasted less than two days, the jury giving their verdict without retiring from the court room. There was, they said, no case for the missionary society to answer: William Parker Snow had not been unfairly dismissed and he was not owed any money or any compensation for the way in which he had been treated. Fresh allegations that the Lloyd's agent in the Falklands had suggested he scupper the *Allen Gardiner* for mutual profit were laughed out of court.

The publicity, however, had not flattered the Society. On the day after the verdict *The Times* lambasted its behaviour: 'One would suppose from the way in which he [Snow] calls Heaven to witness against them that his employers were Turks and monsters, instead of being enthusiastic and devoted missionaries burning with the love of human souls . . . As it is, the Patagonian Mission has ended very ill, and can show a list, not of heathen converted, but of a number of excellent Christians quarrelling and abusing one another.' The Society clearly had work to do to restore its reputation, but it was a great relief for the ordeal to be over. The first *Voice of Pity* for 1860 boasted,

> Most hopeful are the present prospects of the Mission abroad. At no time in the history of our work did ever such signs of blessing appear. The Christian mind will not fail to appreciate the mercy of the Lord in permitting us to report of natives of Tierra del Fuego, outwardly at least, joining in work, and in worship, and in prayer, and praise, with our Missionary brethren.

Unknown to anyone in England on 8 December 1859, the day that Snow's case reached its final verdict, eight missionaries had been lying dead in Tierra del Fuego for over a month.

The *Allen Gardiner* had been expected back at Keppel Island on 1 December 1859. By February of the next year those at the mission station were growing increasingly alarmed at its failure to return and Despard took the Society's second boat, the *Perseverance*, to Stanley, where he commissioned the American seafarer William Smyley, owner of the brigantine *Nancy*, to go in search of the missing ship.

Smyley was a rumbustious Rhode Islander in his late sixties, whose reputation as a seal and cattle hunter had earned him the nickname 'Fat Jack of the Bone House'. He was a maverick sea-farer, whose legitimate dealings in the South Atlantic occasionally verged on the piratical. In 1854 he had supported an American corvette threatening Port Stanley with bombardment in a dispute over the power of the British authorities there. Nevertheless, in spite of his notoriety in the eyes of some of the local establishment, it was recognised that he had a great streak of humanity and an unrivalled knowledge of both the Falklands and the Fuegian archipelago. It had been Smyley who had discovered the bodies of the missing Gardiner expedition in 1851 and this, combined with his unmatched knowledge of the South Atlantic and its islands, made him the man most likely to find the lost schooner.

Smyley arrived at Wulaia Cove on 1 March 1860 and discovered the *Allen Gardiner* at anchor. As the *Nancy* drifted it was surrounded by canoes. On one of them a white man stood and waved – Alfred Coles. The crew hauled him aboard, and behind him Jemmy Button clambered onto the ship then headed off to the galley for bread and water. Smyley welcomed the mission party's cook, gave him food and blankets and asked him for his story.

Coles, trembling with relief and holding his head to one side from the pain of a huge boil under his right ear, told how in November 1859 he had rowed the *Allen Gardiner*'s gig away from the massacre. Over his shoulder he had seen the killers climbing into their canoes and racing towards the ship, one canoe peeling off in his direction. He had paddled hard, and within minutes was scrambling ashore and dashing into the dark security of dense woodland. The three small loaves he had placed in his Guernsey had fallen out during his panic-stricken flight. From the upper branches of a tree, he had watched his pursuers land their canoe nearby. He had seen them climb out of their boat, run ashore and look around for him before abandoning their pursuit, and settling for his small boat, which they took in tow.

When it seemed safe, Coles had descended from the tree and stolen away in the direction of the sun across open countryside.

Over the next few days he had wandered to the east, through a land teeming with guanaco and geese, living off berries and sleeping at night under makeshift shelters of sticks and grass. After four days he had arrived, cold and hungry, at a river too wide and deep to cross. He followed the water's course to a beach where he found limpets and mussels, but without matches he could not make a fire to warm himself or dry his sodden clothes. A short while later, despite everything that had passed, he hailed a passing canoe steered by Tellon's eldest son.

The murderous rage of a few days earlier had gone, replaced by the hand of friendship and the offer of a lift. Coles climbed into the canoe and warmed himself by the fire at its heart. For over a week as the two men drifted from island to island, he was forced to fend off gangs of locals who begged and robbed him of almost everything he possessed. All of his clothes were taken, except his belt and earrings, his beard and eyebrows were plucked out by their roots or shaved off with sea shells. Among the inhabitants he had seen one wearing a Mission Yacht Guernsey and another sporting Captain Fell's blue coat. Despite their rough treatment of him, the Yamana had shared their food with him, and after ten days he was taken back to Wulaia, where, out at sea, the *Allen Gardiner* rode at anchor. She was little more than a carcass: masts, deck lights, rigging poles, steps and anything metallic had been stripped from her. The Fuegian mob had dispersed, and among the few that remained were Jemmy Button, his brothers Macooallan and Macalwense, Schwaiamugunjiz and the boys Ookoko and Lucca, all of whom were sympathetic, feeding him with mussels, shellfish and occasionally fish. They gave Coles stockings, his own hat and trousers, and a pair of boots belonging to the dead captain. They had even handed over one of the ship's muskets, a nightcap full of powder, some shot and percussion caps, with which he hunted geese and became known as a 'very good fellow'.

For almost four months Coles had been treated as one of the Yamana, and the women looked after him with particular kindness — one of those who had been at Keppel Island even selected him to attend her during her confinement, owing to the special skills he was believed to possess. Every day he had taken his share of the food when the men returned from their fishing expeditions, and as the sun went down he had joined in the native wrestling matches that had filled the nights. He had gone to Button Island in a canoe and had visited the *Allen Gardiner* a dozen times, but found her rifled of everything. On some days he had searched from dawn to dusk without success for the bodies of his dead comrades. One Fuegian told him that the corpses had been thrown into the sea, another that they had been buried at a secret location.

As Coles spoke, Smyley wrote down his testimony. The twenty-three-year-old cook recounted the events leading to the slaughter, the awful sight of the killings, the screams, the blood and the merciless brutality. He concluded with some serious allegations:

> The boys of the tribe told me that Jemmy Button and the others went on board the *Allen Gardiner* the evening of the massacre and that Jemmy Button slept in the captain's cabin. There was no one living on board when I got back.
>
> My belief is that the cause of the massacre was Jemmy Button being jealous that he did not get as much as he thought he had a right to, and that he was at the head of the whole proceedings.
>
> As to what became of the bodies I don't know, the boys told me that they saw Jemmy Button fight; I did not see him from the nest, I could not tell him. I could only tell Billy Button; he was a little on one side from the rest when he knocked Mr Phillips down.

Smyley heard out Coles with great seriousness. The *Nancy* only had a crew of six: to stop would be dangerous and the man Coles accused of being the chief assassin was still below in the galley. Without putting down anchor, he cut the painter of Jemmy Button's canoe adrift and sailed out of Wulaia. The unsuspecting Fuegian had been abducted and was once again on his way to the Falklands.

The people of Port Stanley greeted the news of the massacre with shock and anger. Volunteers queued up to go to Tierra del Fuego and exact revenge; the commander of the marines, Captain Abbott, proposed taking twenty of the Falklands' garrison to Wulaia to punish the culprits by force. Smyley wanted to take a posse of vigilantes on board the *Nancy*. However, the governor, who harboured misgivings about the activities of the Patagonian Missionary Society, withheld permission for reprisals. He was unwilling to rush into harsh and potentially unjust action to avenge something he considered as tricky and dishonest as the mission station at Keppel Island. At the time, to have voiced such sentiments would have been unfeeling and controversial. Instead he argued that the killings were beyond his jurisdiction; only one Indian had been identified as involved, and the various tribes had dispersed after the murders. The innocent were as likely to be hurt by reprisals as the guilty. Nevertheless, when he wrote to the Secretary of State for the Colonies with news of the deaths, he conceded that

> If in calmly reviewing all the circumstances of the case you think it right to send a small vessel of war to visit the scene not to revenge the fate of the murdered men so much as by a salutary display of force to ensure the safety of any seamen hereafter cast ashore on those islands . . . I am bound to say that such a demonstration would be very useful.

Jemmy was taken from the *Nancy* neither as a prisoner nor as a free man, but his life was in danger. No official report records it, but the people of Stanley wanted him strung up as the supposed architect of the killings. George Packenham Despard later remembered that as Jemmy was taken to Government House he was lucky to survive, 'hardly escaping Lynch-law execution . . .' Here in the colonial secretary's office on 12 March 1860 he was cross-questioned on the massacre.

In the presence of Governor Moore, the Colonial Chaplain, Captain Smyley and the undersigned, James Button Terra del Fuegian states:

I staid at Keppel Island 4 moons with wife and children – did not like to stop, don't want to, don't like it. Despard say go back Jemmy your old, your children stop – would like children to stop at Woollya – want to go back with you (Captain Smyley). All like to go back to Woollya, Mr Despard ask you to go to Keppel, Mr Despard said go two time, Keppel two time a year. Woollya no work at Keppel. Cask of water in big hut at Keppel, spear fish at Keppel, no catch seal. Catch fish big fish, I did not see them search the bags. Oens country boy very angry boy, when Despard look in bags. Oens country men killed Captain Fell – all same as Patagonias bow and arrow men – my country in small channel, others from big waters, my country at Woollya their's near Patagonia – Oens country boys say we no kill you you go away we kill them – Captain Fell was killed with stone by Oens country – I see Captain Fell killed – Carpenter another man saw and killed – I no see Mr Phillips killed – I put four in the ground, I no see the others – I will show Captain Smyley – I no see one live. I think one get away in the field run away – I bury Captain Fell and the Carpenter and two others Swedes. I no sleep in schooner run about on mainland – no more sleep run about – I have been all round island no see white man, me look for body Captain Fell my brother say – all by ground near house – my brother dig. Every tribe speaks differently –

woman at Woollya is 'keeper' my tribe has 15 canoes (counting on his fingers) plenty canoes other side over water plenty. Your people no speak Woollya Oens country no speak (Lennox Island described) they no speak. Yorks country two ships broke long time ago – York man eat man – Scratch country. My brother perhaps go back to Keppel. I had plenty of it – no want to go back – been away three times – country men perhaps go back (accompanied by look to say no) – (afterwards added) my country boy no want to go back to Keppel.

Taken down the day and year before mentioned from Jemmy Button's lips as far as he could be understood or made to understand the questions.

J.R. Longden Colonial Secretary
Charles Bull Colonial Chaplain

There were inconsistencies, contradictions and some outright lies in the Fuegian's statement, but amid these, and his memories of conditions at Cranmer – the cask of water, the fishing, the lack of seal – there emerged another version of events leading to the massacre. Jemmy had resented his time on Keppel Island: he had not wanted to go there in the first place and did not want to return. Moreover, it was clear that he had not believed the enterprise was viable – 'Woollya no work at Keppel,' he said. There had been great anger at the searching of the bags, but the killers had not been from among his people; instead they were the much demonised Oens-men, the deadly enemies of the Yamana. He added that he had buried four of the dead men and had not slept in the captain's cabin of the deserted schooner. He finished with a quick snipe at York Minster and his cannibalistic people and added that he had had enough of Keppel Island. Perhaps his brother would go back, he suggested, but then immediately reconsidered this: 'my country boy no want to go back to Keppel'. His people had had their fill of the mission station.

News of the massacre reached London on 4 May 1860, two days short of six months after the event. It came in the form of a despatch from the Falklands' governor, Thomas Moore. It detailed everything he knew about the circumstances of the unhappy affair: the work of the mission station; the searches of the Fuegians; the names of the dead; the evidence and rescue of Alfred Coles; the indignant response in Port Stanley; his refusal to seek reprisals; and the few details known of the bereaved. Moore threw in a note of personal opinion: 'I am bound to say that I do not think Mr Despard's measure of searching the men in any way judicious, nor do I think that the natives were contented with their enforced residence at Keppel, and I must note that those natives were foremost in the murders.' He had, he added, also banned the further importation of natives by the Society and instituted an inquiry into the slaughter under the 433rd clause of the Merchant Shipping Act.

The following day the story emerged in the press. 'HORRIBLE MASSACRE OF A MISSIONARY SHIP' was the headline in the *Daily Telegraph* which, along with the *Morning Advertiser* and the *Western Daily Press*, was the first to pick the story up. By Monday 7 May the news won wider circulation: the *Observer* and the *Morning Star* were among those that printed the story, and the *Daily Record* carried a letter from the secretary of the Patagonian Missionary Society, Waite Stirling. In this he attempted to put a positive gloss on the killings. He praised the work of the missionaries and, after vowing to keep up the struggle with the heathen, finished with a flourish:

From one who speaks out of a warm heart, and with a strong

faith, but who utters sentiments held by one, at least, high in the Church's ranks, we have received these words, 'We are Englishmen – not to say Christians – and must not give up.' Oh, Sir, speed these words forth. They may be the rallying cry of a thousand sorrowing hearts.

In Bristol, the home of the Society's headquarters and the *Allen Gardiner*'s port of embarkation, all the local papers covered the story, and in the region's only daily newspaper, the *Western Daily Press*, Waite Stirling was given space on 8 May to issue a long and melodramatic call for support on behalf of the organisation:

We have, indeed, to lament the cruel treachery of a supposed friendly people, but do we not thereby recognise the urgent duty of making known to them the word of truth and righteousness? If Christian missionaries are mere romantic enterprises, it is time to give them up in Tierra del Fuego at least. But if they are great and serious matters, undertaken in order that the Grace of God may be brought to bear upon and change the fallen hearts and consciences of mankind then is the treachery of Woollyah a more imperious call than ever to continue the work of this society . . .

Is the faithfulness unto death of the men whose loss we now deplore, a signal for us to forsake the work they loved? Assuredly not. The work must go forward.

Other papers were less generous. The liberal weekly the *Bristol Gazette* scolded the Society from its leader column, reminding its readers of the claims made in a recent court case:

Without entering into the question of the squabbles between Captain Snow and the Society, this is established, that nothing was done towards converting the Fuegians. Mr Despard was set up as a grazier or cattle-breeder at Falkland, and a few Fuegians were enticed or entrapped into becoming his servants, or rather his slaves, but we never heard or read that any of them were made Christians . . . Now, we do ask what has been done by this Society to compensate for the loss of so many brave Englishmen? These Fuegians are, perhaps without exception, the lowest in the scale of humanity certainly not above the Bosjesmen of Africa or the Mousemen of Australia. For more than a quarter of a century we have been trying to Christianize and civilize them, and we see the result. We have spent treasure, we have sacrificed many valuable lives, and yet the Society cannot show us one single native whom they can confidently point out as converted. Is it not time, then, that this Quixotic enterprise should be abandoned? It is all very pleasant for gentlemen who stay comfortably at home to make eloquent speeches on platforms, to fair and sympathizing auditors, but they should remember that a vast responsibility rests upon them.

The London correspondent of the *Bath Chronicle* speculated on the cause of the killings when he repeated the rumour doing the rounds in the capital that the Fuegians, 'it seems, had been made so thoroughly miserable by being washed, clothed, pulled about, pawed over, and preached at, that they resolved on revenge, and when they found themselves once again in their wigwams, happy, naked, and free, they caught the unhappy Christian party . . . and killed them with clubs and stones . . .'

The most furious debate was reserved for the letters columns where the killings unleashed a torrent of emotion in both the national and local press. It was a foregone conclusion that the disaster would pitch the prolific and increasingly vitriolic William Parker Snow against the increasingly defensive Society. In the *Morning Post* of Friday 11 May, Snow demanded a full inquiry into both the massacre and the activities of the Society, adding that 'it may be thought that these natives are so savage as to make all precaution useless against them. If so, all I can say is that I did not find them so; and my wife as well can testify to their kind and friendly disposition, even at the very place where this massacre has occurred.'

In the *Western Daily Press* of 12 May, an anonymous correspondent, hiding behind the alias 'Scrutator', joined the attack, accusing the Society in picturesque language of not only being responsible for a reckless loss of life, but also of being complacent in their response. A searching inquiry was needed into the instructions given to the dead men and the means provided to avoid catastrophe.

> That such a dreadful announcement should be made, and then allowed to pass over in silence, as the secretary fondly thinks it will, or result in increased efforts in the same direction, is to suppose us deaf to the cry of the bereaved widows and orphans. No quack doctor would think of heading the placard announcing the virtues of his nostrum with the device of a Death's head and cross bones. Nor should the society, as I take it, commence a fresh appeal to the public without at first satisfying them that their efforts will be more wisely and prudently directed and the public secured, humanly speaking, from again being horrified by such sickening details.

It was strong stuff and the Society was stung by the criticisms. Waite Stirling, rapidly becoming the organisation's whipping boy, replied to Scrutator by admitting that there may have been over-confidence on the part of the party aboard the *Allen Gardiner*, but if that was so then it was because the treachery of the Fuegians had been masked and unknown. This was a mistake, but the missionaries had not been the only ones to make such an error in the face of 'barbarous people'. Britain was still reeling from the 'glorious' bloodbath of 1857's Indian Mutiny: was there not a direct parallel?

It is not very long since we deplored the frightful slaughter in India of whole companies of Christians. Lucknow, Cawnpore, Merut, and Delhi are names written in letters of anguish on the hearts of thousands of our countrymen. Does 'Scrutator' want to know why? I will tell him. The blood of Englishmen and Englishwomen – the blood of martyrs – has been shed there – shed because of the over-confidence of Britons and the treachery of a too trusted native soldiery.

The dispute raged on. Scrutator retaliated, accusing the Society of kidnap, of disregarding the native disaffection and of lack of precaution. Stirling countered that, naturally, some might find cause for the massacre in the bad temper of three or four natives four days before the slaughter, but 'reflecting minds will scarcely accept as satisfactory such an explanation of events'. He attacked the correspondent for hiding behind an alias, and concluded with the words, 'I will not gratify "Scrutator" by any further remarks. His gross insinuation that I have invented "an interesting episode in the dark story" is sufficient reason for his writing under a mask.'

But Scrutator was not the only one who hid behind a pseudonym to take up cudgels: in the *Western Daily Press* of 29 May A.B. joined the fray:

GENTLEMEN, – I have read with interest the very able letters of 'Scrutator' on the late massacre in Patagonia, and with pain the feeble and evasive replies of the Secretary.

The object of my intruding on your columns is to inquire if any provision is being made for the widows and orphans of the sufferers, for although the committee have been reminded

— is it not a disgrace that they should require to be reminded?
— by the Rev. Mr Bull and 'Scrutator' of its necessity, yet
they seem to have taken no steps in the matter, and it was
not mentioned at the prayer meeting held some time since in
St Paul's Schoolroom.

The letter encapsulated the widespread annoyance at and
dissatisfaction with the behaviour of the Society, and its apparent
unwillingness to accept responsibility.

In government circles the news of the massacre sparked off a
serious debate, in which little sympathy was shown towards
the Patagonian Missionary Society. Stirling had alluded to the
notorious tragedies of the Indian sub-continent, and it was fair to
say that the scale of the deaths on Wulaia paled into insignificance
in comparison with the hundreds slaughtered on Indian streets,
in Indian rivers and thrown down Indian wells. Nevertheless,
the issue aroused serious concern at the Colonial Office. The
murder of Britons abroad was always vexatious, and missionaries
were generally backed by powerful lobbying organisations. As a
consequence set procedures had to be followed and appropriate
responses calculated. The actual discussions in the Colonial Office
are not recorded, but the tenor of the arguments may be construed
from the minutes scribbled on the back of documents as they
passed from civil servant to junior minister to minister to Secretary
of State — the Duke of Newcastle.

Some of the notes written on Governor Moore's initial despatch, received on 4 May 1860, are revealing. It is clear that the
most immediate priority of the office was to scotch the possibility
of reprisals. A.B. (most probably A. Blackwood, senior clerk of the
Colonial Office) noted that the idea of avenging the catastrophe by
an onslaught on the Yamana was 'preposterous':

It is indeed open to doubt whether we could possess ourselves of the actual offenders we should be justified in applying to Barbarians that measure of retribution which is dealt out to criminals in Christian countries. The Patagonians probably slay any person who offends them without much regard to the degree of the offence, and for us to punish them in the same way as they have treated our intruders – who offered the first affront – would be descending, on our parts, to their scale of morality.

The Assistant Under Secretary of State, T.F. Elliot, launched a scathing attack on the Society. His comments were for private viewing only and his vitriolic assault leaves no doubt as to where his sympathies lay. His jottings talk of a 'gratuitous waste of life' arising from 'folly and obstinacy . . . and carelessness'. Despard, he says, 'acted badly throughout' and then, most startlingly,

Captain Snow has always asserted that the natives were retained at Keppel against their will, to work for the missionaries. His evidence is doubtless to be perceived with caution, but the present testimony of the man called Button tends to its confirmation. If the Chief Missionary kidnapped natives, and then kept them to forced labour, it is not surprising that murder should follow.

In its frankness and its acknowledgement that events in the South Atlantic were illegitimate, this last phrase, '. . . it is not surprising that murder should follow', is a remarkably powerful indication of the way high-ranking members of the government were thinking. Elliot followed it up by hammering home this message to his colleagues: 'The poor men who have perished cannot with truth be represented as sufferers for religion: they have paid the penalty of the wilfulness of one gentleman who still lives and of their own subsequent rashness – They are victims, but not martyrs.'

This was extraordinary stuff, and Elliot's fellow Assistant Under Secretary, Chichester Fortescue, concurred, adding that it had been the right course of action to prevent the importation of any more natives by 'this foolish mission scheme'. With the Duke of Newcastle's agreement, no further action should be taken until the results of a promised inquiry were received, and until HMS *Buzzard*, which had been despatched to the Falkland Islands, reported back.

The impression that the Colonial Office really did not want any reprisals against the Fuegians is reinforced by a minute to the Admiralty of 4 June. Alfred Coles had positively identified one of the Fuegians, Billy Button (Macalwense), as the killer of Garland Phillips. It had been his stone that had crashed against the fleeing catechist's head. A note on the draft letter reads,

> Whilst indiscriminate revenge is a thing not to be thought of, both on account of its injustice and of the future evil it would produce, it certainly is a different question whether, if he fell into our power, the very individual who murdered an unarmed and unresisting Englishman should be suffered to escape with impunity. The important point to weigh would be the probable future effect on these natives, on which a great deal might be said on both sides. I have intentionally omitted the topic from the letter to the Admiralty, as being at all events premature.

The Colonial Office waited for over a month before communicating with the Patagonian Missionary Society. It wanted the results of the governor's inquiry in its hands before making any public pronouncements on the massacre, but when news failed to arrive, the Duke of Newcastle decided that there should be no more delay. On 19 June his office forwarded the governor's correspondence to the Society with a covering note explaining that statements in the accompanying letter 'seriously impugn

The young fly-catcher, or stone-pounder, Charles Darwin in 1840,
painted by George Richmond.

Above: An Indian family glide across the still waters of Tierra del Fuego in their canoe.

Right: 'their hair hanging down on all sides, like old thatch. . .' a Yamana couple pose for the camera.

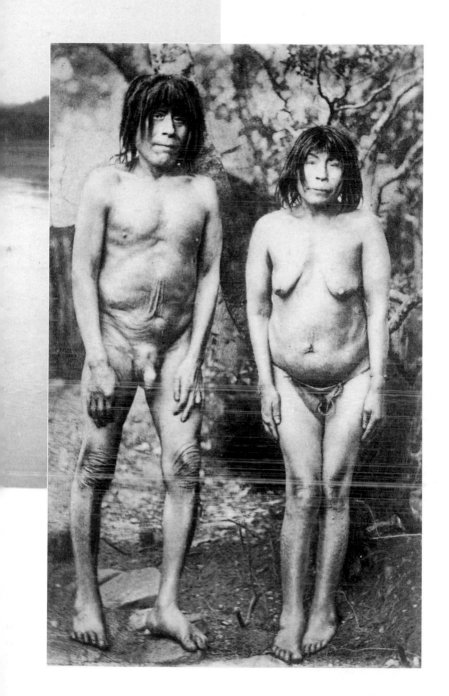

HOPE DEFERRED NOT LOST

ALLEN GARDINER

SEELEYS, FLEET ST.; J. NISBET & Co. BERNERS' ST.
LONDON: & J. WRIGHT, BRISTOL.

Above: The Patagonian Missionary Society's great hope, the Cranmer mission station on Keppel Island, the Falklands.

Right: The thorn in the side of the Patagonian Missionary Society, William Parker Snow in 1867.

Left: The ill-fated vessel, the Allen Gardiner.

Above: Alakaluf women rounded up to work in the mission station on Dawson Island.

Above left: Waite Stirling, the first bishop of the Falklands, with the four Fuegians – Threeboys, Uroopa, Mamastugadegenes, (Jack) and Sesoienges – he brought to England in 1865.

Left: Fuegian men dressed in European clothes pose while building a traditional wigwam.

Right: A source of amusement. . . a Fuegian man wanders the deck of a European ship, smoking a cigarette.

Below: 'Muerto en el terreno de honor' – dead in the land of honour. Fuegians were mercilessly hunted down by European settlers.

Muerto en el terreno de honor.

the prudence of part of the proceedings which preceded this calamity', and requested explanations. The note also demanded to know whether the missionary superintendent was indeed forcibly holding Fuegians at Cranmer, because if so, it was 'scarcely necessary to say that Her Majesty's Government could not sanction the detention of any people on a British territory against their will'.

Waite Stirling responded for the Society on 26 June, emphatically denying that natives had been taken to Keppel Island against their wish. He argued that Jemmy Button's deposition was far from clear, that it had been made under duress, and that his responses resulted from leading questions put to him by people unacquainted with his language, with preconceived opinions about the cause of the killings. In fact, he went on, not only had Jemmy Button agreed to go to Keppel Island for 'four moons', he also gave such a good report of it that nine more of his compatriots had agreed to go there for ten months. Furthermore, the searches of the Fuegians might have been injudicious but that did not mean that they were wrong: they had to be taught not to steal.

Stirling went on to address the frequently heard accusation that insufficient precaution had been taken by the men on the day of the massacre, but said that this could only have arisen because captain, catechist and crew had been confident of the friendliness of the people at Wulaia. As to the actual causes of the massacre, the committee believed they had been 'sought within too narrow a limit, such that consequently mere incidental circumstances have been invested with a fictitious importance, and have been magnified so as to assume the character of primary causes'. As reluctant as they claimed to be to apportion blame, they felt that, despite Alfred Coles's assertion that Jemmy was the culprit, those responsible were most likely the Oens-men who had flooded the area and whom Jemmy had accused.

In the Society's opinion the Fuegians of Wulaia were almost certainly accessories to the attack and to the subsequent plunder: 'In the excitement of the attack it would have been remarkable if men, who knew little of the restraints of Christian civilisation, should have wholly abstained from acts of violence.' Nevertheless the governor had acted correctly in repressing the feelings of revenge that had boiled over in Stanley, but Stirling hoped that the government would send a warship to patrol the channels of Tierra del Fuego as an occasional show of force and would also lift the prohibition on Indians going to Keppel Island.

The Colonial Office received a further barrage of letters from William Parker Snow. Just five days after the colonial secretary, the Duke of Newcastle, heard of the deaths, on 9 May, Snow was writing with the scent of victory in his nostrils and, as he said, in the character of a person 'having the rights of Kings'.

> A fearful massacre of a whole ship's Company has taken place. I foretold it: I warned the authorities; I pointed it out to the Government at home; and I entreated for interference to prevent the natives being taken away by those men who under the name of 'Missionaries' were reckless of consequences so long as they could carry on the system and thus obtain money from an easy public. I offered to clearly prove that the whole plan was not only deceptive but dangerous to others as well as to the poor subordinates engaged in it. But my voice was of course unheeded. The result is now seen!

Once again Snow spelled out what he had been through, what he had predicted and how he had been ignored. Yet again he demanded an inquiry and insisted that the authorities at Port Stanley be punished for their handling of his misfortune and the corruption that permeated their dealings. In private the officers of the Colonial Office agreed. A minute appended to one of Snow's letters on 11 May read, 'It cannot be denied that Mr Snow has a sort of triumph. He foretold sad consequences from the course of this mission and his predictions have been verified. There is something moving in his earnestness . . .' Another minute exposed the quandary that the department found itself in:

> The difficulty is to know what Mr Snow wishes to be done. A great calamity has happened, – the worst of his prophecies of evil has been fulfilled, – and it really seems, by some of the latest evidence, as if a new addition has been made to the instances in which religious zeal has lately taken the shape of kidnapping. But granting all this, what is it that this Department can do?

More letters from Snow followed, reiterating his case, demanding responses and urging action. He wrote on 22, 26 and 30 May, finally threatening to publish all the letters and communications that had passed between him and the government over the course of the previous four years. He said he would have the facts printed up and distributed throughout the country so that 'people may know how true it is our Rulers utterly despise and trample the People under foot when certain individual interests connected with government are to be considered.' Government officers were unimpressed by the threats, and after a week or two in which they had felt a certain grudging respect for the Society's former skipper, they clearly began to tire of him. They decided to put an end to their side of the correspondence. On Snow's letter of 30 May Elliot jotted,

> Two more rhapsodies have arrived from Mr Snow. I think with a loud adventurer of this kind, the boldest course is the safest, and after taking care, for upwards of a year and a half, to exhibit ample patience and supply full explanations I should recommend

administering to him now such a letter as will stand well in his way in any passionate and one-sided representation that he may contemplate publishing . . .

One last letter was issued. It declared that the Colonial Office had no right to interfere in properly constituted court cases and should Mr Snow wish to spend vast sums of money publishing his correspondence, then so be it.

The attacks from Governor Moore, the government and William Parker Snow had not been entirely unexpected, but the Society would have been more surprised by the comments of the colonial chaplain in the Falklands that appeared in the Anglo-Catholic weekly the *Guardian* on 9 May. The Reverend Charles Bull accused the Society of lamentable mistakes in its operations with the Fuegians, criticised the searches that were carried out, and suggested a major rethink by the missionaries: 'Would it not be well to establish a body of missionaries on the spot – say, at this very Woolya; give them an iron house to live in, placing firearms in their hands to use on an emergency, and visiting them regularly from Stanley or Monte Video?' In this way, Bull suggested, the seed of a Christian church could be planted in Fuegian soil, allowing constant intervention in the lives of the people there while providing a measure of security for the missionaries on the spot.

In early May the Society was reeling from the events and the criticism. It realised that its initial response – Stirling's first letter to the *Western Daily Press* of 8 May – had not been good enough; a more robust defence was needed. The detailed response to the Colonial Office and its declaration of innocence were part of this. On 11 May a public meeting was held in the schoolroom of St Paul's church, at Clifton near Bristol. It was a Friday afternoon, but the room was packed with local worthies. The meeting began with the singing of a psalm and a reading of the second chapter of Zechariah, after which Waite Stirling rose to make a statement on the massacre. He confessed that when he had first heard the news he had doubted that the mission could survive. But he had received seventy or eighty letters, all but one supportive, and he now felt that it was the Society's duty to continue. The massacre had been a test set by God that the Society must pass. He argued that the depot at Keppel Island was the only way forward, that it had been the *Allen Gardiner*'s inspiration and that the public would not have supported any other course of action. He added that though the Society had been guilty of shortcomings it had made progress with the Fuegians and now understood impressive amounts of their language. To give up would be to throw away so many hard won gains.

Stirling's audience that afternoon was not entirely sympathetic. The mysterious Scrutator might have been sitting among the crowd for, in a letter to the *Western Daily Press*, he renewed his attack:

And now, Gentlemen, let me remark, after the above facts, upon the strange consolation derived from this disaster by the good people assembled at the prayer meeting in Upper Park Street, to wit 'that it happened on the Sabbath day,' and 'it seemed as if God pointed out that it was Satan raging against His work;' but I have proved that it was produced by the recklessness of the society and their agents, and therefore I must conclude that Satan is much maligned in this matter.

To the outside world the Patagonian Missionary Society presented a united front, but some senior figures — and they may have been in the majority — harboured grave misgivings about

277

its operations. The committee meeting of 5 May, at which the tragic news was broken, triggered general discussions about the missionary schooner, and how to ensure the safety of Mr Schmidt, who had gone off on his own to set up a mission in Patagonia, as well as examining ways of defraying the expenses of the widows Mrs Phillips and Mrs Fell. An interesting discussion resulted in an intriguing minute: 'The present impression of the Committee was to the effect that Cranmer had failed to produce the advantages which were expected from it.'

The massacre caused the Society committee to meet more frequently than normal during May and June. It had to agree a response to the tragedy, a public stance with which to go forward, and a strategy for both the immediate and long-term future. On 16 May the committee minutes record a shift in its thinking on policy:

> The question as to whether it would be expedient to renew the work in Tierra del Fuego was answered in the affirmation. The proper subject for consideration was how to conduct future operations? Keppel Island had been unavailing to prevent the most terrible of disasters. Was not the right principle to work on the mass, not on the few? A vessel with a screw propeller, would perhaps give reasonable security to the Mission party hereafter engaged in the work. Or a station either at Picton Island or at Elizabeth Island might perhaps be advantageous. To get amongst the natives as much as possible with as great security as possible was the problem to be solved.

A week after Charles Bull's letter had appeared in the *Guardian* suggesting greater integration of the Society's work with the lives and lands of the Fuegians, the committee, despite publicly rejecting the option, was privately moving in that direction.

However, the most interesting discussion took place at a

meeting on 7 June. The vagaries of the mail from South America meant that the committee had received two letters from George Packenham Despard in the same delivery. His first had been written on 10 February, when he was concerned about the delayed return of the *Allen Gardiner* but did not yet know what had happened. The second was written on 6 March, soon after Smyley had returned from Wulaia Cove with the bad news.

For some reason that is not mentioned in the minutes of the meeting of 7 June – and the original letter no longer exists – the first letter from Despard offered his resignation. With the massacre as yet undiscovered, the idea of Despard standing down is intriguing. As has been seen, the official publications of the Society for that period are uniformly optimistic: Despard had been portrayed in the *Voice of Pity* as a man fulfilled, carrying out good and highly successful work at Cranmer and Wulaia, surrounded by a family happily settled into their Falkland Island home. Was his offer to resign an admission that things were not going as well as planned and publicly stated, and that members of the committee were as unhappy with their missionary superintendent as had been a number of their people in the field? It is possible that William Parker Snow's criticisms had been privately acknowledged by members of the Society. If so Despard might have been told this. It would have been costly and inexpedient to get rid of him while the court case dragged on, but by February the chief missionary would have been informed of the Society's legal victory against its former skipper and might have felt under pressure to go.

A number of influential members of the committee were unable to attend the meeting that day, most notably Society stalwarts the Reverends E.G. and J.W. Marsh, in-laws of Allen Gardiner, and Captain Bartholomew Sulivan (Retired). However, each supplied their thoughts on the resignation in letters to the meeting. The Marshes advised Despard not to act hastily, and to consider the circumstances of the mission. Sulivan was more controversial: his letter announced that he 'scarcely thought it expedient to continue the services of Mr Despard'. A general discussion broke out, and it soon became clear which way the debate was going.

It was well known in Committee that Mr Despard had exceeded their wishes in some particulars, and that he had conceived plans, and wished to develop them beyond what the Committee deemed necessary, or expedient. To ask Mr Despard to reconsider his resignation would be to commit the Committee to all his plans.

The contents of the letters were discussed. In his first missive Despard had resigned giving six months' notice; from the tenor of the second the committee deduced that he still intended to resign, but the fact that he put in a request for more men and supplies suggested that he would not leave in August at the end of his notice period. A resolution was passed:

The Rev. G.P. Despard BA having tendered to the Committee his resignation as Superintendent of the Patagonian Mission abroad, under date of Stanley Feb 10 1860 – and the circumstances of the Mission having undergone a material change since the massacre of the Catechist, and the ship's crew in Tierra del Fuego, on Nov 6 1859 – the Committee deeply regrets being compelled to accept his resignation and desire the Secretary to communicate their decision to him. At the same time the Committee think it incumbent upon them to express their admiration, and gratitude to the Rev. G.P. Despard BA for the untiring devotion of himself, and his family to the work from the commencement, and they most heartily wish himself and his family every blessing.

The decision was that Despard would leave, and his departure would be handled so that it tied in neither with the Snow case nor with the missionary massacre. Damage to the Society would thereby be limited. At some later date, Despard's removal might be attributed to his having completed his stint on the station.

The rather downcast gentlemen of the committee turned to discuss matters that, if carried out in the field, would lead to the winding down of the mission's affairs in the Falklands and Tierra del Fuego. They agreed the sale of the *Perseverance*. They agreed that all stores at Cranmer that were not needed should be sold off. They gave the go-ahead to refit the *Allen Gardiner*, if she was recovered from Wulaia, so that she could be brought back to England, with Despard and his family (unless they preferred to be dropped off on mainland South America). And finally they decided that, for the moment, they should hang on to their Keppel Island outpost until new plans could be drawn up. Thirty-nine years after Allen Gardiner had founded the Patagonian Missionary Society defeat was once again staring it in the face.

Chapter 22

The delay in communications between Britain and its South Atlantic outpost meant that by the time news filtered through to London of the menace, events had moved on several stages in the Falklands and Tierra del Fuego. Smyley had wanted to return for the *Allen Gardiner* with the islands' garrison to wreak revenge and teach the natives a painful lesson they would not forget. This could not be countenanced by the authorities in Stanley, but when the *Nancy* left to return Jemmy Button and retrieve the abandoned schooner, the captain did so with a crew of double its normal complement, six carbines and a supply of ball cartridge loaned him by the Falklands' governor.

He had a rough passage to what was a tough job. Ice and snow greeted him at Wulaia, as did a small fleet of thirty-eight Fuegian canoes. It was natural that recent events would instil a greater sense of caution into the ship party's dealings with the Indians, and although Smyley needed no reminding of this, the fact that many of the latter wore European clothes, necklaces of shillings and half-crowns, and in one case the back of a watch underlined it. The Fuegians seemed friendly, but for the week that it took to salvage the *Allen Gardiner*, Smyley took no risks: Jemmy Button was placed under house arrest on the ship. He was allowed visitors and treated with respect, but while he was in custody the Fuegians were unlikely to turn violent.

The *Allen Gardiner* had dragged her anchor and drifted some way from Wulaia, but with Jemmy acting as interpreter the *Nancy* traced her course. The schooner had been fortunate: although she had nearly been dashed and wrecked against the rocks her chains had been trapped under a submerged boulder shortening her leeway. It took a full day to raise the chain and several more to patch up the ravaged ship sufficiently for the journey ahead. As Smyley had already ascertained from Coles, she was little more than a shell, all her ironwork gone, her sails stripped and the instruments stolen. Across the deck were black scorch marks where fires had been lit.

As work continued the Fuegians maintained their good spirits. Macooallan paddled a full day to fetch the *Allen Gardiner*'s longboat, which he returned undamaged. He also organised transportation of a cargo of wood for the *Nancy*. Short forays ashore by the crew in search of the bodies of the massacre victims proved fruitless, but they learned that six of the party were buried at the foot of a rock and Ookoko said that the other two were somewhere behind the house, but that many foxes had feasted on their flesh.

Before setting off for Wulaia, Despard had asked Smyley to bring back more Yamana for Keppel Island. It was an insensitive and impolitic request that the governor refused immediately, but while they were repairing the ship Ookoko had come on board and demanded to be taken back to Cranmer. This sounds too convenient to be credible, but it is probably true. Ookoko had not come from Wulaia; on the day of the slaughter he had been visibly distressed by the slayings and now, he said, he feared for his life. He described the aftermath of the tragedy, how two Fuegian men had died after eating the ship's soap thinking it was meat, how when the ship's clock stopped they had thought it was dead and smashed it up. He said he was married and would like to bring his sixteen-year-old wife, Camilenna-keepa, with him to Keppel Island. Smyley agreed to take the pair, knowing that although the governor would be annoyed, there was little he could do to stop Ookoko and spouse being transported to Cranmer. Smyley was an American citizen and could claim that he was helping two young people escape apparent danger.

On 11 April 1860 the *Allen Gardiner* was ready to move. Both ships got under weigh, and Jemmy Button was helped into a waiting canoe and allowed to paddle ashore. The ships reached Port Stanley five days later, where the waiting Despard said she presented 'a mournful sight, with all her furniture broken, and damage everywhere, through wanton mischief'.

With Jemmy Button in Tierra del Fuego and the *Allen Gardiner* back in the Falklands a chapter in the tragedy had been closed, but the question of who had carried out the killings and why remained open. There had only been one eye-witness, and Alfred Coles remained firm in his conviction that he had seen Billy Button (Macalwense) throw the stone that killed Garland Phillips, and that Jemmy Button had been at the head of the mob because he had been envious of the presents that others were receiving. However, Coles had seen the massacre from the deck of the ship, which had been anchored more than 300 yards out to sea: how reliable was his report of the mayhem ashore and the bloody confusion? After all, there had been 300 Indians involved in the attack.

One man who agreed with the ship's cook was Smyley, who knew these parts and who, when he arrived to rescue Coles, was quick to assess the scene. From a more distant perspective others were quick to muddy the waters. They asserted that things were not so clear cut. Emotions ran high, but despite the early desire of Port Stanley's inhabitants for revenge, as evidenced in the attempt to lynch Jemmy Button and the suggestion of sending a force against the guilty Fuegians, it is remarkable how quickly Coles's testimony came to be disregarded. Jemmy's willingness to go to

Port Stanley and give evidence – and just how willing he actually was is open to conjecture – impressed the authorities there, as did his statement that the killings had been perpetrated by outsiders. Another puzzling factor was that if he and his people had been responsible, why had they treated Alfred Coles with such care and compassion for four months? They had fed him, clothed him and even given him a gun. Why had they not destroyed the *Allen Gardiner* and dismantled the evidence? Some said it was because they were afraid of reprisals and that they hoped in saving the cook and the ship that the white man would look kindly on them. However, if the people at Wulaia had been the assassins a more logical course of action would have been to wreck the ship, burn it, kill Coles, then claim that the *Allen Gardiner* had been in the area but had sailed on to the west.

The identities of the assassins were a mystery and there seems to have been a disinclination on the part of the government and the Patagonian Missionary Society to get to the truth. Positive identification of guilty parties would lead to difficult choices and unwanted consequences. When Jemmy Button came to Stanley and pointed the finger at the Oens-men it was seized upon by both sides as a convenient solution to a tricky problem. In private Jemmy even told Despard that he had been in the house when the attack was launched, he had remonstrated against the assailants, but given up through fear of men who 'no sabby God'. It was not very convincing – he surely did not go to the house unaware of what was about to happen – yet Despard wrote, in a letter of reassurance to Jemmy's old mentor, Robert FitzRoy, 'James Button, and Tom (Macooallan), Ookokko and Lucca, I am persuaded, had no hand in the deed.'

After conducting the official interview with Jemmy at Port Stanley, the colonial chaplain Charles Bull wrote, 'I may add my own impression that Jemmy Button did not take part in the awful tragedy; that afterwards he joined in the plunder; but his kindness to Alfred Cole, and his coming voluntarily on board the *Nancy*, prove that it was not a premeditated act.' Yet how true was this? How likely was it that the Oens-men were the protagonists of the drama at Wulaia?

It is true that there were many more Indians on the cove that week than was normally the case, but past experience showed that Yamana numbers swelled quickly in response to the news of potential booty, even without the presence of the Oens-men. To believe Jemmy's story was not only to ignore Coles's eye-witness report and his accounts of Jemmy and other Yamana Fuegians coming on board the *Allen Gardiner* in the days leading up to the tragedy (confirmed, in Fell's diary, as being 'troublesome'), but to accept that the Yamana and the Oens-men could co exist peacefully in the same enclave for almost a week. Judging by Jemmy's known fear of these people and the historic ferocity of their exchanges, such as that experienced when York Minster and Fuegia Basket were at Wulaia, this was unlikely.

Another element does not ring true: the Oens-men were expert archers, yet there was no suggestion that any of the mission party was killed other than by bludgeoning or stoning. Whenever Jemmy had had problems in the past and white men had been present, he had accused the Oens-men. They were a convenient peg on which to hang the blame, and this was probably so with the tragedy at Wulaia Cove. Jemmy Button might have woven a tale to save his neck.

But why was his explanation championed by so many people? Throughout the empire the British had established a reputation for avenging ills inflicted upon their own, for pulling the trigger before asking questions, for doling out lessons in morality and eth-ics to those they deemed lesser mortals. In this instance, however, everybody in authority from the governor to the colonial chaplain to the Secretary of State removed their fingers from the trigger before the gun could go off. There can be no doubt that they were uneasy about the course of events in Tierra del Fuego and the Falkland Islands: they had never approved of the Patagonian Missionary Society and only ever given it lukewarm support. To have acknowledged the culpability of Jemmy Button would have necessitated action they were unwilling to carry out: they were far from sure that he and his people had been responsible and thought that harsh revenge against ignorant 'savages' would not only be pointless but counterproductive to future relations. This, of course, had never stopped the British in the past, but something else was going on here: a feeling of disquiet at the activities of the mission, a suspicion that it had not been straight with the authorities, that it was up to no good, and that although the deaths could not be justified, they might have been foretold.

In private they chose to blame the chief missionary: as the scribbled minute in the Colonial Office read, the dead had 'paid the penalty of the wilfulness of one gentleman who still lives.' That gentleman was George Packenham Despard. In short, the authorities in Port Stanley and London believed it would be unfair to attack the Yamana. The governor summed up the feeling in his despatch of 8 May:

> The statements of Jemmy Button, the discontented and threatening language which has been used by the natives who have already been taken to Keppel and the bloody revenge which they took instantly on their return to Tierra del Fuego are my tangible evidence that their residence at Keppel Island was enforced and irksome, and I submit to Your Grace that it is practically impossible for Mr Despard or his agents, only acquainted with a few words of the language of one tribe, to make a contract which could for a moment be considered equal or fair with the savages.

The Society's motivation was completely different. If its work was to continue – and that, of course, was not certain – then it had to present an optimistic face by propagating the message that significant progress had been made and that lives had not been frittered away. If it had been admitted that the Indians they had taken to Keppel Island had turned against them, whether for plunder or revenge, all their efforts would have been halted in their tracks, their past work written off, their hopes for the future untenable. If Jemmy Button and his brothers had killed the missionary party despite all the education and time that had been invested in them, they were obviously beyond the pale. Not only was the Society unable to justify taking more Fuegians to Keppel Island, it would receive neither support at home nor the permission of the Port Stanley authorities to do so. If it admitted that Jemmy had been the ringleader it was signing its own death warrant. Thus when it might have been expected to believe its own ship's cook, the Society's representatives, both in the South Atlantic and in Bristol, seized the explanation that other Indians had been responsible.

Stirling set out its public position in a letter to the Duke of Newcastle:

> With respect to other members of his [Button's] tribe, with the exception of one who was seen to hurl a stone at Mr Phillips, we have no proof at all that they continued or even shared in the fatal attack on the mission party. All that is really known is that it took place at Woollya the headquarters of the tribe to which the natives who had been at Keppel belonged . . . the great majority of the natives assembled at Woollya belonged not to the tribe usually located there, and which is but a very small one, but to the larger, and more powerful tribe called Oens men. To these Jemmy Button attributes the massacre and if the Committee from their previous knowledge of the habits of

these people may hazard an opinion in so uncertain a matter, they would venture to suggest that jealousy of the peculiar favours bestowed upon the little tribe at Woollya and a desire to enrich themselves by the plunder of the mission vessel stimulated the Oens men to seize the remarkable opportunity for the massacre presented by the defenceless condition of the missionary party; on the morning of Nov 6 1859.

Not everyone subscribed to the view that Jemmy Button and his people were innocent. Alfred Coles stuck unswervingly to his account, which he related on several occasions. Captain Smyley cleaved to that view too, but it was William Parker Snow who once again attempted to nail the lie. He recognised the advantage to the Society of Jemmy's exoneration and that any other version would cripple their operation. In a letter to the *Western Daily Press* published on 28 May 1860 he spelled it out:

Mr Stirling can dare say that 'Jemmy Button acquits his own people entirely' of the massacre! How contemptible such an argument is on the part of a minister of the Gospel! Far better for these gentlemen to honestly and manfully admit the truth, acknowledging the error done, and trying to make amends. But, no, that would not suit Mr Stirling, nor his missionary, nor those that back them up in law. Nevertheless, it is evident that they are wrong, and that Mr Stirling does not give the clear truth. It was Jemmy Button's brother, and Jemmy Button's family and tribe that massacred the party at Wollyah, for Coles distinctly says so. Besides . . . it was from these very men I had the most trouble, causing me the most anxiety.

He reiterated his familiar demand: 'That blood demands from a Christian community like this of England that an immediate and most searching investigation — full, fair and without being perverted by legal quibbling – be made into the doings of the "Patagonian Society".'

By coincidence, the same day that his letter appeared in the newspaper an inquiry into the massacre was opening in Stanley. It seemed that there was going to be a genuine attempt to get to the bottom of the catastrophe. The Reverend George Packenham Despard had been summoned to the Falklands' capital and had arrived there on 25 May. He immediately engaged the services of the islands' only professional lawyer, Mr Lane, an action that is automatic in the present age but which back then, considering the circumstances of the investigation, caused frowns then among the authorities. On Monday 28 May the investigation began in Port Stanley's court house before the justices of the peace, Arthur Bailey and John Dean. The colonial secretary J.R. Longden conducted the proceedings.

Alfred Coles was the first called and sworn in. In response to questions from Longden he repeated his version of events at Wulaia. When asked if the natives had been searched in Tierra del Fuego, he responded that they had because many things had been lost. Mr Lane jumped to his feet and objected: the hearing could not extend to the cause of the loss of life on shore at Tierra del Fuego, he argued, as it was being carried out under the 432nd and 433rd sections of the Merchant Shipping Act, and could only deal with the causes of the abandonment of the *Allen Gardiner*.

The magistrates looked sceptical. Mr Longden resumed. Was the loss of life on shore the cause of the abandonment of the vessel? he asked. Coles affirmed that it was. A legal debate broke out between Longden and Lane, and after some minutes of technical arguments the bench ruled that they had full power to inquire into any matters occurring aboard the vessel and also into the cause of the loss of life on shore.

Longden continued his questioning, eliciting the now customary responses from Coles on what had happened to him after he had escaped from the ship. In cross-examining Coles, Lane asked whether Captain Fell and the men returned safely after taking Tommy Button and his wife ashore in the hours after the search. Coles agreed that they had, and that in fact many trips ashore had been made over the next few days.

The bench asked if, during the week, the men had gone armed. 'They were only armed with axes for cutting wood,' replied Coles. Then, in answer to further questioning by Lane, he reiterated that he had been kindly treated by the Fuegians at Wulaia in the four months that he had lived there, and concluded,

'Before the massacre none of the natives in my hearing ever remarked about any violence towards them. I saw one man who had been at Keppel join in the outrage, it was William Button. I am certain I saw him. I was on board the vessel, about 300 or 400 yards distant; he flung a stone at Mr Phillips and hit him on the side of the head.'

Despard was called, but at the witness stand he refused to be sworn in. The magistrates were startled. Mr Lane rose and told his client that he had no choice, he must take the oath. Despard raised his hand and swore to tell the truth.

The colonial secretary asked if he had in his possession any of the ship's papers. Despard produced the crew list and said that this was all he had. The names of the dead were read out. Longden asked if he could give any evidence as to the cause of the abandonment of the vessel. Despard replied, 'I cannot.'

'Are you aware,' Longden asked, 'of any threats or threatening language used by the natives at Keppel Island on board the vessel before she embarked?' Despard refused to answer. Longden announced that he would not be asking any more questions.

The magistrate Mr Dean asked again if the missionary had heard threats made by the natives. Despard replied with a curt, 'I have no distinct recollection of hearing any.'

'Did the natives at Keppel ever attempt any outrage or threats towards the colonists there?'

'No.'

Arthur Bailey asked, 'Did you search the bags of the natives at Keppel?'

Despard objected to the question. Lane rose again and explained that this question was not permitted, it was outside the remit of the inquiry. Further proceedings were futile and the magistrates had no choice but to close the inquiry.

Uproar followed. On 29 May Charles Bull, who had taken a close interest in the Society's affairs, wrote to the Falklands' governor expressing his 'deep anxiety, for the sake of the natives, for the sake of the character of the Missionary Operations generally . . .' He said he had new and damning information on the appalling way the missionaries had treated the Fuegians. Mr Turpin, the former catechist of the mission, who was now living in Port Stanley, had told him that on at least one occasion Fuegians had been detained on the *Allen Gardiner* against their will. 'If the natives are brought to Cranmer without any intelligent notion of the object of their long voyage we have at once a key to the massacre of Mr Phillips and the Captain and crew of the *Allen Gardiner*!' Bull wrote. For the sake of one and all – the missionary society, the Yamana and the dead men – for the sake of avoiding future martyrs and for the 'honour of the flag', he urged the governor not to accept the previous day's hearing and to take whatever steps he thought fit to resolve the matter.

Governor Moore had no intention of letting the issue rest, though it was by no means an easy matter for him: Tierra del Fuego fell outside his jurisdiction. He had no authority or responsibility for events there, but he had hoped that for the general well-being of the Falklands' colony and its future progress, Despard would have shown a willingness to get to the truth of the massacre by co-operating with the inquiry. Instead, Moore wrote to Rear Admiral Sir Stephen Lushington, the commander on Britain's Brazil station, that the 'gravest suspicions have been for some time entertained as to the voluntary character of the residence of the Fuegians at the Mission Station'. These suspicions, he added, had been 'greatly aggravated by Mr Despard's conduct', which was a cause for regret, because the mission would suffer.

I believe that the natives are brought over from the finest and most philanthropic motives, but I am afraid they themselves did not appreciate the philanthropy of their benefactors. All the information in my possession tends to prove that at Keppel Island they were disoriented, peevish, anxious to return to their native land and occasionally threatening the mission party with vengeance on their return to Tierra del Fuego.

He wrote in a similar pessimistic tone to the Secretary of State for the Colonies back in London:

I should have hoped that instead of availing himself of every technical objection to defeat the enquiry Mr Despard would gladly have availed himself of this public investigation in open court to have cleared the mission from the grave suspicions which have become current in the colony regarding their dealings with the natives. As it is, those suspicions have been necessarily aggravated by this studied concealment, and in place of establishing the truth the door is left open for conjecture of all kinds.

He included in this despatch a copy of Charles Bull's letter and confirmed that he would not be lifting the ban on the importation of natives to the Falklands until a full and satisfactory inquiry had been carried out.

London had placed great weight on the findings of the inquiry at Stanley. Initial plans to send HMS *Buzzard* to investigate had fallen through and the governor's despatch was eagerly anticipated. It arrived on 6 August, and many minutes were scribbled over it, but the mood in the Colonial Office was united. Blackwood, the senior clerk, was first to pen his thoughts:

> The course pursued by Mr Despard warrants the inference that his proceedings have, to say the least, been extremely indiscreet and disastrous in their results. But his silence and the want of other evidence must, I fear, baffle the government in bringing home to him or the agents in the affair any distinct charge of culpability.

In the Colonial Office the new Permanent Under Secretary of State, Sir Frederick Rogers, agreed. He suggested, in a lengthy note again setting out the known facts, that the department should write to the Society expressing extreme surprise at the conduct of the chief missionary, adding that such behaviour could not 'fail to give rise to the most unfavourable surmises'.

After waiting a month to see whether any more information would arrive from either the governor or the Royal Navy, Chichester Fortescue, Assistant Under Secretary of State, wrote a savagely critical letter to the Society. He enclosed Governor Moore's report and the letter from Charles Bull.

> After the occurrence of so deplorable an event, it might have been supposed that the Chief Agent of the Society on the spot would have been anxious to do all in his power to facilitate inquiry. But the Revd Mr Despard took a different view of his duty . . . It is for the Society to judge whether this was a right or a becoming

line of conduct. The report contains much matter which calls for the grave consideration of the Society, and the Secretary of State cannot doubt that they will weigh it with a full sense of the responsibility which must attach to the conclusion they adopt and to their future proceedings.

The feeling was different at the Clifton headquarters of the Society. Despard had written explaining that his conduct at the inquiry had been motivated by the realisation that the parties conducting it were all prejudiced and had no right to interfere in the Society's business or events away from the Falklands.

The committee of the Society responded to the government's letter on 4 October. Waite Stirling wrote that though the committee regretted the silence of the Society's representative at the inquiry, they could not 'shut their eyes to the fact that their superintendent was summoned from a distance of 150 miles, with a rough sea voyage, to appear before a Court of Enquiry the functions of which were limited, but whose authority was sought to be extended beyond the sphere of its legitimate control'. Had the remit of the inquiry been adequate to the task in hand then Mr Despard would not have had the slightest hesitation in answering all of the questions put to him. Furthermore, Stirling argued, the dice were loaded against Despard. Bull had been misled by partial information, an assumption that the Fuegian party had been mistreated at Keppel Island informed the proceedings, and both the governor and the colonial chaplain had failed to be as assiduous in collecting their evidence as they should have been.

Nevertheless Stirling held out an olive branch. The committee was ready to submit the journals of Despard, Turpin, Phillips and Captain Fell for inspection by members of the Colonial Office, 'so that by a comparison of their contents Her Majesty's Government may be assured how wholly without foundation the suspicions rife at Stanley really are'. He also acknowledged the need for a full and free inquiry 'in order to quell these turbulent suspicions, which parties abroad have become a prey to'. The committee would instruct Despard by the next mail to make himself available at the earliest opportunity for a full examination of all matters related to the deaths at Wulaia.

Although the promise of an unhindered investigation was undoubtedly a step in the right direction it must have seemed in the Colonial Office, with the anniversary of the massacre fast approaching, that the steam was going out of the affair. With a burgeoning empire to look after, the department was one of the busiest in the government and was losing interest in the butchering of a small missionary party on a far-off shore. Blackwood jotted on the back of Stirling's letter, 'I think that to continue a correspondence with this Society on this subject can lead to no profitable result and that an inspection of the journals, as proposed by the writer, would be undesirable on the part of this office.' Frederick Rogers concurred, adding, 'I do not know what more can be done . . .'

On 23 October Chichester Fortescue wrote to Stirling:

I am desired to state, with reference to the Society's offer to allow the journals of Mr Despard and other of their officers to be inspected at this office, that as no enquiry could be effectually conducted in this country no object would be attained by such inspection, but that the Secretary of State will forward your letter to the Governor of the Falkland Islands directing him not to neglect any opportunity which may offer itself of discovering the full truth respecting this disastrous affair.

When Despard himself wrote to the Colonial Office at the end of 1860, expressing the view that it had not been his Fuegians who had carried out the killing but 300 'northern Firelanders', Blackwood wrote on it, 'I should be disposed to treat his present tardy representation as a very lame excuse for what has happened.' As far as the Colonial Office was concerned the matter was closed.

Contrary to many expectations, a fuller inquiry into the massacre did take place in Port Stanley, although it did not open until 24 April 1861. By then Despard's resignation had been acknowledged in January's *Voice of Pity* with some recognition of the difficulties incumbent on the missionary's work:

> It is not without genuine sorrow that the Committee accept the resignation which has been tendered to them . . . It is a growing conviction in the minds of those who watch most narrowly the conditions of the Fuegian branch of our work, that, in future, the Superintendent abroad should be free from family ties; while the Catechists, or at least one of them, should be married. The peculiarly trying nature of the Superintendent's office, in virtue of which it becomes necessary for him to be almost always present in the Mission vessel, during her visits to the natives of Tierra del Fuego, renders it highly expedient that he should be without additional anxiety on the score of his family. On the other hand, the presence of females at the Mission Station is most essential, and must be provided . . .

Despard and his family were expected to settle near Buenos Aires where there was an opening for a clergyman willing to work with the *estancieros*, the large cattle grazers of the pampas. In the meantime he remained in the Falklands, and when requested by the Society's committee went to Stanley prepared to answer any questions, this time without the protection of a lawyer.

The proceedings opened in the council room of Government

House with an examination of Charles Conyngham Turpin, former catechist of the mission station, the man whom Bull alleged had claimed that Fuegians were held against their will on the *Allen Gardiner*. Captain Molony and Mr Longden presided, and Despard asked most of the questions, fifty of which were fired at Turpin. They elicited little new information: Jemmy Button had been happy on Keppel Island and had been returned on time; he had not been forced to work and had not been ill-treated. The same could be said for the second party who, at all times, appeared contented, and only those who were willing to work had done so.

He revealed some interesting snippets, although surprisingly, and rather frustratingly for the historian, they were not followed up by his examiners. Turpin claimed to have been ashore at Wulaia on many occasions and to have spent a great deal of time with the Indians when the second party agreed to go to Keppel Island. However, in answer to a question on the quality of the mission's communication with the Fuegians he agreed that they had had it 'rather imperfectly'. When asked who had arranged for the natives to go to Cranmer, he replied, 'I don't recollect.' Turpin denied telling the colonial chaplain that Fuegians had been detained on the *Allen Gardiner* and said that he had written to Bull to express his displeasure at such an insinuation. Nevertheless, despite his denial, the letter to Mr Bull, which he handed over to the inquiry, admitted that these Fuegians had been kept on board the schooner until they returned clothes intended only for those agreeing to go to Keppel Island.

Alfred Coles followed Turpin and repeated his much-told story. Next followed John Betts, a former seaman on the *Allen Gardiner* turned labourer at the mission station. On the day the second party had boarded the ship to go home he had been present at the search and admitted that the Fuegians had not seemed pleased at the goings-on; he had seen Schwaiamugunjiz 'shake his fist at Mr Despard's back'.

With Betts's testimony complete, Despard offered himself for examination. He handed over extracts from his journals, then answered plainly and directly the eighteen questions put to him by Molony and Longden. It was a disappointing anticlimax: the questions were far from searching and, under the circumstances, it is curious that the former missionary had been so reluctant to comply with the first inquiry. His two examiners went through the motions, neither cajoling nor pressing him on any particular issue. The final question was, 'Do you attribute the massacre to any feelings of revenge on account of the search?'

Despard answered, 'No, I ascribe it entirely to covetousness to be gratified by plunder of the vessel.'

Apart from a written submission by the absent Smyley – in which, incidentally, he wrote, 'I feel certain that Jemmy Button was at the head of the massacre' – that was it, and the inquiry was over. Governor Moore received the transcripts, took a little while to analyse the evidence and having done so wrote to Despard offering him thanks that he 'so candidly and fairly answered every question put to you. Allow me to remark that much of my personal annoyance to yourself would have been spared had you shown the same willingness to satisfy the public interest in May last year.' The massacre, he said, could only be partly explained by the desire to plunder. The most important reasons, he felt, were

the enforced search of the natives at Keppel Island, which was most unwise, and does not seem to have been followed up by the commonest precautions; the detention and rough treatment of the natives for eight days at Keppel Island, during which the man Coles knocked a native into the hold; the neglect of observing due faith by returning the natives before the commencement of their egg season, and the want of precautionary measures even after perceiving the gathering of the natives, and their troublesome behaviour, as appears from Captain Fell's journal, and from the final search, and scuffle, which took place.

Only when Governor Moore was satisfied that Fuegians were to be brought to the Falklands for Christian education and practical instruction and that they understood the term of months for which they were to stay, and only when he was sure that the captain of the transport vessel had received such precautionary instructions as were needed to guard against further disasters, would he remove the ban against importation.

In the end, the inquiry did not put names to the killers – other than the already identified Billy Button – but it did tackle possible motivations. The question of how far Jemmy Button was involved in murder will never be resolved. The fact that so many influential people said that he was not should be weighed against their vested interests and their need to clear him. The balance of evidence suggests that there was some complicity in the events by Jemmy and his family. Moreover, there is little doubt that he joined in the plunder of the ship. However, the important issues hinge not so much on the culpability of FitzRoy's Fuegian, but on how far the killings could be justified, whether they might have been predicted and therefore avoided.

From the British point of view it would never be possible to justify such a brutal massacre. The dead men were all largely innocent – certainly the six crew members who died were mere sailors carrying out instructions, with very little involvement in the day-to-day affairs of the Indians, either in Tierra del Fuego or on Keppel Island. Whether the killings might have been anticipated is a different matter. With hindsight even if the Fuegians had not been detained at the Cranmer mission station against their will, they had been unhappy about going there and far from content to stay. Despite claims by Despard that he and his missionary foot-soldiers had mastered the Fuegian language, it is obvious that this was not so. And with the Fuegians capable of speaking only a few words of English, how much did they truly understand about what was expected of them?

There were elements of their existence on Keppel Island that they might have appreciated – the food, the warm accommodation, the clothes – but the long-term effects of the sudden changes the missionaries were trying to impose brought avarice, servility and covetousness in their wake and did little to advance them towards the missionary goal. Added to this, missionary arrogance compounded the problems. Despite repeated warnings that accusations of thievery were insulting to the Fuegians – no matter how true – the missionaries continued to make an example of them. The lesson that theft is bad, theft was unChristian, was valid to the missionaries, but to a people who did not understand property it was meaningless. The missionaries had several opportunities to adapt their behaviour: the reaction of the Indians to the search on the quayside at Keppel Island was alarming; that they were unsettled for days and had to be punished physically should have been a warning. That the crew would search them again at Wulaia was astonishing. When the Fuegians acted with violence it was almost certainly in response to what they perceived as a threat to their livelihoods.

The missionaries had engendered an atmosphere of greed that contributed to their downfall. When the natives left the *Allen Gardiner* for the last time they did so viewing the ship as not only home to their tormentors but also as the source of boundless treasure. The missionaries had fostered a demand for booty that was stronger and more frenzied than they could comprehend and which, in the end, they failed to guard against.

PART SIX

The Fall

Chapter 23

For the Patagonian Missionary Society the 1861 inquiry into the Wulaia killings signalled that the worst was over. Interest at home in the organisation's activities waned, registered by a drop in income, but nevertheless there was renewed enthusiasm among the Society's committee members for the work to be continued and consolidated. In October 1861 George Packenham Despard left the Falklands for England on board the *Allen Gardiner*, having failed to find a suitable position anywhere in South America (he eventually settled in Australia). His replacement was to be the no-nonsense robust former secretary of the Society, Waite Stirling.

Behind him at Keppel Island, Despard left his eighteen-year-old adopted son Thomas Bridges, the Fuegian Ookoko and wife Camilenna, along with their baby son. Free of his stepfather's autocratic and deadening control, an invigorated Bridges revived the mission station. He realised that many of its problems lay with its failure to come to terms with the Indian language. He pumped Ookoko and Camilenna for words, for grammatical rules and for accuracy of pronunciation. By the time Stirling arrived, in January 1863, Bridges could claim both to have mastered Yamana like no white man before him, and to have collected and recorded over 7,000 words.

The two men made a formidable team. As missionary, Stirling approached his work aggressively and frequently trampled over local protocol and even some of its laws – most notably the Alien Ordinance and the specific ban on the mission importing natives. Within three months of his arrival at Keppel Island he and Bridges were at Wulaia Cove. It was the first time that either man had been there and they found the Fuegians sheepish and apprehensive of reprisals. They also discovered that their numbers had mysteriously dwindled. Jemmy Button was well, though, and he came on board to explain that a strange illness had killed many of his people. Stirling listened, and promised him presents if he would organise the repair of the house on the beach, which was now a mere skeleton. He would also give Jemmy two hatchets, four knives, two buckets and ship's biscuits if he would fetch wood for the *Allen Gardiner* before she left for the Falklands. It seems that sound relationships were established because the two missionaries sailed out of Wulaia with seven Fuegians on board: Jemmy's son Threeboys, Luccaenche, a fourteen-year-old boy called Uroopa, Macooallan and his wife Wendoo, along with their twenty-year-old son Pinoiense and an infant. Jemmy and his family towed the ship out of the cove and demanded a chorus of three cheers for old times' sake. The crew obliged.

This was the first of many breaches of the Alien Ordinance by the Society. In the course of the next four years Stirling oversaw the transportation of more than fifty Fuegians to and from Keppel Island. An abrasive correspondence ensued with the Falklands' new governor, Mackenzie, but nothing was done to enforce the law. In the end the governor settled for the missionary's agreement to supply a list of the Fuegians present at Cranmer, and the understanding that although he had not stopped the importation, neither had he approved of it.

On 18 February 1864 the *Allen Gardiner* left Keppel Island with the intention of returning the latest party of Fuegians to their homes. Joining them were Ookoko, Camilenna, their children (Camilenna had recently given birth to a daughter), seven goats and a collection of tools. Ookoko was to attempt to break away from the nomadic life of the Fuegian Indian by cultivating a smallholding. Camilenna would relinquish fishing and idle wanderings in her canoe for, the *Voice of Pity* reported, her life was from now on to 'resemble that of an English wife; she was to stay at home, take care of the children, and present to her people an example of domestic life'.

However, as the ship reached the outlying islands of Tierra del Fuego an air of despondency fell over the party. Rumours reached the Fuegians on board that, this last summer, another terrible disease had cut down swathes of their people. Every Yamana on the ship was said to have lost somebody – mothers and fathers, brothers, sisters, uncles and aunts. The native passengers became downcast and many cried openly at the news. Saddest of all was Threeboys, who had heard an unconfirmed report that his father Jemmy Button had been among the victims. Stirling reported back to the Society that 'loud and melancholy sounded the tidings of death'.

On 7 March the ship reached Wulaia Cove and, the *Voice of Pity* disclosed, 'The approach of the vessel was the signal for a burst of mournful news . . . There had been a malignant sickness, and old and young, very many, had been swept away by it. James Button was dead.'

The *Allen Gardiner* dropped anchor and those on board sat and waited for news. The following day Jemmy's wife Lassaweea arrived in a canoe with eleven young people. Stirling wrote in his journal, 'Her face was visibly impressed with sorrow; and, pointing with her finger toward the sky, she gave me to understand by looks, more than words, the cause of her grief, and how great it was. A majority of the natives had the hair cut short on the crown of the head, and other evidences of mourning were frequent . . .'

Early the next morning a boat was lowered and Ookoko and Pinoiense were rowed across the bay to Button Island, where it was intended they would set up a farm. Stirling came across a grim scene as he walked along the beach: the remains of a still smouldering funeral pyre on which the body of one of Macooallan's brothers had recently been incinerated. Nearby stood a feeble wigwam of wickerwork branches where the corpse had been kept until the pyre was ready. Ookoko whispered to the missionary that Jemmy Button had been interred, and had yet to be cremated. The Fuegians had waited for Macooallan and Threeboys to return before proceeding.

Stirling expressed no interest in seeing the body of the man who had done so much to change the relationships of white man and Fuegian, who had been half-way around the globe and had met the King and Queen of England. There was to be no special funeral for this once sought-after and good-natured man. The mission had moved on, and Jemmy Button had outlived his usefulness. When he died, the man for whom Allen Gardiner and his six companions had starved to death, and for whom eight men had later perished on Wulaia Cove, was no longer important to the Society's plans. The missionaries were conquering the Yamana language, and the bridge that FitzRoy's Fuegian had built between two worlds had been superseded. With his demands and occasional rages, and his probable involvement in the 1859 massacre, Jemmy was now considered something of a problem. He had died a heathen, unchristened and unwanted by the missionaries who had so exploited him. He would be cremated by his own people, but Stirling did not wait to watch. He returned to the boat and headed back to Wulaia Cove.

Here more chilling news awaited him. From the deck of the *Allen Gardiner* Lucca had pointed to the spot where the bodies of the massacred crew had been hidden. He had talked confidently about the burial, about when it had happened and how he had helped carry one of the corpses. He told how he and Ookoko had covered it with large stones to protect it from foxes. Ookoko confirmed the story and was left on the ship in a state of distress, as Stirling, Lucca and the new catechist, Jacob Rau, rowed out to the base of an overhanging cliff where smashed rocks lay in a huge pile. The three men scrambled ashore and found traces of the bodies scattered among the boulders. Stirling noted:

> The remains of Mr Phillips and Captain Fell are unmistakable, Lucca tells us that Mr Phillips, and Captain Fell, were both cast into the same chasm of rocks. We can collect only a part of the remains. But I have no doubt now that six of the bodies of our beloved friends were placed where we sought them in their entirety, that they were placed there in their clothes, – (for the signs are unmistakable) – and that not even their pockets were rifled.

Stirling marvelled at Alfred Coles's failure to find the remains of the murdered men, especially considering how much time he had spent at Wulaia. He speculated that perhaps Coles had assumed that the cadavers had been flung into the sea, or perhaps he had been afraid of mentioning the massacre to the Fuegians who had been so kind him.

Next day, 11 March 1861, a funeral service was conducted, partly on board the *Allen Gardiner* and partly on the rocks under which the dead men lay buried. The flag was hung 'half-mast high' and they sang the hymn

When our heads are bowed with woe
When our bitter tears o'erflow
When we mourn the lost, the dear,
Jesu, born of woman hear.

The ship's two guns fired a brief, but dramatic salute over Wulaia, signalling the end of the service. Then, the crew set to building a new home and goat house for Ookoko, on the cove itself near the dilapidated manse. The *Allen Gardiner* set sail a week later carrying a new party of eight Fuegians, plus Lucca and Threeboys. It was reported that the latter was in such deep grief at the loss of his father that he asked if he could live at Keppel Island for the rest of his life.

Over the next year more trips were made to Tierra del Fuego and more Indians transported in both directions. The experiment with Ookoko on Wulaia failed when, after months of harassment from fellow Fuegians, his house was burned down and most of his goats slaughtered. He was taken back to Keppel Island where Stirling debated whether he was ready to become the first Fuegian to be christened. It seems the missionary was torn between the desire to baptise Ookoko and the fear of being accused of doing it prematurely simply to gain kudos. For the moment he held off, though a letter from the Society's old adversary Charles Bull suggested that the young man was ready:

> I think [Stirling] is a little impelled to delay Ookokko's baptism, because he does not wish for a single moment to be the instrument of doing that which might have the appearance of being only an empty show to parade results. I have seen many a catechumen not near so promising as all the natives I have mentioned baptized at the Cape of Good Hope . . .

On 10 June 1865 Stirling left for England on the *Allen Gardiner*, accompanied by four young Fuegian men: Threeboys and Uroopa, both in their late teens, Mamastugadegenes, an orphan, aged twelve, who went by the name Jack, and Sesoienges, an eleven-year-old. With hindsight, this episode raises the question of whether the lessons of the last thirty-five years had been learned. The removal of Jemmy, York, Boat and Fuegia to Walthamstow had not been successful, but Stirling was keen to impress both supporters and detractors of the Society at home. He was anxious to show the progress that had been made since the tragedy of November 1859. The aims of the exercise, as reported by the Society, had a familiar ring:

> Care was taken to place them under the protection of those who could teach them to read and practise the holy lessons of the Bible, but they were shown, as opportunity offered, not only the sights which are most surprising to a stranger, but the arts and manufactures, the fruits of actual industry and trade, which render a civilized country such a startling contrast to a land wholly devoid of them.

On 11 August 1865 the *Allen Gardiner* sailed up the river Avon, under Brunel's new suspension bridge at Clifton, and then into Bristol, where it was met by Bishops Anderson and McCrae. At a thanksgiving service on board the singing was led by the four Fuegian boys.

The time these Fuegians spent in England was to be significantly more productive than the stay of their predecessors three decades earlier. There was less sense of abduction and the whole affair seemed freer. Each of the boys had been properly vaccinated, their understanding of English, English ways and culture was far greater than that of their predecessors. Moreover, the network of support awaiting them was more sophisticated, and their visit was longer, enabling them to acclimatise more satisfactorily.

They also travelled about more. In the years since the last visit by Fuegians to Britain the country had driven its way into the modern age on the back of nineteenth-century industrialisation. Roads were better, railways were swifter, steam ships no longer a novelty, and the Fuegian boys were taken the length and breadth of the country. In September they attended the annual conference of the British Association in Birmingham and one session on geology was interrupted so that the BA's president Sir Rodney Murchison, who had dined with Button, Basket and York back in 1831, could introduce them to the conference. The Fuegians saw the Crystal Palace, went to Ireland, had their photograph taken in York, attended discussions in private homes and participated in missionary meetings. They roamed around independently, finding their way around large cities and towns and even braving the country's steam locomotives, as one Society member noted:

> The two eldest boys quickly accommodated themselves to the perplexing difficulties even of railway travelling, and if either of them failed, when travelling by himself, to understand which of several trains he was to enter, he contrived to make the porters understand his difficulty; or, if he gave up his ticket before his journey's end, he would settle that difficulty by 'buying another ticket,' and travelling on.

On days without formal business they passed their mornings in lessons given by a friend of the Society, much of the time spent reading the Bible aloud, and their afternoons in the carpenter's shop. Dr John Beddoe, who was the 'Foreign Associate' of the Anthropological Society, examined them and reported that the measurements of the two eldest boys' heads showed an intelligence that was 'above the averages yielded by the population of Bristol and its neighbourhood'.

Their stay in Britain proved longer than anticipated. The *Allen Gardiner* was undergoing a complete refit, and the Society was embroiled in a legal dispute, which delayed their departure further. In January 1866 the organisation had renamed itself the South American Missionary Society, partly to deflect attention from its earlier notoriety but also to reflect its extended field of operations in other parts of the continent, and had moved its headquarters from Bristol to London. Some members were unhappy at this and fought the changes, most notably over ownership of the missionary schooner. In the meantime, the Fuegians charmed all who met them. At a big meeting in Ireland, Threeboys had made a brief speech in Fuegian and then sung the first verse of 'How Sweet The Name Of Jesus Sounds' in English. The Bishop of Cork was moved:

> Of the addresses which I have heard tonight [he wrote], the one which I shall longest remember is the address written on the face and form of this youth and in the tone of his voice 'warbling his native wood-notes wild'. There is a softness and sweetness in it that shows that he can say with us, 'God is my Father, Heaven is my home, and Eternity is my lifetime . . .'

The Society's annual general meeting in London, in February 1866, was presided over by the Right Reverend the Lord Bishop of Rochester, who thirty-five years earlier had gone by the simpler title of the Reverend Joseph Wigram — one of the original sponsors of Jemmy Button and his colleagues. He was delighted to see that the work pioneered by Robert FitzRoy had continued. He told Threeboys that he had known his father, and shook hands with him vigorously.

Their stay became even more drawn-out as the dispute dividing the Society became more convoluted. In anticipation of an imminent departure in June 1866 the four Fuegians stepped up their speaking activities. A fragment from their appointment diary for a five-day period in that month shows a hectic schedule:

11.6.66   Annual Meeting of the Christ Chapel Association, Maida Hill
12.6.66   Marylebone Meeting at Edwards Street Institution
Drawing room meeting at Mrs Grautoff's, 8 Foulis Terrace, Brompton
13.6.66   Streatham Common Association for two meetings
14.6.66   Annual Meeting for Battersea and Wandsworth at the Freemasons' Hotel
15.6.66   Meeting in Wimbledon
Drawing room meeting at Mr Ridsdale's, Clapham
16.6.66   Lawn meeting at the Rectory, Beckenham

And this was only part of it. As it became increasingly obvious that they were not about to go home, they attended meetings and gave addresses and lectures in Redhill, Reigate, Putney, Spring Grove, Rochester, Blackheath, Cheltenham, Dover, Folkestone, Exeter, Sundridge, and Tunbridge Wells. Eventually the problems in the Society were resolved, Stirling was reappointed as missionary for Tierra del Fuego and, on 8 December 1866, sixteen months after they had arrived in England, the four boys began their journey home.

The visit had been a success, and the South American Missionary Society hoped that it represented the beginning of a new era, but the voyage back to the Falklands had lamentable consequences. Storms lashed the missionary ship and by the time they reached Monte Video, Uroopa, who had suffered constant sea-sickness, was racked with consumption. Nine days ashore did little to alleviate his agony. He was placed back on the ship, which was kept in port so that he did not have to suffer the rolling of waves. As his condition deteriorated he began to pray 'like one verging on eternity' and handed out his few possessions to those around him. On 23 March, in the presence of the whole crew and a Reverend Mr Adams, Stirling baptised Uroopa, giving him the name John Allen Gardiner. The next day the ship pulled out of Monte Video for a dreadful passage to the Falklands. On the afternoon of 1 April the Fuegian called for the captain and Stirling in the belief that he was dying, but the pain eased temporarily. However, at just before one the next morning his body gave in. Three days later he was buried in the cemetery in Port Stanley.

In June, Stirling, Threeboys and Ookoko went to Tierra del Fuego with the dual purpose of scouting land for a possible settlement and of breaking the bad news to Uroopa's father. One day four canoes came alongside the *Allen Gardiner* and a man stood up, gesticulating with a spear, and shouting abuse at the missionary party. It was Uroopa's father. He had heard that they had murdered his son and he had come for revenge. Thomas Bridges placated him and persuaded him to come on board. In the captain's cabin Threeboys and Ookoko told him of his son's illness, and also of how he had become a Christian. Uroopa, they convinced him, had died happy. The father accepted their explanation.

Now, though, misfortune struck again. The seemingly healthy Threeboys came down with an excruciating kidney complaint. As the pain got worse, he became delirious and screamed and rambled for hours. Stirling ordered that the ship turn tail and make haste for Port Stanley. On 18 June, in a moment of lucidity, Threeboys agreed to be baptised and to take the name George, but he died three days later while the *Allen Gardiner* was still a full day's sailing from the Falklands' capital. A post-mortem carried out by a surgeon in the town diagnosed Bright's disease, a malady unknown among the Fuegian peoples.

In 1867 Stirling and Bridges felt confident enough of their relationship with the Yamana and their knowledge of the terrain to undertake a more ambitious scheme. Ever since the massacre at Wulaia, one of the Society's goals had been to move in among the Indians in their homeland. Stage one was the founding of the small settlement of Laiwaia here at the mouth of the Murray Narrows. Ookoko, Pinoiense, Lucca, Jack and their spouses were settled with building materials and agricultural implements brought over in the *Allen Gardiner*. At the same time the missionaries surveyed the area for a site suitable for settlement by the white man – the area around the Murray Narrows, with its rush of water, made for difficult access and, besides, they wanted more open pastureland and a good harbour. The location they chose was called Ushuaia, which means 'inner harbour to the west'. It was a large open bay on the northern shore of the Beagle Channel that promised both good shelter and fertile land.

In 1868 Thomas Bridges was recalled to England to take holy orders. Early the next year, with Bridges still absent, Stirling took a three-room prefabricated shack to Ushuaia on the *Allen Gardiner* and, once it was erected, ordered the crew of the missionary schooner to leave him there on his own. This was extraordinarily brave, some would say foolhardy, but when the ship came back a month later, in February 1869, its company found a small settlement of wigwams belonging to friendly Indians radiating out from the shack. In the building, Stirling had been joined by the Fuegian Jack and his wife, both of whom had fled from Laiwaia where things had been going significantly less well. There, the small community was on the edge of collapse in the face of attacks from groups of marauding Indians.

Stirling remained at Ushuaia for six months before he himself was recalled to England, where he was consecrated Bishop of the Falklands (a diocese that encompassed the whole of mainland South America). Development of the new settlement continued over the next two years. More Fuegians, including all of those who had been at Laiwaia, moved under its aegis and began the gradual transformation to a sedentary, agricultural life. Bridges, who was now married, returned from Europe and oversaw the construction of a new and larger building – Stirling House – at Ushuaia, and the transfer of materials to the area from Keppel Island.

On 1 October 1871, Thomas Bridges, his wife Mary and their young daughter disembarked from the *Allen Gardiner* at the Beagle Channel settlement that would be their home for the next thirteen years. Mary Bridges had not stepped outside her native Devon until recently, and her initial impressions must have been both powerful and stark. Ushuaia consisted of a double peninsula. To the south, small hills rolled, clothed in scrub and grassland, and to the north dramatic mountains, covered with dense beech trees, deep gullies and glaciers, climbed from the water's edge. She must have been stunned by the beauty of what confronted her and a little frightened by the isolation and mystery of the landscape and its inhabitants. Her as yet unborn son Lucas, who was to grow up in Ushuaia, speculated on this moment of his mother's life in his book *Uttermost Part of the Earth*:

> As they were rowed ashore from the *Allen Gardiner*, this Ushuaia, of which she had heard so much, was new, strange and rather frightening. Behind the shingle beach the grassland stretched away to meet a sudden steep less than a quarter of a mile from the shore. Between shore and hill were scattered wigwams,

half-buried hovels of branches roofed with turf and grass, smelling strongly, as she was to find later, of smoke and decomposed whale blubber or refuse flung close outside. Round the wigwams dark figures, some partially draped in otter skins, others almost naked, stood or squatted, gazing curiously at the little boat as it approached the beach.

Some canoes lay hauled up on the shingle, and in others women were fishing or paddling alongside the schooner, trying to barter fish or limpets for knives or those great delicacies introduced by foreigners, biscuits and sugar. These Paiakoala [beach people] were wanderers, attracted by the wish to see what the white men were doing at Ushuaia.

On the summit of the thornbush-covered hill in the background she saw her future home, Stirling House, a five-roomed bungalow of wood and corrugated iron. It was not yet completed, and looked very lonely perched up there all by itself.

The presence of white settlers among the Yamana led to a much closer understanding of a native people so easily dismissed by past explorers as grim, base, primeval specimens – the 'miserable barbarians', as Darwin had called them. In addition to building the settlement – constructing new homes, and laying out roads – Bridges devoted much time to working with the Yamana, learning their customs and traditions, watching them hunt, analysing the relationships of one Fuegian to another, transcribing their language. He taught them English, encouraged them to work, preached Christianity and occasionally got involved in serious disputes. This sometimes led him into danger and Bridges was threatened more than once.

Not long after he had made Ushuaia his home, one of the local inhabitants had been murdered. Bridges intervened in the resulting dispute between relatives of the deceased and the killer. As he stood between the squabbling parties a spear was jabbed at his chest. Another time, after he had harangued a native called Tom Post for laziness, he was walking away when his dog viciously attacked the Fuegian. Bridges dragged it off and smacked it, only to be told later by other Indians that the dog had saved his life. 'Tom Post was going to kill you with his axe,' they informed him.

When a man called Harrapuwaian stole another's wife, Bridges reprimanded him. The situation appeared to resolve itself with the return of the wife, but Harrapuwaian was bristling with anger. He told a friend that he was going to knock on Bridges' door and ask for a biscuit, then, when the missionary turned to get one, he would whip out an axe and crack open his head. The friend informed on him, but Bridges would not believe the story until, one evening, the Fuegian turned up on his doorstep, and duly asked for the biscuit. Without turning his back, the missionary lunged at his visitor's arm and shouted, 'Why do you come here with a hatchet? Give it to me.' Harrapuwaian was stunned by the missionary's prescience and handed over the specially sharpened weapon without question. He was even more surprised when, after a short chat, Bridges handed back the hatchet, asking him to leave it at home next time he called.

Bridges came to know the Yamana better than anyone previously; he understood their habits and emotions, their superstitions and rituals, and was able to dispel important myths that had become enshrined as given truths about them. Most notably he put an end to the centuries-old story that the Yamana, and indeed all of the Fuegian tribes, were cannibals. This story had persisted since the times of Magellan and Drake, and had been further propagated by the stories of Jemmy, York and Fuegia. It was completely without foundation. Fuegian people never devoured their enemies or their old women and never cooked the cadavers of shipwrecked sailors. Bridges found that nothing could be further from the truth. That death was distressing to them was already well known. In a paper Bridges read to the English Literary Society of Buenos Aires in 1888 he stated that the Yamana had always been misunderstood:

> They have been called cannibals and the sketches of them have been caricatures rather than the truth. They will eat neither fish nor meat in its raw state . . . Cannibalism is utterly impossible among these aborigines by the laws of their society of living, in which human life is considered sacred and every relation of a murdered man considers himself bound to avenge the death. There have been times of extreme famine when on account of the bad weather it has been impossible for them to obtain provisions from the ships, from the coasts, or from the sea. At such times I have known them to eat their foot-gear and their raw-hide thongs, without a suggestion that they should eat human flesh. The lives of the old men, which according to Darwin, were those fixed upon for the purpose of cannibalism, are as sacred to them as those of any other person, for they are protected by their relatives.

All of this begs the question why, if it was false, Jemmy, York and Fuegia were so keen to perpetuate the myth. In his later years Jemmy often said that York's people were cannibals and that they had eaten marooned crews, but he was probably using an opportunity to slander his old colleague and adversary. The claims of the three when they were in England and when they were on the *Beagle*, when they convinced even Darwin with their stories, are more intriguing and more difficult to answer. In *Uttermost Part of the Earth* Lucas Bridges asks the same question and offers what can be the only remotely plausible solution: FitzRoy's Fuegians had answered questions in the way they felt was expected of them. In the early days of their abduction their English would have been poor and when asked, 'Do you kill and eat men?'

their responses would have been limited to 'Yes' or 'No'. As their English improved they might have embellished their story to a point where, as Bridges noted, 'This delectable fiction once firmly established, any subsequent attempt at denial would not have been believed, but would have been attributed to a growing unwillingness to confess the horrors in which they had formerly indulged.'

In the 1880s, when Lucas Bridges read a report of Fuegian cannibalism carried in the *Liverpool Weekly News* to a group of Yamana Indians, he observed that the

> gruesome story lost nothing of its horror when I translated it for the benefit of my companions. They fairly rocked with mirth. Then the face of one of them, Halupaianjiz, became grave 'Why,' he asked me, 'do these people tell lies about us? We do not say bad things about them. You ought to write and tell them the truth.'

Thomas Bridges' most significant contribution to the understanding of the Fuegian peoples was his English Yamana dictionary. He had been compiling a vocabulary of Fuegian words ever since his earliest days on Keppel Island. What he discovered about the Yamana language contradicted the belief of European visitors to Tierra del Fuego — including Darwin and FitzRoy — that Yamana consisted of barely a few hundred grunted words. It also exposed as sham the claims of the missionaries at Cranmer under Despard that they had had a great understanding of the language.

Bridges' dictionary brought together 32,000 Yamana words. The language, he found, had more inflections than Greek, more words than English and when constructed phonetically the structure suggested the possibility of two or three more characters than the Roman alphabet. A single short word could describe what in English would need a short sentence; additional letters to the word could mean an additional sentence. A letter prefixed to a word could give a different tense or sense. For example,

Ta	To fix a bird spear on a shaft
Tia	To use anything for fixing a bird spear on a shaft, such as a bit of line
Katia	I use a bit of line to fix a bird spear on a shaft
Katior	I shall use a bit of line to fix a bird spear on a shaft
Katide	I did use a bit of line to fix a bird spear on a shaft

Distant family relationships that took a sentence in English to unravel could be explained succinctly in the native tongue. Yamana had sixty-one words for relations, in comparison to the twenty-five English words. It had a host of pronouns that indicated not only the person or object but also their location in relation to, for example, their wigwam or to the person being addressed: different words were used if the speaker was in a canoe, on land, or in a wigwam. The word for beach depended on its position in relation to the speaker – the direction it faced and whether there was land or water between the speaker and it. There was a precision to the language that lent it a slightly bizarre feel: the word *hatanisanude* meant 'I thought so' when to do so was correct, *hayengude* meant 'I thought so' when to do so was a mistake; there were five words for snow and, Lucas Bridges recalled, among the many words employed by the Yamana for the verb 'to bite', one meant 'coming unexpectedly on a hard substance when eating something soft' – a pearl in an oyster.

The language was far more sophisticated than had been thought. It had certainly fooled the Europeans, whose errors in comprehension were frequently egregious. Perhaps the most striking and most common mistake was over the word *yammerschooner*. This had been screamed, shouted, chanted and mumbled at every foreign visitor to the area. Traveller after traveller had commented on the irritating repetition of '*yammerschooner, yammerschooner . . .*' that had greeted their arrival on Fuegian islands and that had echoed from the flotillas of canoes that had come to trade. Some Europeans had even invented a verb for it: the natives had been 'yammerschoonering', they commented. It was usually said with one hand outstretched, as if in begging, and it was believed that it meant 'give me'. It did not. Down the centuries, Fuegian Indians had been abused by the crews of passing ships and had come to fear the presence of strangers, and the potential for violence that they brought. *Yammerschooner* did not mean 'give me' but 'be kind to me', or 'be kind to us'.

Another example of radical misinterpretation came from the mission station at Cranmer. Despard had boasted a number of times in his journals and letters home that he had translated the Doxology into Fuegian:

> Praise God from whom all blessings flow.
> Praise him all creatures here below.
> Praise him above, ye Heavenly Host.
> Praise Father, Son and Holy Ghost.
> Amen.

He said that the Indians were now able to repeat it in their own tongue. What Bridges discovered was comical. Despard had been unable to unearth the word for 'praise', so to try to get over the problem he had complimented one of the Fuegians on his progress in English, and told him that he wished to 'praise' him for it. As he said this he tapped the Indian on the shoulder. The Indian gave him the word that he thought was wanted. Despard completed his translation. Bridges discovered that not only were most of the words of the Doxology incorrectly rendered, but for three years the native version, sung every day by Fuegians taking Christian education, began with the words 'Slap God . . .'

Ushuaia began to take on the appearance of a more settled community. Bridges was joined by Robert Whaits, a skilled handyman who was a blacksmith, joiner and wheelwright rolled into one, John Lawrence, a market gardener, and James Lewis, a carpenter. Each brought his wife and children, and soon the settlement, with its four British couples, its 100-plus Yamana residents and its shifting population of transient Fuegians could rightly be called a village.

The settlement stirred interest among native peoples right across Tierra del Fuego. They were not only interested in the activities of the missionaries and the behaviour of their fellow Fuegians but also saw it as a place to attempt barter and trade. One day in 1873 a party of Alakaluf Indians paddled their canoes into the bay. They were an especially hardy, wild-looking group and among them was Fuegia Basket.

Since her betrayal of Jemmy Button on Devil Island, and her escape with York Minster, there had been few sightings of the young woman who had so charmed the English court. In 1841 an English ship cruising the Straits of Magellan had met a native woman who had asked of the crew, 'How do? I have been to Plymouth and London.' Ten years later the governor of a Chilean outpost in the area had pointed her out to two English captains, but Darwin in his *Journal of Researches*, published in 1845, sounded the alarm bells:

Capt Sulivan, who, since his voyage in the *Beagle*, has been employed on the survey of the Falkland Islands, heard from a sealer in 1842, that when in the western part of the Strait of Magellan, he was astonished by a native woman coming on board, who could talk some English. Without doubt this was Fuegia Basket. She lived (I fear the term probably bears a double interpretation) some days on board.

Thomas Bridges found the legendary Fuegia in good spirits, strong and healthy. She was 'short, thickset and with many teeth missing from a mouth that was large even for a Fuegian'. She had some memories of London and Mrs Jenkins, as well as the *Beagle* and Captain FitzRoy. She could also remember the words 'knife', 'fork' and 'beads', but seemed to have forgotten how to sit in a chair because when one was brought out for her she squatted beside it. In Yamana she told Bridges that York Minster had been killed in retaliation for murdering a man, and that though she was now in her fifties, the teenager who accompanied her was her husband.

Mary Bridges brought her two children, Mary and Despard, to meet Fuegia who said, with a big grin, 'Little boy, little gal.' Bridges tried to recover any remnants of her Walthamstow religious education, but to no avail. She stayed at Ushuaia for a week before setting off back to her own land in the west, where her own two children, by York Minster, were waiting for her. There was one more recorded sighting of Fuegia before she died: in February 1883, while Thomas Bridges was exploring the western flank of Tierra del Fuego, he learned that she was nearby. He found a fragile old woman in her early sixties, visibly nearing the end of her life. She was physically frail and unhappy. Bridges read to her from the Bible and left her in the care of her daughter and two brothers.

Chapter 24

One person who had watched the work of Thomas Bridges with interest was Charles Darwin. The young 'flycatcher' or 'stone-pounder', as he had been known on the *Beagle*, had grown into something far more important than the unassuming character of his early days. In the years since the *Beagle* had docked at Plymouth in 1836, he had suffered frequent bouts of crippling ill-health and the strains and stresses of raising a family of ten children. Nevertheless, by the late 1850s he had reached the heights of the Royal Society, become famous for his writings on the *Beagle*'s journey and renowned among scientists for his groundbreaking work on barnacles. In November 1859 Darwin published a book that would be among the most famous, enduring and controversial of the nineteenth century.

He first came to public notice after contributing the third volume of the *Narratives of the Voyage of the Beagle*, in which he described his experiences and many of the natural phenomena he encountered on the journey around the world. When published in May 1839, it was his section that proved the most popular. Darwin's account, with its details of fossil records, extraordinary geological formations and strange animals, captured the popular imagination and, before the year was out, had been reprinted separately from the rest of the *Narratives* (though without Darwin's permission). Several editions of the volume were released, under a number of different titles, the most notable of which was its 1845 best-selling version *Journal of Researches into the Natural History and Geology of the countries visited during the Voyage of HMS Beagle round the world under the command of Captain FitzRoy RN, by Charles Darwin, 2nd Edition, corrected with additions.*

His days at sea had a profound impact on Darwin's life: he had seen the world, examined rock formations, mountains, cliffs and river-beds, scrutinised the flora and fauna of three continents, communicated with strange and 'savage' peoples, and filled notebook after notebook with astute observations and beautiful descriptions. His chance inclusion on the *Beagle*'s roster had been the defining moment of his life, as he wrote to FitzRoy in February 1840:

> However others may look back to the *Beagle*'s voyage, now that the small disagreeable parts are well nigh forgotten, I think it far the most fortunate circumstance in my life that the chance afforded by your offer of taking a naturalist fell on me . . . These recollections and what I learnt in Natural History I would not exchange for twice ten thousand a year.

The journey had left many indelible images in his mind: his first sight of the 'barbarians' of Good Success Bay, earthquakes and volcanoes in Chile, the wondrous isles of the South Pacific and the giant tortoises of the Galapagos Islands. But the voyage had also raised many questions: the age of the earth, the age of life, the relationship of the Fuegians and other aboriginal peoples to 'civilisation', and the development of different species. It was after he returned to London and realised that finches he had examined in the Galapagos were distinct to their particular island that he began to question how this could be. As early as 1837 he started collecting facts on the variations of domestic and wild animals and plants, in a notebook set aside for what he called 'the transmutation of species': 'I soon perceived that selection was the keystone of man's success in making useful races of animals and plants. But how selection could be applied to organisms living in a state of nature remained for some time a mystery to me.'

The journey on which he had set out took him twenty years to complete. Inspired by the writings of the political economist Malthus on population and the over-production of offspring, Darwin's notebooks took him straight to the heart of natural selection:

In October 1838, that is, fifteen months after I had begun my systematic inquiry, I happened to read for amusement Malthus on Population, and being well prepared to appreciate the struggle for existence which everywhere goes on from long-continued observation of the habits of animals and plants, it at once struck me that under these circumstances favourable variations would tend to be preserved, and unfavourable ones to be destroyed. The results of this would be the formation of a new species. Here, then I had at last got a theory by which to work.

In 1842 he pencilled a thirty-five-page essay on the subject, which he expanded three years later to 230 pages. It was essential that he now began to accumulate evidence. The family home at Down in Kent became a seething, stinking laboratory, as he boiled up cadavers of wild and domesticated ducks to compare the dimensions of their skeletons. Vats of brine filled all available shelves as he tested the idea that the sea could transport seeds which would germinate on reaching land. Other rooms were littered with the corpses of animals ready to be skinned and measured.

As he had spent much of the early 1840s engaged in the microscopic examination of barnacles – producing a much-praised three-volume work on his findings – so he passed much of the latter half of the decade, and on into the 1850s, observing fancy pigeons. The skill with which pigeon owners bred and cross-bred their birds, and the expert eye with which they judged their beauty, fascinated Darwin and bolstered his belief in the evolution of species. He befriended pigeon-fanciers, went to their shows and conventions, and drank with them in their pubs. He built his own pigeon house at Down and introduced tumblers, fantails and almond runts but then, having become attached to them, he proceeded to boil them down for their skeletons.

Darwin knew the implications of what he was coming to understand about natural selection, and the fury his thesis would arouse. Not by nature a bold or provocative figure, and plagued by a weak stomach and a frequently debilitating lethargy, he ran scared of publishing his findings until he was prompted to act by the fear of being beaten to the draw by a young biologist, Alfred Wallace. In November 1859, just days after the massacre at Wulaia, *On the Origin of Species by means of Natural Selection or the Preservation of Favoured Races in the Struggle for Life* was published. 'It is no doubt the chief work of my life,' he wrote later in his autobiography.

Origin had an explosive impact and became the basic evolutionist text. It argued that species were not fixed, but adapted, transmuted and diversified in a blind struggle for survival. It contended that organic beings were descended from one stock, and that the continuation of life depended on the continual modification and push away from that stock. The greater the diversification, the better the chance of living. Weaknesses were discarded by nature, strengths preserved. Environment had little to do with the process: evolution was down to the chance variable of competition among closely associated groups. 'Thus, from the war of nature, from famine and death, the most exalted object which we are capable of conceiving, namely, the production of the higher animals, directly follows,' Darwin wrote in the conclusion to *Origin*.

> There is grandeur in this view of life, with its several powers, having been originally breathed into a few forms or into one; and that, whilst this planet has gone cycling on according to the fixed law of gravity, from so simple a beginning endless forms most beautiful and wonderful have been, and are being, evolved.

Grandeur there might have been, but Darwin knew that not everybody would see it that way. He wrote to Alfred Wallace, 'God knows what the public will think . . .' It was not long before he found out. The book polarised the worlds of science and religion, and redefined the boundaries of both. Though natural selection had been discussed by others before Darwin, here in *Origin* it was clearly articulated, concisely and brilliantly argued, and backed up with compelling evidence. The scientific and religious establishments were dominated by creationists who believed that species did not evolve but were created whole and fully formed by the hand of an all-powerful superbeing. This God was also responsible for any and all variations from the original. There was no common stock from which life had been derived, just creation itself. They threw up their hands in horror at Darwin's book and called it treacherous, even blasphemous. It undermined the basic doctrines of Christianity and science, they protested. Where was the hand of the maker in natural selection? they asked.

Origin sold all 1,250 printed copies on its first day and became a powerful weapon in a battle that had been spoiling for years between a group of feisty, but frustrated young turks anxious to seize the reins of scientific power from the grip of the theologians and old-school creationists. Reviews in the country's most important newspapers and periodicals lambasted one another in their support for or antagonism for *Origin*. *The Times* gave Darwin's favourite acolyte, Thomas Huxley, more than three columns to praise the new philosophy on Boxing Day 1859. By April Huxley had coined the enduring term 'Darwinism' and was heralding it a 'Whitworth gun in the armoury of liberalism'.

Across the battlefield Richard Owen, the influential superintendent of the natural history collections at the British Museum, vilified natural selection in the *Edinburgh Review*, and one of Darwin's old professors at Cambridge wrote to him that he had caused more pain than pleasure and asserted that 'You have deserted the true methods of induction, and started in machinery as wild, I think, as Bishop Wilkins's locomotive that was to sail with us to the moon.'

Darwin was a timid man, who stood back and let the controversy rage. He knew the logical conclusions that would be drawn sooner or later from a thesis that suggested all life emerged from the same soup, namely that humankind was not superior to the beast but was related to it. Aware that there was mischief to be made from his work, he had therefore deliberately made as few references to humankind as possible. In *Origin* he used anything else as an example: brachiopods and cirripedes, humming-birds and dogs, pigeons and Scotch fir trees. Nevertheless his critics were only too pleased to pinpoint the central heresy. The *Athenaeum* magazine was the first to highlight what it called the evolutionary nonsense of men from monkeys – an idea that captured the public imagination. In Oxford in June 1860, at a meeting of the British Association for the Advancement of Science, more than 700 people witnessed Samuel Wilberforce, Bishop of Oxford, round on Thomas Huxley and ask him whether he was descended from an ape on his grandmother's side or his grandfather's. There was uproar, and one lady fainted. Huxley retorted that he could not see what difference it would make and that if he was asked which he would rather have, 'a miserable ape for a grandfather or a man highly endowed by nature and possessed of great means and influence and yet who employs these faculties and that influence for the mere purpose of introducing ridicule into a grave scientific discussion, I unhesitatingly affirm my preference for the ape.' Laughter ricocheted around the room.

In the middle of the auditorium a man stood waving a Bible, imploring those present to believe the word of God. He was shouted down by those around him. The man was Robert FitzRoy.

The ghastly spectacle of the *Beagle*'s former captain being heckled and hooted on the floor of an Oxford debating chamber discloses an unfortunate tale, for as Darwin's star rose so FitzRoy's had faded. Once destined for greatness, the brightest student of his year, his career had peaked with the circumnavigation of the globe. In the years since the voyage he had veered from disappointment to controversy, frustration and tragedy.

Five years at sea, with his liberal upbringing, had shaken Darwin's Christian faith to the roots, but FitzRoy's high Tory, Anglo-Catholic conservatism had led him to see the experience as an affirmation of the literal truth of the Bible. Over the years his inflexibility and intolerance had hardened, as did the frequency of his bouts of melancholia, the 'blue evils', as he called them. In 1841 he was invited to stand for Parliament in a vacant seat in County Durham, but the election saw a dirty campaign during which he fell out with a fellow Tory candidate, whom he challenged to a duel. The scandal hit the press, the duel was botched, but the two men brawled away their dignity outside the United Services Club in the Mall.

FitzRoy was elected nevertheless, but remained an MP for only two years before he accepted the governorship of New Zealand. Here, he found himself between Scylla and Charybdis and, more importantly, popular with no one. There was trouble in the new colony over the issue of land for settlers and the rights of the native Maoris. FitzRoy's sympathies lay with the hard-pressed Maori peoples, but they were not looking for sympathy, they wanted solutions. The settlers were even more unhappy with their colonial chief, troubles broke out, minor rebellions erupted and, in 1845, he was removed from office. In the town of Nelson the departing governor's effigy was carried around the streets and burned by a triumphal mob.

In 1850 FitzRoy was elected a fellow of the Royal Society and in 1853, a year after his first wife Mary died, he was appointed meteorological statist at the Board of Trade. He invented a new barometer, which he issued with instructions to fishing ports all around the country, and went on to establish twenty-four weather stations from which information could be gathered and analysed. Using all the resources to hand, he systematised the collection of data on winds, pressures, temperatures and humidities, which he recorded on charts. FitzRoy became the father of weather forecasting and brought about a revolution in meteorology. There was much for him to be proud of, and a great debt is owed to him by modern meteorologists. But for him it was not enough. His moods were darkening. In 1857 he applied for the job of chief naval officer in the Board of Trade's maritime department, but found himself losing out to his former lieutenant on the *Beagle*, Bartholomew Sulivan. The publication of *Origin* two years later mortified him. Its atheistic theory of natural selection was abhorrent to him; that it had been written by his former cabin mate on the *Beagle*, a man he had chosen to take on board and for whom he was therefore responsible,

horrified him. Amid the controversy over *Origin*, news arrived of
the massacre at Wulaia and the possible culpability of his favourite
Fuegian, Jemmy Button. It was hardly surprising that a debilitated
FitzRoy succumbed to a growing despondency.

By 1865 his work on the weather was met with wounding
shafts of criticism. FitzRoy was accused of being unscientific, and
forecasting was damned as foolishness. Ill-health began to take its
toll – FitzRoy's second wife wrote to a relative in April 1865 that
he had been out of sorts for a good while and the 'doctors unite in
prescribing total rest, and entire absence from his office for a time.
Leave has been given him, but his active mind and oversensitive
conscience prevent him from profiting from this leave . . .'

On 30 April 1865 FitzRoy awoke at six in the morning and
lay still beside his wife. At seven thirty the maid called them
for breakfast. They lay there for another fifteen minutes before
FitzRoy pulled back the blankets and walked to his dressing room.
On his way he went to see his daughter Laura and kissed her
cheek. In his dressing room he closed the door without locking
it, took out a razor, held it up and then, in a deliberate arc,
slit his throat. A little more than a year after Jemmy Button had
died in a foreign-borne epidemic on a beach in Tierra del Fuego,
Robert FitzRoy lay crumpled and lifeless on the floor.

Darwin was greatly saddened by the untimely demise of his old
mentor. During the voyage, the two men had had their ups and
downs, and even the occasional serious confrontation, but Darwin
had recognised and respected FitzRoy's many admirable qualities
and strengths. The time they had shared among the Fuegians had
clearly influenced Darwin, which was evident from the opening
paragraph of the *Origin*:

When on board HMS *Beagle*, as naturalist, I was much struck with certain facts in the distribution of the inhabitants of South America, and in the geological relations of the present to the past inhabitants of that continent. These facts seemed to me to throw some light on the origin of the species — that mystery of mysteries, as it has been called by one of our greatest philosophers.

This was further confirmed in a letter of 1862 to the author Charles Kingsley, who had written to offer his support for the theory of natural selection. He also informed Darwin of a weekend he had spent with the Bishop of Oxford and the Duke of Argyll, during which *Origin* had been the main topic of conversation. Darwin's reply makes it clear that the unearthing of a common thread between himself and the Fuegians had been a far from easy discovery:

> That is a grand and almost awful question on the genealogy of man to which you allude. It is not so awful and difficult to me, as it seems to be most, partly from familiarity and partly, I think, from having seen a good many Barbarians — I declare the thought, when I first saw in Tierra del Fuego a naked, painted, shivering hideous savage, that my ancestors must have been somewhat similar beings, was at that time as revolting to me, nay more revolting than my present belief that an incomparably more remote ancestor was a hairy beast. Monkeys have downright good hearts, at least sometimes, as I could show, if I had space. I have long attended to this subject, and have materials for a curious essay on Human expression, and a little on the relation in mind of a man to the lower animals. How I should be abused if I were to publish such an essay . . .

Revolting as it had been to him, Darwin had made the link between barbarity and civilisation; he had set personal feelings aside and followed the logic of his theory. Soon after the publication of the *Origin* he realised that, like it or not, he would have to place man in the picture and explain the lineage, the process and the context of humanity. The resulting work – *The Descent of Man* – drew widely on the memories and notes he had stored away about his time with Jemmy, York and Fuegia, and the experiences in Tierra del Fuego among their people. Published in 1871, the *Descent*'s central tenet held that 'man is descended from some less highly organised form' and was essentially the 'monkey theory' writ large. In setting out his argument Darwin recalled many of the peoples he had met and conversed with as the *Beagle* had circumnavigated the globe. However, it was clear that the contrast between civilised England and the primitive Fuegians had had the greatest impact on him, not least because they were the first raw savages he encountered but also because on the ship he had become acquainted with Jemmy, York and Fuegia.

The Fuegians rank amongst the lowest barbarians; but I was continually struck with surprise how closely the three natives on board HMS *Beagle*, who had lived some years in England, and could talk a little English, resembled us in disposition and in most of our mental faculties. If no organic being excepting man had possessed any mental power, or if his powers had been of a wholly different nature from those of the lower animals, then we should never have been able to convince ourselves that our high faculties had been gradually developed. But it can be shewn that there is no fundamental difference of this kind.

The Descent of Man is dotted with references to the Fuegian Indians: how different subsistence patterns in eastern and western Tierra del Fuego influenced the stature of the various Fuegian peoples; the way they had perfected their stone and spear-throwing; their ability to live in harsh conditions without clothes.

Darwin described Fuegian courtship rituals, how this people appeared to have no belief in God, but were superstitious, and that Jemmy Button had, with 'justifiable pride, stoutly maintained that there was no devil in his land'. Observing the Fuegians had brought home to Darwin that for civilisation to flourish it needed an understanding and an accumulation of property, settled homes and a tribal chief. In the conclusion to the book, Darwin refined the thoughts he had expressed to Kingsley nine years earlier:

there can hardly be a doubt that we are descended from barbarians. The astonishment which I felt on first seeing a party of Fuegians on a wild and broken shore will never be forgotten by me, for the reflection at once rushed into my mind — such were our ancestors. These men were absolutely naked and bedaubed with paint, their long hair was tangled, their mouths frothed with excitement, and their expression was wild, startled, and distrustful. They possessed hardly any arts, and like wild animals lived on what they could catch; they had no government, and were merciless to every one not of their own small tribe. He who has seen a savage in his native land will not feel much shame, if forced to acknowledge that the blood of some more humble creature flows in his veins. For my own part I would as soon be descended from that heroic little monkey, who braved his dreaded enemy in order to save the life of his keeper, or from that old baboon, who descending from the mountains, carried away in triumph his young comrade from a crowd of astonished dogs — as from a savage who delights to torture his enemies, offers up bloody sacrifices, practices infanticide without remorse, treats his wives like slaves, knows no decency, and is haunted by the grossest superstitions.

Darwin had begun preparing for *The Descent of Man* as early as 1860 when he had sent a list of questions on Fuegian habits and expression to Thomas Bridges on Keppel Island. These had included such queries as

> Do the Fuegians or Patagonians, or both, nod their heads vertically to express assent, and shake their heads horizontally to express dissent?
>
> Do they blush? and at what sort of things? Is it chiefly or most commonly in relation to personal appearance, or in relation to women?
>
> Do they express astonishment by widely open eyes, uplifted eyebrows and open mouth?
>
> Do they evince anger or fear by same expression of countenance and actions as we do?

Bridges had responded with answers to most of the questions, but in 1867, when Darwin began to order his notes in preparation for drafting *The Descent of Man*, he found that he needed more information and wrote to his old colleague and friend Bartholomew Sulivan, who was still playing a leading role in the missionary society.

> Your letter has interested me exceedingly all about S. America and the Fuegians. I never thought the latter cd have been civilized, but it appears that I shall be proved wrong.
>
> I wish poor FitzRoy was alive to hear the result of his first attempt for the civilization of the Fuegians. Do you know Mr Stirling well enough to ask him to grant me a great favour? Namely to observe during a few months the expression of countenance under different conditions of any Fuegians, but especially of those who have not lived much in contact with Europeans, and to take the trouble to write me a letter on the subject.

It is clear that Darwin had retained an interest in the behaviour of the Fuegians, but his work on *The Descent of Man*, along with his friendship with Sulivan, rekindled a curiosity in their affairs that remained with him for the rest of his life. In 1867 he donated £5 to the general funds of the South American Missionary Society. There seems to have been no conflict in his mind about his being the advocate in chief of what many viewed as an atheistic doctrine and his association with the missionaries. Three years later, on 30 January 1870, he wrote to Sulivan: 'The success of the Tierra del Fuego Mission is most wonderful, and charms me, as I had always prophesied utter failure. It is a grand success. I shall feel proud if your Committee think fit to elect me an honorary member of your society.'

When Darwin began work on *The Descent of Man* he had intended to write a chapter on the ways different animals and races express emotion, but as the project grew he realised that there was need for a separate book. *The Expression of the Emotions in Man and Animals* was published in 1872 and incorporated the answers he had received from Bridges and Stirling. It did not stop him, however, firing off more inquiries. In 1873 he wrote to Stirling, through Sulivan, asking whether he felt that the process of civilising the natives harmed their health. His concern may have been prompted by long-standing qualms Darwin had about such work with the Fuegians. It may have been prompted by the deaths of Threeboys and Uroopa, or it may have been because in 1872 another former colleague from the *Beagle*, Arthur Mellersh, who had been mate on the second voyage, wrote to him: 'Sulivan tells me there is a mission established in Tierra del Fuego, I hope it will succeed in preventing the poor people from being "improved" off the face of the earth.'

Stirling's answer to Darwin, again through Sulivan, was reassuring, though hardly convincing. Threeboys had died of Bright's disease, which was unknown among the Fuegians but which might have been caused by deficiencies in the food on the long voyages to Britain and back. Jemmy and Fuegia had not suffered any ill-health as a consequence of their three years in civilised company and York had been murdered. 'The Bishop tells me that he does not think the Fuegians suffer in health through increased civilization. That if at all it was at first when their mode of life was changed; but they soon got accustomed to it, and seemed to enjoy as good health as others . . .'

In April 1878 Sulivan wrote to Darwin that the mission was anxious to raise and train two orphan grandsons of Jemmy Button, currently living at the station in Ushuaia. Each child would cost £10 a year to maintain, but the Beckenham branch of the Society had undertaken to pay for one of the two, who would henceforth be known as William Beckenham Button. Would Darwin be willing to join in a subscription, to be raised among former *Beagle* crew members, to pay for the care of the other orphan? Sulivan asked. The child would be called James FitzRoy Button in honour of the old captain, and it would cost the sponsors £1 each a year.

Darwin replied with enthusiasm, but also with a note of concern:

I shall be happy to subscribe £1 annually as long as I live for Jemmy FitzRoy Button; and to save trouble I enclose subscription for next two years. I suppose that you have thought of the Boy's future, and whether it is a real kindness to him to educate him; and secondly that we Beaglers are growing old . . .

Some confusion followed when Sulivan discovered, to his great disappointment, that Jemmy's grandson had already been adopted and named by a daughter of one of the Society's committee members. He returned Darwin's cheque, but a year later he found that Thomas Bridges had set the child aside for the *Beagle* crew. Sulivan wrote on 13 October 1879,

> My Dear Darwin
>
> I find that after all Mr Bridges reserved Button's grandson for Beagles by getting the lady who had taken on herself to provide for him to take another orphan and though he did not write to me about it he has sent them the list of orphans for publication and forgetting that I told him the boy should have FitzRoy's name added, and be called 'James FitzRoy Button' he had put my name instead of FitzRoy's and called him 'James Button Sulivan'.
>
> This I will have altered as Mrs FitzRoy likes the name I proposed and so we all did.
>
> She and her daughters wish to give £3 a year towards the £10 required. I am going to give £2 and will ask you again to give the £1 you gave when it was first mentioned. I have no doubt Hamond, Mellersh, Usborne and Stokes will do the same. Johnson is so ill, his memory was so weak the last time I saw him that I will not say anything to him about it . . .

Sulivan and Darwin corresponded many times in the next two years, frequently discussing the mission at Ushuaia and their adopted orphan. From the naturalist's responses it is indisputable that Sulivan had succeeded in stoking his old friend's enthusiasm. On 3 January 1880 Darwin wrote that journals Sulivan had sent on the mission were very interesting and that 'I have often said that the progress of Japan was the greatest wonder of the world but I declare the progress of Fuegia is almost equally wonderful.'

In March 1881 Sulivan attended a lecture given by Thomas Bridges on the language of the Fuegians. Afterwards he scribbled a quick letter to Darwin giving him the details of the talk. Writing from Down House, on 20 March, Darwin replied with unequivocal pleasure: 'The account of the Fuegians interested not only me, but

all my family. It is truly wonderful, what you have heard from Mr
Bridges about their honesty and about their language. I certainly
should have predicted that not all the Missionaries in the world
could have done what has been done.'

On 21 November 1881 Darwin received a communication
from a surprising source. William Parker Snow wrote to him
with the news that he was revising his *A Two Years Cruise in Tierra
del Fuego* and that, in looking over his material, he had found
that he was at variance with the opinions and researches of the
famous evolutionist. It had been twenty-two years since his case
against the Patagonian Missionary Society had been heard, but
the same themes recurred in his letter: 'I still propose and have
submitted (uselessly to our Government though more favourable
to Foreign Powers) the establishment of a small settlement and
Harbour of refuge etc about Cape Horn . . .' There was the
same element of discontent in his words, the same grumbling
tone and a sense of having been wronged. There was also a
tantalising hint (unrecorded elsewhere) that Darwin had helped
him out in the past:

> In my heavy literary labours, unaided, and much opposed by
> officials and the Missionary Society, my old days are far from
> easy, and it will be a question if I can ever bring to fruition and
> publication what I have for so many years laboured upon, but if
> I do, a copy shall be sent.
>
> I do not forget a temporary aid you rendered a few years
> ago.

He offered to visit Down House and bring with him some
specimens he had collected in Tierra del Fuego, but his letter
seems to have gone unanswered and it is doubtful that the
encounter ever took place. Darwin was growing old and, on 1

December 1881, he sent his last letter about Tierra del Fuego to Sulivan. It enclosed two years' subscription for Jemmy FitzRoy Button. 'Judging from the missionary journal,' he noted, 'the mission in Tierra del Fuego seems going on quite wonderfully well . . .'

Sulivan contacted him a couple of days later to let him know that he had paid two shillings too much, but he would put it towards some extra warm clothing for the boy. He had some sad news and a plan:

> My youngest son when on his way to visit his agents at North German ports and Riga saw a party of poor Fuegians exhibited in Zoological at Berlin about ten I think men women and children brought from western Tierra del Fuego by a German vessel. They seem to have been shown around like wild beasts. He wrote a long letter to the society describing them and urging that they should be got from their master and brought to England for the purpose of sending them back through our mission station.
>
> It is difficult to advise, but I have suggested that if they can get them when the owner has exhibited them at Hamburg, to which place he was going – they might keep them here long enough to teach them a little cleanliness, decent dress etc and then send them out direct to Sandy Point [Punta Arenas] to go to Ooshwaia. I think they must be from Fuegia's tribe. I have no doubt that friends of the mission would provide the necessary funds.

Darwin's view on the matter is not recorded. He died on 19 April 1882 and was buried amid great ceremony in Westminster Abbey. There is no record of what became of the Fuegians of Berlin Zoo.

Chapter 25

On a sunny Sunday afternoon in September 1884 four warships of the Argentine navy sailed along the Beagle Channel. Their presence came as a surprise to the settlement of Ushuaia on its northern bank and, as the three steamers and one sail-ship dropped their anchors in the port, there was agitation on shore. Thomas Bridges wandered to the quayside. Yamana settlers poured out of their huts and wigwams and surrounded the forty-one-year-old Englishman, chattering and gesticulating, shouting and crying from fear and torment at what dangers the newcomer brought.

Bridges, his assistants John Lawrence and Robert Whaits, and a native crew climbed into a whale-boat and rowed to the largest of the flotilla, the *Villarino*. As they came alongside, its captain greeted them with an instruction, 'The other ship, Mr Bridges,' pointing at the *Parana*. The crew rowed on and found Colonel Augusto Lasserre waiting for them with a handshake, a smile and an explanation: he had come to claim Ushuaia for the newly created sub-prefecture of Tierra del Fuego, in the republic of Argentina.

The missionary had no complaints. He had known that one day the 'civilised world' would reach this far, and he promised to co-operate with the new government of the small town. For his part, Lasserre promised not to interfere in the continuing operations of the mission settlement. They went ashore together and, amid a mass of Yamana Indians, the colonel handed Bridges an Argentine flag. The Englishman lowered the missionary flag that had flown over the settlement for sixteen years – a flag similar to but different from the Union Flag, so that imperial ambitions could not be misconstrued – and then raised the pale blue and white standard of the Republic of Argentina. Out at sea the four ships fired a twenty-one-gun salute and the Yamana raised a loud cheer.

The congenial souls of the Argentine Navy were welcomed; they built a new office, set up two reflecting beacons and left behind a small force of twenty men. Disastrously they also brought with them something far less desirable: the measles virus. Within a month over half of the Yamana people were dead. They fell in such numbers that it was impossible for the strong and unaffected to dig graves quickly enough: bodies piled up everywhere. On the outskirts of town corpses were dumped at the entrance to wigwams or dragged to the nearest bushes. Within two years half of the survivors had also died. Exactly a quarter of a century on from the massacre at Wulaia, the Yamana people were staring extinction in the face.

Whether accidental or deliberate, what followed was a final cruel twist in the tale of the Fuegian Indians. It came in the disguise of convicts, gold and sheep.

These days, one has only to turn on the television or open a newspaper to find slaughter on a grand scale: in Kosovo, Rwanda, Bosnia-Herzegovina, Croatia, East Timor. In modern times the terms 'genocide' and 'ethnic cleansing' have, sadly, become common currency. The massacre of the innocents in these tragic countries has been appalling, but occasionally, whether for added effect or through journalistic sloppiness, the labels are misapplied. When dealing with the Fuegian Indians they are entirely appropriate: anyone unfortunate enough to have witnessed events in that far-off corner of the planet during the latter half of the nineteenth century and the first decades of the twentieth would have been observing the total extermination of a race.

For Thomas Bridges it was too much to bear. Two years after the arrival of the Argentine ships at Ushuaia he abandoned the mission station. The epidemic had sapped his spirit, and the continuing growth of the settlement, which had by now acquired a governor and many of the trappings of government, led him to a decision to break out on his own. With a grant of land forty miles east of Ushuaia he took up ranching, and by 1894 he had enclosed a farm of more than 2,000 acres that he called Harberton, after his wife's home village in Devon.

As Bridges had long feared, the success of Ushuaia brought with it the darker side of civilisation: alcohol, guns and greed. More importantly, every new influx of settlers brought with it disease and infection. After an Argentine penal colony on Staten Island, at the extreme limit of Tierra del Fuego, suffered a bloody uprising among the inmates, the prison was moved to Ushuaia. The result was another epidemic which, in 1888, killed every Yamana Indian within thirty miles of the settlement.

When gold was discovered in the early 1890s small communities of prospectors from Eastern Europe, Spain, North America and Argentina sprang up in locations from Lennox Island and Dawson Island to the eastern coast of Tierra del Fuego as far north as Rio Grande. The first two prospectors had arrived in the area after a three-month ride across the main island during which they had shot every Fuegian they encountered. For the Selk'nam – Jemmy's Oens-men – the miners' presence was like a cancer. From them the Selk'nam stole or traded guns and with these the fragile tribal balance of the area was unhinged. The guanaco, their main food source, was driven into extinction and local feuds were transformed into homicidal rampages, as Indian wiped out Indian. Lucas Bridges relates a number of these incidents in his book *Uttermost Part of the Earth*, as when the Indian Kiyohnishah – which meant guanaco dung – and a band of sixty followers fell upon a larger party of Selk'nam as they feasted on a stranded whale. Kiyohnishah's party carried with it a number of stolen firearms and the slaughter was appalling, men and women randomly gunned down. Later, Bridges describes an attack in which Kiyohnishah was the victim. A Selk'nam by the name of Ahnikin got hold of three Winchester .44 repeating rifles and, with a small party, launched an attack on a camp near Lake Hyewhin.

As day dawned the attackers advanced on the sleeping encampment. The dogs began to bark, but their warning came too late. Taken completely by surprise, Kiyohnishah sprang to his feet. As he looked over the top of his kowwhi to see what the dogs were barking at, a bullet from Ahnikin's rifle blew his brains out. This was followed by a fusillade of shots that brought down six or seven more, among them Chashkil, who died as swiftly as his brother. Kawhalshan fell with a broken leg, Kautempklh, Kilehehen, the boy Teorati, Kilkoat with his rifle and a few others dived into the woods, while the women hid their heads and wailed.

Kawhalshan, lying helpless on the ground, was prodded slowly to death with a blunt arrow by young Kautush, who, as he despatched the wounded man, shouted at him again and again: 'You killed my father.'

A murderous pursuit continued into the woods at the end of which Ahnikin returned to the scene of his triumph, only to find the women hacking the body of his dead uncle Yoknolpe into bits and feeding them to the dogs. Ahnikin levelled his rifle and shot seven women dead.

Even worse news for the Fuegians was the arrival of the sheep farmers who began to colonise Tierra del Fuego. Huge expanses of pastureland were sold off by the Argentinian and Chilean governments, but the enclosure of vast ranches was anathema to the nomadic ways of the native population, who now crossed their own heartlands as trespassers. Plunged into near starvation by the disappearance of the guanaco they inevitably killed sheep, for which the ranchers exacted a terrible toll. The new settlers quickly came to see the Indians as vermin, and vermin had to be eradicated. They put a price tag on Fuegian heads – as little as £1 was paid for each one killed – and packs of horseback gauchos hunted them down and wiped them out.

Lucas Bridges told of the exploits of one particular brute he called McInch, the self-styled 'King of the Rio Grande'. McInch was a heavy-drinking Scotsman with broad, ruddy features, wispy red hair and green-blue eyes. As a young man he had gone with Kitchener to Khartoum, and later in life had tried to establish a sheep farm in northern Tierra del Fuego. When it failed he blamed the Selk'nam and vowed revenge.

On one occasion he heard that a large party of Selk'nam were heading across wide open grasslands towards Cape Penas where they would hunt the thousands of seal that landed there. Bridges took up the story:

> Armed with repeating rifles and eager for excitement, Mr McInch and a band of mounted white men encircled the headland, thereby cutting off the retreat of the luckless sealers, who, when the tide rose, were driven from their refuge at the foot of the cliffs into the range of the enthusiastic manhunters.
>
> I do not know how many natives were killed that day. Mr McInch claimed afterwards that they had shot fourteen. He maintained that it was really a most humanitarian act, if one had the guts to do it. He argued that these people could never live their lives alongside the white man; that it was cruel

to keep them in captivity at a mission where they would pine away miserably or die from some imported illness; and that the sooner they were exterminated the better.

Such barbarous acts in Tierra del Fuego often set off small chain reactions. One example of this occurred after McInch's bloody attack. The Selk'nam Indian Kilcoat successfully escaped into the woods with his wife and child. A few days later, after he had been hunting, Kilcoat returned to find his wife lying dead, face down in a swamp, her child tied to her back. She had been shot from behind with a bullet that had skimmed the child's ribs. The child was still alive. Kilcoat was devastated and sought vengeance against the first white man he came across. He hid behind a rock and when a lone miner passed by he shot him in the back with an arrow. He then stole the dead man's repeating rifle and ammunition. This was one of the firearms used subsequently to such deadly effect when Kiyohnishah massacred his fellow Selk'nam feeding on the stranded whale, and was used again during the killings at Lake Hyewhin.

The missions of which McInch spoke were Roman Catholic Salesian projects on the main island and on Dawson Island. In the face of the land-grab that was going on throughout Tierra del Fuego, these missions were the only concessions granted to the indigenous population, their only refuge from the Winchester rifle. In the eyes of many they provided a humane alternative to the lives the Indians were living, and the destruction they were facing in the wild. Some sheep farmers offered £5 a head for the capture of natives and their placement in the missions; others tried to persuade them that it was for their own good. More than a hundred Selk'nam were transported to Dawson Island, where they learned new skills alongside Alakaluf Indians who had been similarly rounded up. For the men there was work in the saw mill, in forestry and sheep shearing, for the women there was spinning and weaving. Another attempt at establishing an Anglican mission near to Cape Horn came to nothing when its founder, Leonard Burleigh, drowned off the coast of Hoste Island.

There can be little doubt that those who ran the Catholic missions in Tierra del Fuego did so with the best of intentions for the indigenous population. In their eyes it was the latest chapter in the age-old story of bringing God and civilisation to a savage people. They brought with them clothes, warm accommodation and good food, but in their own way the Salesian missions were as efficient in killing off the Fuegians as the gunmen at their perimeter. Wool, blankets, immigrant priests, nuns and supply ships brought disease to the heart of the stations. The change of climate ruined the immune systems of the Selk'nam who were taken to Dawson Island. The effects on a free and nomadic people of being corralled and regimented into close, confined quarters was depressing: their spirit was broken, their resistance crushed.

Few ever understood the Fuegians, or saw beyond their naked, primitive appearance. The racial attitudes of Europeans towards people of non-European descent are appalling to modern eyes. To attempt an assessment of the lives of Fuegians, or indeed other tribal peoples around the world, without condescension, was not part of the nineteenth-century psyche. As 'civilisation' expanded, whether through secular empire-building or religious missionary endeavours, the need to 'save' the rude savage became imperative. To white European imperialists, or missionaries, these people were crude, barbarous aborigines. They were generally black, unclothed, apt to live in poor shelter, content to dine on sub-standard food and prone to violent outbursts. They communicated through a limited number of grunts, exhibited little curiosity and no knowledge of God or Christ. European visitors could see that there was need to regiment, to organise, to fill their lives with order, work and religious joy. The fact that the Fuegians had survived in their habitat for centuries was irrelevant to the European mind: that it transpired that their language was, in some respects, more sophisticated than English only exposed the intruders' ignorance. What was important was saving them for God and heaven.

Alternatively, if they could not save the 'savage' they could always destroy them — though often the effect was the same. The Europeans, and later the Argentines and Chileans, judged those Fuegians unwilling to play the game — those who were less acquiescent to the white man's demands, those who were troublesome, less adaptable to change, and more assertive — to be worthless primitives who could be dismissed with the click of a trigger. It is difficult to put numbers on the scale of the tragedy that befell the Fuegians because there are no precise records. When the *Beagle* carried Jemmy Button back to the Yahgashaga in 1833 there were probably three thousand Yamana Indians. In the early 1850s, there were 7,000–9,000 Fuegian Indians, of all tribes. By 1908 there were barely 170 Yamana Indians alive; by 1947 there were only 43, and less than 150 surviving pure Fuegians of any tribe, with roughly the same number of mixed race. It is doubtful that there are any pure Fuegian Indians today.

In the story of Jemmy Button the notion of what was savage or barbarian and what was civilised is of great importance. Civilisation was defined by the apparently civilised, who also designated what was savage. Yet there was no lack of paradoxes. What was civilised about the abduction of native peoples, their removal from their families and their transportation across the world? Or about men hunting down packs of Indians and wiping them out without fear of reprisal? Or the forced herding of Fuegians into mission stations and their coercion into work programmes and the trappings of European societies? It is worth bearing in mind that Jemmy Button, along with York, Fuegia, and four more Fuegians in the 1860s, went to England, were indulged in polite society and survived; they proved adaptable, intelligent and understanding. The same could not always be said for Europeans going the other way.

It is possible to speculate on how close the Fuegians came to avoiding their miserable end. Tierra del Fuego was a forsaken corner of the world, important only for its location on a major shipping route. By the second decade of the twentieth century it had been made largely irrelevant by the construction of the Panama Canal. As there was no longer reason for ships to risk a rounding of Cape Horn, there would have been little reason for the clash of cultures, and nobody would have had to worry about the fate of marooned sailors in these parts. Had the canal been built half a century earlier one could fairly ask whether or not some living remnant of the Fuegians would still be with us.

It is also important to consider the role, no matter how unwitting, that Jemmy Button played in his people's downfall. It was he who unlocked the final catastrophic floodgates, though he was hardly to blame. For over three centuries European ships had passed through these waters, had traded with the Fuegian Indians and had moved on. They had passed along the Magellan Straits, through the many channels of the archipelago, or even round the Horn. There had been the occasional skirmish, an isolated violent death, and certainly when a ship was wrecked here, sailors had as much to fear from the people as they did from the raging seas. But the balance of Fuegian Indian life and their relationships with the environment and each other were not challenged irrevocably until FitzRoy abducted the four Fuegians and brought them back to England for their education and betterment.

In a nineteenth-century context it is difficult to question his motives: once again, here was a person who genuinely believed he was doing good, that with luck and God's will he would improve the lot of all Fuegian Indians, transform their nomadic existence into some form of settled society. FitzRoy failed, but the return of Jemmy, York and Fuegia to Tierra del Fuego drew the attention and raised the hopes of future missionaries.

The presence of Jemmy near Wulaia, with his ability to speak and understand English, his rudimentary grasp of Christianity and his awareness of English cultural expectations was too much to resist. He was a magnet to colonising missionaries and the nature of contact between Fuegian and foreigner was transformed; the white man no longer arrived, hunted seal and perhaps traded fish before moving on, he came to stay, and in his wake came trouble.

Of course, it was in the nature of nineteenth-century exploration and colonial expansion that if it had not been Jemmy it would have been another Fuegian. Sooner or later a European was bound to have seen the region as ripe for colonisation. It was always certain that 'civilisation' would spread south from the burgeoning republics of Chile and Argentina, but Jemmy was the catalyst. His abduction opened up a period of unprecedented interference in the lives of Fuegian Indians and within a few decades of his death on Button Island the rest of his people had been eliminated.

In *Uttermost Part of the Earth*, Lucas Bridges (who, it should be remembered, was the adopted grandson of George Packenham Despard) wrote that the plans of the missionary martyr Allen Gardiner had been 'followed as closely as possible through trials and disasters to a successful conclusion. Though I am well aware that, within less than a century, the Fuegians as a race have become almost extinct, I deliberately use the word "successful".'

This success, which Lucas Bridges heralded so triumphantly, was bittersweet indeed. When considering the Fuegian people and the tragedy that engulfed them it is natural to view their existence with sadness and no little anger at the treatment meted out to them. On 30 September 1889 *The Times* carried the following story about an exhibition held at the Royal Aquarium in Westminster. Seven Selk'nam Indians — one man, two women, two girls and two boys — had been taken from their homeland by a gold-digger who wished to show them off at the Paris Exhibition. He had arrived too late for the show, and instead passed them on to a Mr Farini for exhibiting in London. The newspaper reported that a tent had been erected for them in the aquarium and that

> They are of a dark, swarthy brown colour, and their hair, which is of a blueish black tinge, is arranged so as to form a large fringe which almost entirely covers the eyes . . . only one of the party, a boy, showing any signs of cheerfulness, the rest maintaining a sullen demeanour. In stature they are small, but their limbs are well developed and show signs of considerable muscular power. Their dress consists merely of a skin, and it is said that they prefer their meat raw. They are unable to understand anything beyond a few signs, and their language has apparently little resource, as their communications seem to consist almost entirely of a few low ejaculations . . . At present they sit about round a large stove, cowering in their skins, apparently contented with the warmth. They will be on view at the Aquarium for some time to come.

It was a sad spectacle, a human zoo, typical in its unfeeling, arrogant and ill-judged representation of a soon-to-disappear people — a people deep in crisis. Without Jemmy Button this would have been the abiding image of the native inhabitants of Tierra del Fuego. But in his life we are left with a powerful contradiction to it. Jemmy's existence and his reaction to his experiences throw open a different window on the Indians of Tierra del Fuego, which offers a far more interesting and revealing view.

At the opening of his odyssey there was nothing that marked out Jemmy as more competent or more intelligent than his friends and family. Yet in his life we see his strength — both mental and physical — and his bold response to his English captors. Orundellico was transformed from the primeval child, out fishing and bartering with his uncles, into the hybrid creation Jemmy Button, neither completely Fuegian nor remotely English. Kidnapped, used and abused in his early life, harassed and troubled in his later years, he emerged nevertheless as a man of character and fortitude. He was a battler, a survivor, a child and man of good nature. He was a boon to FitzRoy's project, someone who adapted to and thrived in the hothouse of London, who adored dressing up and preening like the most narcissistic of dandies. He grew into something respectable enough to present not only to the aristocratic friends of the young captain, but also to the pinnacle of English society, royalty itself. From FitzRoy's own observations on the Fuegian peoples, this was more than he could realistically have expected when he began seizing Fuegian Indians. In the end the captain's experiment with his Fuegian missionaries failed, but that had little to do with the abilities of Jemmy, York and Fuegia and more to do with its ill conception, half thought-out design and poorly resourced execution.

It is true that in his later years Jemmy became more fractious, less helpful and was at times a thorn in the side of those who sought him out. It is also distinctly probable that he was involved, and possibly led, the massacre at Wulaia Cove in November 1859. Yet Fuegians lived by different rules and values and this was their customary response to the threat of foreign incursion, the fear of further kidnappings and, it is important to remember, to a twice-repeated insult in the form of the searches imposed on them by the missionary and the captain of the ship. Moreover, as with other victims throughout history, it shows that they offered some resistance and were not willing just to lie down and die.

Many years before, Jemmy Button had been used and discarded like flotsam, abandoned to the vagaries of his people, the selfishness and cravings of York Minster, and the self-doubts that grow in the heart of the exile. With hindsight it was hardly startling that, when the white man came calling once more, he would be reluctant to help. As he stated in his testimony at Port Stanley in 1860, he had 'had plenty of it – no want to go back . . .' and, in the words of the assistant secretary in the Colonial Office, when the missionaries started to force the issue it was 'not surprising that murder should follow'.

Orundellico was an unremarkable boy, whom fate picked out for an extraordinary life. His drama was one of human resilience and unquenchable spirit, throughout which it is possible to recognise his abilities and intelligence as a sign of the potential abilities and intelligence of the wider Fuegian peoples. The natives of Tierra del Fuego are lost now to the world, but it is better to remember them in the person of Jemmy Button, whether hunting seal and guanaco on the shores of the Yahgashaga, toying with the inhabitants of Good Success Bay, repeating scriptures in the classroom at Walthamstow, or dining with the friends of FitzRoy, than those shadows of Tierra del Fuego who were exhibited in the Royal Aquarium in 1889.

Bibliography and Sources

British Library Manuscripts Room

British Library Add MS 35309   Snow correspondence

Public Record Office (Kew)

ADM/1/5736   Qa50
              Qa55
              Qa68

ADM/1/5744

ADM/1/1817   Letters 1830;
              Letter 114
              Letter 117

ADM/1/2031   Letters of PP King
              Letter 35
              Letter 40

ADM/1/1818   Letters 1831

ADM/53/236

ADM 102.637   Plymouth Hospital muster

CO78/40   Letter 171
              /9227

CO78/41	/3743
	/4508
	/6664
	/7744
	/7574

CO78/42	/4780
	/5571
	/6288
	/6752
	/6715
	/9692

CO78/44	/6022

CO78/45	/Letter 6861
	/Letter 9397
	/Letter 3410

CO78/46	The Falkland Islands 1862
CO78/47	Volume 2 of 1862, Falkland Islands
CO78/48	Falkland Islands, 1863
CO78/49	Falkland Islands, 1863, volume 2
CO78/50	Falkland Islands, 1864, volume 1
CO78/51	Falkland Islands, 1864, volume 2
CO78/52	Falkland Islands, 1865
CO81/15	Falkland Islands Blue Book for 1860

LC 10/7	Bills of the King's Messengers

University of Birmingham – Special Collections: archive of the Church Missionary Society

C N/O/36/19 Letter from Richard Matthews, 20.12.1841. Kaitaia.

C N/O/36/20 Letter from his brother Joseph, Kataia.
C N/O/36/24
C N/O/36/25
C N/O/36/33 Replies from Hadfield and Mason
C N/O/36/36 Long letter from RM to Davis, 17.8.1842
C N/O/61 Letter from Joseph Matthews 28.12.1835
C N/O/62
Correspondence Committee 16 November 1830
Correspondence Committee 14 February 1832
Correspondence Committee G/AC3 1.11.1830, Letters of JL Harris and R Fitzroy

South American Missionary Society

Minutes of the Patagonian Missionary Society
SAMS Minute Books
SAMS General Committee Books

Wellcome Institute

Murchison letters 5220/895220/93
Robert MacCormick's diary '*Voyage to Rio Janeiro and South America in 1831–32*' mss 3559 MacCormick

WC Trevelyan Collection, Robinson Library, University of Newcastle

Letters of WP Snow: WCT 229–1860
WCT 230–1861
WCT 231–1862
WCT 232
WCT 234–1868

Barlow, N (ed). 1967. *Darwin and Henslow: the growth of an idea (Letters 1831–1860)*. Bentham-Moxon Trust. London.

Darwin, CR. 1997. *The correspondence of Charles Darwin, volumes 1–10*, editors: F Burkhardt, S Smith et al. Cambridge University Press. Cambridge.

Darwin, CR. 1945. *Charles Darwin and the Voyage of the Beagle [Letters and notebooks]*. Edited with an introduction by Nora Barlow. Pilot Press. London.

Darwin, CR. 1933. *Charles Darwin's Diary of the Voyage of H.M.S. 'Beagle'*. Edited from the MS. by Nora Barlow. University Press. Cambridge.

Darwin, CR. 1839. *Journal of Researches into the Geology and Natural History of the Various Countries visited by H.M.S. Beagle, 1832–1836*. Henry Colburn. London.

Darwin, C. 1871. *The Descent of Man, and selection in relation to sex*. 2 vol. John Murray. London.

Darwin, C. 1872. *The expression of the emotions in man and animals*. John Murray. London.

Darwin, C. 1859. *On the origin of the species by means of natural selection, or the preservation of favoured races in the struggle for life.* John Murray. London.

Darwin letters in the Darwin Archive at Cambridge University, including:
— Letter from John Henslow to Charles Darwin, 24 August 1831. DAR 97 (ser 2): 4–5; *Darwin and Henslow:*29; *Life and Letters of Charles Darwin* 1:192.
— Letter from Charles Darwin to Susan Darwin, 3 December 1833. DAR 154.
— Letter from Charles Darwin to Robert FitzRoy, 20 February 1840. DAR 144.
— Letter from Charles Darwin to Thomas Bridges, 6 January 1860. DAR 185 and DAR 189.
— Letter from Arthur Mellersh to Charles Darwin, 25 January 1872. DAR 171.
— Letter from Bartholomew Sulivan to Charles Darwin, 23 February 1874. DAR 177.
— Letter from Bartholomew Sulivan to Charles Darwin, 12 October 1879. DAR 177.
— Letter from WP Snow to Charles Darwin, 21 November 1881. DAR 177.
— Letter from Bartholomew Sulivan, 3 December 1881. DAR 177.

Darwin letters belonging to English Heritage:
— Letter from Charles Darwin to Caroline Darwin, 12 April 1833. DAR 223:16; *Charles Darwin and the Voyage of the Beagle:*79
— Letter from Charles Darwin to Catherine Darwin, 6 April 1834. DAR 223: 21; *Life and Letters of Charles Darwin:* 1:251; *Charles Darwin and the Voyage of the Beagle:* 96.
Letters from Robert FitzRoy dated 4 December 1832 and 4 April 1834, to his sister Frances in the Darwin Archive at Cambridge University — Ms add 8853.

Letter to Charles Darwin from John Henslow, dated 11 April 1833, in the Archives, Royal Botanic Gardens, Kew (Henslow letters: 17); *Darwin and Henslow: 71.*

Letter to Charles Kingsley from Charles Darwin, dated 6 February 1862 in the Dittrick Medical History Center. Cleveland Medical Library Association/Case Western Reserve University, Cleveland. Ohio.

Letters to Charles Darwin from Bartholomew Sulivan in the private collection of Mrs E Sulivan.

Darwin, F (ed). 1887. *The Life and Letters of Charles Darwin, including an autobiographical chapter. 3 vols.* Murray. London.

Hamond, R. Private diary, in the Ursula Mommens deposition, Darwin Archive, Cambridge University.

File in Vestry House, Walthamstow museum on the Wigram family.

Newspapers and journals

Bath Chronicle, Bristol Mercury, and Western Counties Advertiser, Bristol Daily Post, Bristol Gazette, Bristol Mirror and General Advertiser, Bristol Observer, Bristol Times and Felix Farley's Bristol Journal, British Baptist Reporter, Clifton Chronicle, Daily Telegraph, Essex Standard, Falmouth Packet, Guardian, Hampshire Telegraph and Sussex Chronicle, Morning Advertiser, Morning Chronicle, Morning Herald, Morning Post, Morning Star, Observer, Record, Royal Devonport Telegraph, The Times, Western Daily Press, Woolmer's Exeter and Plymouth Gazette.

Secondary Sources

Altick, R. 1978. *The Shows of London.* Belknap Press of Harvard University Press.

Barquet, N and Domingo, P. Smallpox: The Triumph over the Most Terrible of the Ministers of Death, *Annals of Internal Medicine*, 15 October 1997. 127:635–642.

Beer, G. 1997. Travelling the other way: travel narratives and truth claims in *Patagonia: Natural history, prehistory and ethnography at the uttermost end of the earth* edited by McEwan, C, Borrero, LA and Prieto, A. British Museum Press, London.

Besley, H. 1845. *The Route Book of Devon: A guide for the stranger and tourist to the towns, watering places, and other interesting localities of this county. With a route map of the roads and plans of Exeter, Plymouth, Devonport, and Stonehouse.* Henry Besley, Exeter.

Borrero, LA and Prieto, A. 1997. The origins of ethnographic subsistence patterns in Furego Patagonia in *Patagonia: Natural history, prehistory and ethnography at the uttermost end of the earth* edited by McEwan, C, Borrero, LA and Prieto, A. British Museum Press, London.

Borrero, LA and McEwan, C. 1997. The peopling of Patagonia: The first human occupation in *Patagonia: Natural history, prehistory and ethnography at the uttermost end of the earth* edited by McEwan, C, Borrero, LA and Prieto, A. British Museum Press, London.

Bosworth, G. 1916. *A history of St Mary's Church, Walthamstow,* Walthamstow Antiquarian Society, Official publication no. 2.

Bosworth, G. 1920. *A history of Walthamstow charities,* Walthamstow Antiquarian Society. Official publication no. 8.

Bosworth, G. 1924. *Some Walthamstow houses and their interesting associations,* Walthamstow Antiquarian Society. Official publication no. 12.

Bosworth, G. 1933. *Some more Walthamstow houses and their interesting associations*, Walthamstow Antiquarian Society. Official publication no. 29.

Bridges, EL. 1948. *Uttermost part of the Earth*. Century, London.

Bridges, Rev T. 1933. *Yamana—English: a dictionary of the speech of Tierra del Fuego, edited by Dr Ferdinand Hestermann and Dr Martin Gusinde*. Printed for private circulation: Mödling.

Brindley, R. 1830. *The Plymouth, Stonehouse and Devonport Directory*. W. Byers: Devonport.

Browne, J. 1995. *Voyaging Darwin* Pimlico, London.

Burkhardt, FH, Smith, S A [eds]. 1985. *Calendar of the correspondence of Charles Darwin, 1821–1882*. Garland London.

Carrington, HE. 1828. *The Plymouth and Devonport Guide*. Byers: Devonport.

Chapman, A. 1997. The great ceremonies of the Selk'nam and the Yamana: a comparative analysis in *Patagonia: Natural history, prehistory and ethnography at the uttermost end of the earth* edited by McEwan, C, Borrero, LA and Prieto, A. British Museum Press, London.

Chatwin, B. 1977. *In Patagonia*. Jonathan Cape, London.

Chatwin, B and Theroux, P. 1985. *Patagonia Revisited*. Jonathan Cape, London.

Clarke, E. 1980. *Clarke's history of Walthamstow [Walthamstow Antiquarian Society]*. Walthamstow.

Desmond, A and Moore, J. 1991. *Darwin*. Michael Joseph, London.

Despard, GP. 1852. *Hope deferred, not lost; a narrative of missionary effort in South America in connection with the Patagonian Missionary Society,* edited by the Rev. G. P. Despard. *[Consisting mainly of extracts from journals by Allen F. Gardiner, Robert Hunt and Richard Williams.]*. Seeleys; J. Nisbet, & Company. London.

Despard, GP. 1863. Fireland or Tierra del Fuego in *Sunday at Home, Vol X,* London.

Drake, Sir F. 1926. *The World encompassed and analogous contemporary documents concerning Sir Francis Drake's circumnavigation of the world.* Editor: N. M. Penzer, with an appreciation of the achievement by Sir Richard Carnac Temple. Argonaut Press. London.

Ferguson, B. J. 1971. *Syms Covington of Pambula, assistant to Charles Darwin on the voyage of H.M.S. Beagle round the world, 1831 to 1836.* Imlay District Historical Society.

FitzRoy, R. 1839. *Narrative of the surveying voyages of His Majesty's ships Adventure and Beagle between the years 1826 and 1836. Volume I. Proceedings of the first expedition, 1826–30, under the command of Captain PP King.* Edited by Robert FitzRoy. *Volume 2. Proceedings of the second expedition, 1831–36, under the command of Captain R FitzRoy. Volume 3. Journal and remarks, 1832–36.* By Charles Darwin. 4 vols. H. Colburn. London.

Fox C. 1882. *Memories of old friends; being extracts from the journals and letters of Caroline Fox from 1835 to 1871.* Edited by H. N. Pym. Second edition. 2 vol. Smith, Elder & Company, London.

Gollock, GA. 1909. *The story of the CMS: being a popular sketch of the history of the Church Missionary Society.* Church Missionary Society. London. 1909.

Gusinde, M. 1977. *Folk literature of the Yamana Indians, Martin Gusinde's Collection of Yamana Narratives* [translated from the German], Johannes Wilbert [editor]. University of California Press. Berkeley.

Hobsbawm, EJ. 1968. *Industry and Empire*. Weidenfeld and Nicolson. London.

Hough, R. 1971. *Blind Horn's Hate*. Hutchinson and Company. London.

Houghton, W. 1937. Walthamstow: its highways and byways, Walthamstow Antiquarian Society, Occasional Publications No. 1.

Keevil, JJ. Benjamin Bynoe, surgeon of HMS Beagle in the *Journal of the History of Medicine*, 1949, 4:90–111.

Law, AD. 1978. *St Mary's Infant School, a brief history*. Typescript produced for St Mary's Infant School. Walthamstow.

Law, AD. 1996. *Walthamstow Village – an account of Church End – the historic centre of Walthamstow (with maps by WGS Tonkin)*. The Walthamstow Historical Society.

Loudon, I [ed]. 1997. *Western medicine, an illustrated history*. Oxford University Press, Oxford.

MacCormick, R. 1884. *Voyages of discovery in the Arctic and Antarctic seas, and round the world*. 2 vols. Sampson Low & Company, London.

Macdonald, FC. 1929. *Bishop Stirling of the Falklands*. Seeley & Company, London.

McCann, P and Young, FA. 1982. *Samuel Wilderspin and the infant school movement*. Croom Helm, London.

McCulloch, RD, Clapperton, CM, Rabassa, J and Currant, AP. 1997. The natural setting: The glacial and post-glacial environmental history of Fuegia-Patagonia in *Patagonia: Natural history, prehistory and ethnography at the uttermost end of the earth* edited by McEwan, C, Borrero, LA and Prieto, A. British Museum Press, London.

McEwan, C, Borrero, LA and Prieto, A [eds]. 1997. *Patagonia: Natural history, prehistory and ethnography at the uttermost end of the earth*. British Museum Press, London.

Marsh, JW. 1883. *Narrative of the origin and progress of the South American Mission or 'First Fruits' enlarged*. South American Missionary Society, London.

Martinic, BM. 1997. The meeting of two cultures: Indians and colonists in the Magellan region in *Patagonia: Natural history, prehistory and ethnography at the uttermost end of the earth* edited by McEwan, C, Borrero, LA and Prieto, A. British Museum Press, London.

Mellersh, HEL. 1968. *Fitzroy of the Beagle*. Rupert Hart-Davis. London.

Mena, F. 1997. Middle to late Holocene adaptations in Patagonia in *Patagonia: Natural history, prehistory and ethnography at the uttermost end of the earth* edited by McEwan, C, Borrero, LA and Prieto, A. British Museum Press, London.

Noort, O. 1744. *The voyage of Olivier van Noort round the world, in a complete collection of voyages and travels by John Harris*. London.

Patagonian Missionary Society. 1857. *A brief reply to certain charges made against the Patagonian Missionary Society, or South American Missionary Society, by WP Snow*. Bristol.

Phillips, GW. 1861. *The missionary martyr of Tierra del Fuego: being the memoir of JG Phillips*. London.

Pigafetta, A. 1874. *The first voyage round the world, by Magellan. Translated from the accounts of Pigafetta, and other contemporary writers. Accompanied by original documents, with notes and an introduction, by Lord Stanley of Alderley*. Hakluyt Society. London.

Porter, R. 1997. *The greatest benefit to mankind — a medical history of humanity from antiquity to the present*. HarperCollins, London.

Powell, WR (ed.). 1973. *A history of the county of Essex, vol VI*. (In the series *The Victoria History of the Counties of England* edited by RB Pugh). Published for the University of London, Institue of Historical Research by the Oxford University Press. Oxford.

Sandars, MF. 1915. *The Life and Times of Queen Adelaide*. Stanley Paul & Company. London.

Shankland, P. 1975. *Byron of the Wager*. Collins, London.

Shipton, E. 1973. *Tierra del Fuego: the fatal lodestone*. Readers Union Limited, Newton Abbot, Devon.

Smith, RS. 1938. *Walthamstow in the Early Nineteenth Century* [Walthamstow Antiquarian Society. Occasional Publications no. 2]. Walthamstow.

Snow, WP. 1857. *A two years' cruise off Tierra del Fuegothe Falkland Islands, Patagonia, and the River Plate. 2 vols*. London.

Snow, WP. 1857. *The 'Patagonian Missionary Society,' and some truths connected with it*. London.

South American Missionary Society. 1860. *A brief statement of the rise and progress of the Patagonian Mission*. Bristol.

South American Missionary Society. *The Voice of Pity for South America vol. 1–9 [1854–62].* London.

South American Missionary Society. *The Voice of Pity for South America vol. 10–13 [1863–66].* London.

Stock, E. 1899. *The history of the Church Missionary Society, 4 vols.* Church Missionary Society. London.

Stovel, C. 1860. *Calamity sanctified in the Martyrs of Tierra Del Fuego A sermon [on Heb. vi. 11, 12], etc. [With a letter from Mrs M. E. Fell.]* London.

Strange, IJ. 1972. *The Falkland Islands.* David and Charles (The island series). Newton Abbot.

Sulivan, HN. 1896. *Life and letters of the late Admiral Sir BJ Sulivan KCB, 1810–1890.* John Murray. London.

Taussig, M. 1997. Tierra del Fuego – land of fire, land of mimicry in *Patagonia: Natural history, prehistory and ethnography at the uttermost end of the earth* edited by McEwan, C, Borrero, LA and Prieto, A. British Museum Press, London.

Thomson, KS. 1995. *HMS Beagle – the story of Darwin's ship.* WW Norton. New York, London.

Tonkin, WGS. 1974. *The Lea Bridge Turnpike and the Wragg stage coaches* [Walthamstow Antiquarian Society Monograph (New series) no. 14]. Walthamstow.

Twain, M. 1962. *The Gorky Incident* in *Letters from the Earth.* Harper and Row. New York.

Victoria history of the counties of England – a history of Essex volume VI.

White, GC. 1902. *Glimpses of King William IV and Queen Adelaide in letters of the late Miss Clitherow, of Boston House, Middlesex. With a brief account of Boston House and the Clitherow family.* London.

Wilson, JD. 1969. *Milestones on the Dover Road.* Faber. London.

Wilson, W. 1840. *A Manual of Useful Information for Residents in the Parish of Walthamstow, respecting the Institutions, Benefactions, Charities and other matters of interest in that parish, etc.* W. H. Dalton. London.

Wilson, W. 1825. *The system of infants schools.* London.

Ziegler, P. 1971. *King William IV.* Collins. London.

Acknowledgements

I would like to express my gratitude to the many people who have helped me along the way with this project, in particular to: Adam Perkins at the Department of Manuscripts, Cambridge University Library; Jean Marshall, Mission Education Officer at the South American Missionary Society; Elizabeth Sulivan (to whom many thanks go also for her great hospitality and fascinating labyrinth); Ursula Mommens for the Hamond diary; Dr Sheila Dean and Perry O'Donovan of the Darwin Correspondence Project; Robin Dower; Philippa Bassett, archivist of Special Collections at the University of Birmingham; Dr Lesley Gordon at the Special Collections department of the Robinson Library, University of Newcastle; Lesley Price, archivist of the Royal Botanic Gardens, Kew; Dr Janet Browne of the Wellcome Institute for the History of Medicine; Barbara Schmidt for her knowledge of Mark Twain and persistence in finding the right reference for me; and Luigi Bonomi for his unceasing enthusiasm and dogged goading.

I am grateful to: the Syndics of Cambridge University Library and English Heritage for allowing me to quote from unpublished material in the Darwin Archive; George Pember Darwin for his permission to use the writings of Charles Darwin; the Dittrick Medical History Center, Cleveland Medical Library Association/Case Western Reserve University, Cleveland, Ohio for the letter from Darwin to Charles Kingsley; Hodder Headline for the extracts from Lucas Poridges's Utermost Point of the Earth.

Many thanks also to the following institutions for allowing me to study and in some instances quote from manuscripts in their possession: the British Library, Department of Manuscripts; Carmarthenshire Archives Service; the National Register of Archives; the Public Record Office, Kew; the Archives, Royal Botanic Gardens, Kew; Somerset Archive and Record Service; University College, London, for the Society for the Diffusion of Useful Knowledge; the Vestry House museum, Walthamstow; the Wellcome Institute for the History of Medicine.

Some archives checked out leads for me and saved me the trouble of making a visit, for which I am appreciative. These include: the Church Missionary Society; City of Plymouth Archives and Records; Flintshire County Council archive; Lambeth Palace Library; the London Transport Museum; the National Library of Scotland; the National Library of Wales; the National Maritime Museum; the Royal Archives, Windsor Castle; Suffolk County Record Office; Warwickshire County Council Record Office; West Glamorgan Archive Service; the Yorkshire Archaeological Society.

Finally I would like to give a huge thank you to Caroline Annesley and David Jeffreys for reading through several drafts of the book as it developed – the latter going beyond the call of duty, reading the manuscript while holding the hand of his wife Julia as she gave birth to baby Lorcan.

Index

Index

Index

Index